Hadoop Security

Ben Spivey & Joey Echeverria

Beijing · Boston · Farnham · Sebastopol · Tokyo

Hadoop Security

by Ben Spivey and Joey Echeverria

Printed in the United States of America.

Published by O'Reilly Media, Inc., 1005 Gravenstein Highway North, Sebastopol, CA 95472.

O'Reilly books may be purchased for educational, business, or sales promotional use. Online editions are also available for most titles (*http://safaribooksonline.com*). For more information, contact our corporate/institutional sales department: 800-998-9938 or *corporate@oreilly.com*.

Editors: Ann Spencer and Marie Beaugureau	**Indexer:** Wendy Catalano
Production Editor: Melanie Yarbrough	**Interior Designer:** David Futato
Copyeditor: Gillian McGarvey	**Cover Designer:** Ellie Volkhausen
Proofreader: Jasmine Kwityn	**Illustrator:** Rebecca Demarest

July 2015:   First Edition

Revision History for the First Edition
2015-06-24:   First Release

See *http://oreilly.com/catalog/errata.csp?isbn=9781491900987* for release details.

978-1-491-90098-7

[LSI]

Table of Contents

Part I. Security Architecture

Part II. Authentication, Authorization, and Accounting

Part III.   Data Security

Part IV.   Putting It All Together

Foreword

It has not been very long since the phrase "Hadoop security" was an oxymoron. Early versions of the big data platform, built and used at web companies like Yahoo! and Facebook, didn't try very hard to protect the data they stored. They didn't really have to—very little sensitive data went into Hadoop. Status updates and news stories aren't attractive targets for bad guys. You don't have to work that hard to lock them down.

As the platform has moved into more traditional enterprise use, though, it has begun to work with more traditional enterprise data. Financial transactions, personal bank account and tax information, medical records, and similar kinds of data are exactly what bad guys are after. Because Hadoop is now used in retail, banking, and healthcare applications, it has attracted the attention of thieves as well.

And if data is a juicy target, big data may be the biggest and juiciest of all. Hadoop collects more data from more places, and combines and analyzes it in more ways than any predecessor system, ever. It creates tremendous value in doing so.

Clearly, then, "Hadoop security" is a big deal.

This book, written by two of the people who've been instrumental in driving security into the platform, tells the story of Hadoop's evolution from its early, wide open consumer Internet days to its current status as a trusted place for sensitive data. Ben and Joey review the history of Hadoop security, covering its advances and its evolution alongside new business problems. They cover topics like identity, encryption, key management and business practices, and discuss them in a real-world context.

It's an interesting story. Hadoop today has come a long way from the software that Facebook chose for image storage a decade ago. It offers much more power, many more ways to process and analyze data, much more scale, and much better performance. Therefore it has more pieces that need to be secured, separately and in combination.

The best thing about this book, though, is that it doesn't merely describe. It *prescribes*. It tells you, very clearly and with the detail that you expect from seasoned practitioners who have built Hadoop and used it, how to manage your big data securely. It gives you the very best advice available on how to analyze, process, and understand data using the state-of-the-art platform—and how to do so safely.

—*Mike Olson,*
Chief Strategy Officer and Cofounder,
Cloudera, Inc.

Preface

Apache Hadoop is still a relatively young technology, but that has not limited its rapid adoption and the explosion of tools that make up the vast ecosystem around it. This is certainly an exciting time for Hadoop users. While the opportunity to add value to an organization has never been greater, Hadoop still provides a lot of challenges to those responsible for securing access to data and ensuring that systems respect relevant policies and regulations. There exists a wealth of information available to developers building solutions with Hadoop and administrators seeking to deploy and operate it. However, guidance on how to design and implement a secure Hadoop deployment has been lacking.

This book provides in-depth information about the many security features available in Hadoop and organizes it using common computer security concepts. It begins with introductory material in the first chapter, followed by material organized into four larger parts: Part I, Security Architecture; Part II, Authentication, Authorization, and Accounting; Part III, Data Security; and Part IV, PUtting It All Together. These parts cover the early stages of designing a physical and logical security architecture all the way through implementing common security access controls and protecting data. Finally, the book wraps up with use cases that gather many of the concepts covered in the book into real-world examples.

Audience

This book targets Hadoop administrators charged with securing their big data platform and established security architects who need to design and integrate a Hadoop security plan within a larger enterprise architecture. It presents many Hadoop security concepts including authentication, authorization, accounting, encryption, and system architecture.

Chapter 1 includes an overview of some of the security concepts used throughout this book, as well as a brief description of the Hadoop ecosystem. If you are new to Hadoop, we encourage you to review *Hadoop Operations* and *Hadoop: The Definitive*

Guide as needed. We assume that you are familiar with Linux, computer networks, and general system architecture. For administrators who do not have experience with securing distributed systems, we provide an overview in Chapter 2. Practiced security architects might want to skip that chapter unless they're looking for a review. In general, we don't assume that you have a programming background, and try to focus on the architectural and operational aspects of implementing Hadoop security.

Conventions Used in This Book

The following typographical conventions are used in this book:

Italic
> Indicates new terms, URLs, email addresses, filenames, and file extensions.

`Constant width`
> Used for program listings, as well as within paragraphs to refer to program elements such as variable or function names, databases, data types, environment variables, statements, and keywords.

`Constant width bold`
> Shows commands or other text that should be typed literally by the user.

`Constant width italic`
> Shows text that should be replaced with user-supplied values or by values determined by context.

 This element signifies a tip or suggestion.

 This element signifies a general note.

 This element indicates a warning or caution.

Using Code Examples

Throughout this book, we provide examples of configuration files to help guide you in securing your own Hadoop environment. A downloadable version of some of those examples is available at *https://github.com/hadoop-security/examples*. In Chapter 13, we provide a complete example of designing, implementing, and deploying a web interface for saving snapshots of web pages. The complete source code for the example, along with instructions for securely configuring a Hadoop cluster for deployment of the application, is available for download at GitHub (*https://github.com/hadoop-security/kite-spring-hbase-example*).

This book is here to help you get your job done. In general, if example code is offered with this book, you may use it in your programs and documentation. You do not need to contact us for permission unless you're reproducing a significant portion of the code. For example, writing a program that uses several chunks of code from this book does not require permission. Selling or distributing a CD-ROM of examples from O'Reilly books does require permission. Answering a question by citing this book and quoting example code does not require permission. Incorporating a significant amount of example code from this book into your product's documentation does require permission.

We appreciate, but do not require, attribution. An attribution usually includes the title, author, publisher, and ISBN. For example: "*Hadoop Security* by Ben Spivey and Joey Echeverria (O'Reilly). Copyright 2015 Ben Spivey and Joey Echeverria, 978-1-491-90098-7."

If you feel your use of code examples falls outside fair use or the permission given above, feel free to contact us at *permissions@oreilly.com*.

Safari® Books Online

 *Safari Books Online* is an on-demand digital library that delivers expert content in both book and video form from the world's leading authors in technology and business.

Technology professionals, software developers, web designers, and business and creative professionals use Safari Books Online as their primary resource for research, problem solving, learning, and certification training.

Safari Books Online offers a range of plans and pricing for enterprise, government, education, and individuals.

Members have access to thousands of books, training videos, and prepublication manuscripts in one fully searchable database from publishers like O'Reilly Media,

Prentice Hall Professional, Addison-Wesley Professional, Microsoft Press, Sams, Que, Peachpit Press, Focal Press, Cisco Press, John Wiley & Sons, Syngress, Morgan Kaufmann, IBM Redbooks, Packt, Adobe Press, FT Press, Apress, Manning, New Riders, McGraw-Hill, Jones & Bartlett, Course Technology, and hundreds more. For more information about Safari Books Online, please visit us online.

How to Contact Us

Please address comments and questions concerning this book to the publisher:

> O'Reilly Media, Inc.
> 1005 Gravenstein Highway North
> Sebastopol, CA 95472
> 800-998-9938 (in the United States or Canada)
> 707-829-0515 (international or local)
> 707-829-0104 (fax)

We have a web page for this book, where we list errata, examples, and any additional information. You can access this page at *http://bit.ly/hadoop-security*.

To comment or ask technical questions about this book, send email to *bookquestions@oreilly.com*.

For more information about our books, courses, conferences, and news, see our website at *http://www.oreilly.com*.

Find us on Facebook: *http://facebook.com/oreilly*

Follow us on Twitter: *http://twitter.com/oreillymedia*

Watch us on YouTube: *http://www.youtube.com/oreillymedia*

Acknowledgments

Ben and Joey would like to thank the following people who have made this book possible: our editor, Marie Beaugureau, and all of the O'Reilly Media staff; Ann Spencer; Eddie Garcia for his guest chapter contribution; our primary technical reviewers, Patrick Angeles, Brian Burton, Sean Busbey, Mubashir Kazia, and Alex Moundalexis; Jarek Jarcec Cecho; fellow authors Eric Sammer, Lars George, and Tom White for their valuable insight; and the folks at Cloudera for their collective support to us and all other authors.

From Joey

I would like to dedicate this book to Maria Antonia Fernandez, Jose Fernandez, and Sarah Echeverria, three people that inspired me every day and taught me that I could achieve anything I set out to achieve. I also want to thank my parents, Maria and Fred Echeverria, and my brothers and sisters, Fred, Marietta, Angeline, and Paul Echeverria, and Victoria Schandevel, for their love and support throughout this process. I couldn't have done this without the incredible support of the Apache Hadoop community. I couldn't possibly list everybody that has made an impact, but you need look no further than Ben's list for a great start. Lastly, I'd like to thank my coauthor, Ben. This is quite a thing we've done, Bennie (you're welcome, Paul).

From Ben

I would like to dedicate this book to the loving memory of Ginny Venable and Rob Trosinski, two people that I miss dearly. I would like to thank my wife, Theresa, for her endless support and understanding, and Oliver Morton for always making me smile. To my parents, Rich and Linda, thank you for always showing me the value of education and setting the example of professional excellence. Thanks to Matt, Jess, Noah, and the rest of the Spivey family; Mary, Jarrod, and Dolly Trosinski; the Swope family; and the following people that have helped me greatly along the way: Hemal Kanani (BOOM), Ted Malaska, Eric Driscoll, Paul Beduhn, Kari Neidigh, Jeremy Beard, Jeff Shmain, Marlo Carrillo, Joe Prosser, Jeff Holoman, Kevin O'Dell, Jean-Marc Spaggiari, Madhu Ganta, Linden Hillenbrand, Adam Smieszny, Benjamin Vera-Tudela, Prashant Sharma, Sekou Mckissick, Melissa Hueman, Adam Taylor, Kaufman Ng, Steve Ross, Prateek Rungta, Steve Totman, Ryan Blue, Susan Greslik, Todd Grayson, Woody Christy, Vini Varadharajan, Prasad Mujumdar, Aaron Myers, Phil Langdale, Phil Zeyliger, Brock Noland, Michael Ridley, Ryan Geno, Brian Schrameck, Michael Katzenellenbogen, Don Brown, Barry Hurry, Skip Smith, Sarah Stanger, Jason Hogue, Joe Wilcox, Allen Hsiao, Jason Trost, Greg Bednarski, Ray Scott, Mike Wilson, Doug Gardner, Peter Guerra, Josh Sullivan, Christine Mallick, Rick Whitford, Kurt Lorenz, Jason Nowlin, and Chuck Wigelsworth. Last but not least, thanks to Joey for giving in to my pleading to help write this book—I never could have done this alone! For those that I have inadvertently forgotten, please accept my sincere apologies.

From Eddie

I would like to thank my family and friends for their support and encouragement on my first book writing experience. Thank you, Sandra, Kassy, Sammy, Ally, Ben, Joey, Mark, and Peter.

Disclaimer

Thank you for reading this book. While the authors of this book have made every attempt to explain, document, and recommend different security features in the Hadoop ecosystem, there is no warranty expressed or implied that using any of these features will result in a fully secured cluster. From a security point of view, no information system is 100% secure, regardless of the mechanisms used to protect it. We encourage a constant security review process for your Hadoop environment to ensure the best possible security stance. The authors of this book and O'Reilly Media are not responsible for any damage that might or might not have come as a result of using any of the features described in this book. Use at your own risk.

Introduction

Back in 2003, Google published a paper (*http://research.google.com/archive/gfs.html*) describing a scale-out architecture for storing massive amounts of data across clusters of servers, which it called the *Google File System (GFS)*. A year later, Google published another paper (*http://research.google.com/archive/mapreduce.html*) describing a programming model called *MapReduce*, which took advantage of GFS to process data in a parallel fashion, bringing the program to where the data resides. Around the same time, Doug Cutting and others were building an open source web crawler now called Apache Nutch (*http://nutch.apache.org*). The Nutch developers realized that the MapReduce programming model and GFS were the perfect building blocks for a distributed web crawler, and they began implementing their own versions of both projects. These components would later split from Nutch and form the Apache Hadoop project. The ecosystem[1] of projects built around Hadoop's scale-out architecture brought about a different way of approaching problems by allowing the storage and processing of *all* data important to a business.

While all these new and exciting ways to process and store data in the Hadoop ecosystem have brought many use cases across different verticals to use this technology, it has become apparent that managing petabytes of data in a single centralized cluster can be dangerous. Hundreds if not thousands of servers linked together in a common application stack raises many questions about how to protect such a valuable asset. While other books focus on such things as writing MapReduce code, designing optimal ingest frameworks, or architecting complex low-latency processing systems on

---

[1] Apache Hadoop itself consists of four subprojects: HDFS, YARN, MapReduce, and Hadoop Common. However, the Hadoop ecosystem, Hadoop, and the related projects that build on or integrate with Hadoop are often shortened to just Hadoop. We attempt to make it clear when we're referring to Hadoop the project versus Hadoop the ecosystem.

top of the Hadoop ecosystem, this one focuses on how to ensure that all of these things can be protected using the numerous security features available across the stack as part of a cohesive Hadoop security architecture.

Security Overview

Before this book can begin covering Hadoop-specific content, it is useful to understand some key theory and terminology related to information security. At the heart of information security theory is a model known as *CIA*, which stands for *confidentiality*, *integrity*, and *availability*. These three components of the model are high-level concepts that can be applied to a wide range of information systems, computing platforms, and—more specifically to this book—Hadoop. We also take a closer look at *authentication*, *authorization*, and *accounting*, which are critical components of secure computing that will be discussed in detail throughout the book.

While the CIA model helps to organize some information security principles, it is important to point out that this model is not a strict set of standards to follow. Security features in the Hadoop platform may span more than one of the CIA components, or possibly none at all.

Confidentiality

Confidentiality is a security principle focusing on the notion that information is only seen by the intended recipients. For example, if Alice sends a letter in the mail to Bob, it would only be deemed confidential if Bob were the only person able to read it. While this might seem straightforward enough, several important security concepts are necessary to ensure that confidentiality actually holds. For instance, how does Alice know that the letter she is sending is actually being read by the right Bob? If the correct Bob reads the letter, how does he know that the letter actually came from the right Alice? In order for both Alice and Bob to take part in this confidential information passing, they need to have an *identity* that uniquely distinguishes themselves from any other person. Additionally, both Alice and Bob need to prove their identities via a process known as *authentication*. Identity and authentication are key components of Hadoop security and are covered at length in Chapter 5.

Another important concept of confidentiality is *encryption*. Encryption is a mechanism to apply a mathematical algorithm to a piece of information where the output is something that unintended recipients are not able to read. Only the intended recipients are able to *decrypt* the encrypted message back to the original unencrypted message. Encryption of data can be applied both *at rest* and *in flight*. At-rest data encryption means that data resides in an encrypted format when not being accessed. A file that is encrypted and located on a hard drive is an example of at-rest encryption. In-flight encryption, also known as over-the-wire encryption, applies to data sent from one place to another over a network. Both modes of encryption can be used independently or together. At-rest encryption for Hadoop is covered in Chapter 9, and in-flight encryption is covered in Chapters 10 and 11.

Integrity

Integrity is an important part of information security. In the previous example where Alice sends a letter to Bob, what happens if Charles intercepts the letter in transit and makes changes to it unbeknownst to Alice and Bob? How can Bob ensure that the letter he receives is exactly the message that Alice sent? This concept is *data integrity*. The integrity of data is a critical component of information security, especially in industries with highly sensitive data. Imagine if a bank did not have a mechanism to prove the integrity of customer account balances? A hospital's data integrity of patient records? A government's data integrity of intelligence secrets? Even if confidentiality is guaranteed, data that doesn't have integrity guarantees is at risk of substantial damage. Integrity is covered in Chapters 9 and 10.

Availability

Availability is a different type of principle than the previous two. While confidentiality and integrity can closely be aligned to well-known security concepts, availability is largely covered by operational preparedness. For example, if Alice tries to send her letter to Bob, but the post office is closed, the letter cannot be sent to Bob, thus making it unavailable to him. The availability of data or services can be impacted by regular outages such as scheduled downtime for upgrades or applying security patches, but it can also be impacted by security events such as distributed denial-of-service (DDoS) attacks. The handling of high-availability configurations is covered in *Hadoop Operations* and *Hadoop: The Definitive Guide*, but the concepts will be covered from a security perspective in Chapters 3 and 10.

Authentication, Authorization, and Accounting

Authentication, authorization, and accounting (often abbreviated, AAA) refer to an architectural pattern in computer security where users of a service prove their identity, are granted access based on rules, and where a recording of a user's actions is maintained for auditing purposes. Closely tied to AAA is the concept of identity. Identity refers to how a system distinguishes between different entities, users, and services, and is typically represented by an arbitrary string, such as a username or a unique number, such as a user ID (UID).

Before diving into how Hadoop supports identity, authentication, authorization, and accounting, consider how these concepts are used in the much simpler case of using the sudo command on a single Linux server. Let's take a look at the terminal session for two different users, Alice and Bob. On this server, Alice is given the username *alice* and Bob is given the username *bob*. Alice logs in first, as shown in Example 1-1.

Example 1-1. Authentication and authorization

```
$ ssh alice@hadoop01
alice@hadoop01's password:
Last login: Wed Feb 12 15:26:55 2014 from 172.18.12.166
[alice@hadoop01 ~]$ sudo service sshd status
openssh-daemon (pid  1260) is running...
[alice@hadoop01 ~]$
```

In Example 1-1, Alice logs in through SSH and she is immediately prompted for her password. Her username/password pair is used to verify her entry in the */etc/passwd* password file. When this step is completed, Alice has been *authenticated* with the identity *alice*. The next thing Alice does is use the sudo command to get the status of the sshd service, which requires superuser privileges. The command succeeds, indicating that Alice was *authorized* to perform that command. In the case of sudo, the rules that govern who is authorized to execute commands as the superuser are stored in the */etc/sudoers* file, shown in Example 1-2.

Example 1-2. /etc/sudoers

```
[root@hadoop01 ~]# cat /etc/sudoers
root ALL = (ALL) ALL
%wheel ALL = (ALL) NOPASSWD:ALL
[root@hadoop01 ~]#
```

In Example 1-2, we see that the root user is granted permission to execute any command with sudo and that members of the *wheel* group are granted permission to execute any command with sudo while not being prompted for a password. In this case, the system is relying on the authentication that was performed during login rather than issuing a new authentication challenge. The final question is, how does the system know that Alice is a member of the wheel group? In Unix and Linux systems, this is typically controlled by the */etc/group* file.

In this way, we can see that two files control Alice's identity: the */etc/passwd* file (see Example 1-4) assigns her username a unique UID as well as details such as her home directory, while the */etc/group* file (see Example 1-3) further provides information about the identity of groups on the system and which users belong to which groups. These sources of identity information are then used by the sudo command, along with authorization rules found in the */etc/sudoers* file, to verify that Alice is authorized to execute the requested command.

Example 1-3. /etc/group

```
[root@hadoop01 ~]# grep wheel /etc/group
wheel:x:10:alice
[root@hadoop01 ~]#
```

Example 1-4. /etc/passwd

```
[root@hadoop01 ~]# grep alice /etc/passwd
alice:x:1000:1000:Alice:/home/alice:/bin/bash
[root@hadoop01 ~]#
```

Now let's see how Bob's session turns out in Example 1-5.

Example 1-5. Authorization failure

```
$ ssh bob@hadoop01
bob@hadoop01's password:
Last login: Wed Feb 12 15:30:54 2014 from 172.18.12.166
[bob@hadoop01 ~]$ sudo service sshd status

We trust you have received the usual lecture from the local System
Administrator. It usually boils down to these three things:

    #1) Respect the privacy of others.
    #2) Think before you type.
    #3) With great power comes great responsibility.

[sudo] password for bob:
bob is not in the sudoers file.  This incident will be reported.
[bob@hadoop01 ~]$
```

In this example, Bob is able to authenticate in much the same way that Alice does, but when he attempts to use sudo he sees very different behavior. First, he is again prompted for his password and after successfully supplying it, he is denied permission to run the service command with superuser privileges. This happens because, unlike Alice, Bob is not a member of the *wheel* group and is therefore *not authorized* to use the sudo command.

That covers identity, authentication, and authorization, but what about accounting? For actions that interact with secure services such as SSH and sudo, Linux generates a logfile called */var/log/secure*. This file records an account of certain actions including both successes and failures. If we take a look at this log after Alice and Bob have performed the preceding actions, we see the output in Example 1-6 (formatted for readability).

Example 1-6. /var/log/secure

```
[root@hadoop01 ~]# tail -n 6 /var/log/secure
Feb 12 20:32:04 ip-172-25-3-79 sshd[3774]: Accepted password for
  alice from 172.18.12.166 port 65012 ssh2
Feb 12 20:32:04 ip-172-25-3-79 sshd[3774]: pam_unix(sshd:session):
  session opened for user alice by (uid=0)
Feb 12 20:32:33 ip-172-25-3-79 sudo:     alice : TTY=pts/0 ;
  PWD=/home/alice ; USER=root ; COMMAND=/sbin/service sshd status
Feb 12 20:33:15 ip-172-25-3-79 sshd[3799]: Accepted password for
  bob from 172.18.12.166 port 65017 ssh2
Feb 12 20:33:15 ip-172-25-3-79 sshd[3799]: pam_unix(sshd:session):
  session opened for user bob by (uid=0)
Feb 12 20:33:39 ip-172-25-3-79 sudo:       bob : user NOT in sudoers;
  TTY=pts/2 ; PWD=/home/bob ; USER=root ; COMMAND=/sbin/service sshd status
[root@hadoop01 ~]#
```

For both users, the fact that they successfully logged in using SSH is recorded, as are their attempts to use sudo. In Alice's case, the system records that she successfully used sudo to execute the /sbin/service sshd status command as the user *root*. For Bob, on the other hand, the system records that he attempted to execute the /sbin/service sshd status command as the user *root* and was denied permission because he is not in */etc/sudoers*.

This example shows how the concepts of identity, authentication, authorization, and accounting are used to maintain a secure system in the relatively simple example of a single Linux server. These concepts are covered in detail in a Hadoop context in Part II.

Hadoop Security: A Brief History

Hadoop has its heart in storing and processing large amounts of data efficiently and as it turns out, cheaply (monetarily) when compared to other platforms. The focus early on in the project was around the actual technology to make this happen. Much of the code covered the logic on how to deal with the complexities inherent in distributed systems, such as handling of failures and coordination. Due to this focus, the early Hadoop project established a security stance that the entire cluster of machines and all of the users accessing it are part of a *trusted network*. What this effectively means is that Hadoop did not have strong security measures in place to enforce, well, much of anything.

As the project evolved, it became apparent that at a minimum there should be a mechanism for users to strongly authenticate to prove their identities. The mechanism chosen for the project was Kerberos, a well-established protocol that today is common in enterprise systems such as Microsoft Active Directory. After strong authentication came strong authorization. Strong authorization defined what an individual user could do after they had been authenticated. Initially, authorization was implemented on a per-component basis, meaning that administrators needed to define authorization controls in multiple places. Eventually this became easier with Apache Sentry (Incubating), but even today there is not a holistic view of authorization across the ecosystem, as we will see in Chapters 6 and 7.

Another aspect of Hadoop security that is still evolving is the protection of data through encryption and other confidentiality mechanisms. In the trusted network, it was assumed that data was inherently protected from unauthorized users because only authorized users were on the network. Since then, Hadoop has added encryption for data transmitted between nodes, as well as data stored on disk. We will see how this security evolution comes into play as we proceed, but first we will take a look at the Hadoop ecosystem to get our bearings.

Hadoop Components and Ecosystem

In this section, we will provide a 50,000-foot view of the Hadoop ecosystem components that are covered throughout the book. This will help to introduce components before talking about the security of them in later chapters. Readers that are well versed in the components listed can safely skip to the next section. Unless otherwise noted, security features described throughout this book apply to the versions of the associated project listed in Table 1-1.

Table 1-1. Project versions[a]

Project	Version
Apache HDFS	2.3.0
Apache MapReduce (for MR1)	1.2.1
Apache YARN (for MR2)	2.3.0
Apache Hive	0.12.0
Cloudera Impala	2.0.0
Apache HBase	0.98.0
Apache Accumulo	1.6.0
Apache Solr	4.4.0
Apache Oozie	4.0.0
Cloudera Hue	3.5.0

Project	Version
Apache ZooKeeper	3.4.5
Apache Flume	1.5.0
Apache Sqoop	1.4.4
Apache Sentry (Incubating)	1.4.0-incubating

[a] An astute reader will notice some omissions in the list of projects covered. In particular, there is no mention of Apache Spark, Apache Ranger, or Apache Knox. These projects were omitted due to time constraints and given their status as relatively new additions to the Hadoop ecosystem.

Apache HDFS

The *Hadoop Distributed File System*, or HDFS, is often considered the foundation component for the rest of the Hadoop ecosystem. HDFS is the storage layer for Hadoop and provides the ability to store mass amounts of data while growing storage capacity and aggregate bandwidth in a linear fashion. HDFS is a *logical* filesystem that spans many servers, each with multiple hard drives. This is important to understand from a security perspective because a given file in HDFS can span many or all servers in the Hadoop cluster. This means that client interactions with a given file might require communication with every node in the cluster. This is made possible by a key implementation feature of HDFS that breaks up files into *blocks*. Each block of data for a given file can be stored on any physical drive on any node in the cluster. Because this is a complex topic that we cannot cover in depth here, we are omitting the details of how that works and recommend *Hadoop: The Definitive Guide, 3rd Edition* by Tom White (O'Reilly). The important security takeaway is that all files in HDFS are broken up into blocks, and clients using HDFS will communicate over the network to all of the servers in the Hadoop cluster when reading and writing files.

HDFS is built on a head/worker architecture and is comprised of two primary components: NameNode (head) and DataNode (worker). Additional components include JournalNode, HttpFS, and NFS Gateway:

NameNode

The NameNode is responsible for keeping track of all the metadata related to the files in HDFS, such as filenames, block locations, file permissions, and replication. From a security perspective, it is important to know that clients of HDFS, such as those reading or writing files, *always* communicate with the NameNode. Additionally, the NameNode provides several important security functions for the entire Hadoop ecosystem, which are described later.

DataNode

The DataNode is responsible for the actual storage and retrieval of data blocks in HDFS. Clients of HDFS reading a given file are told by the NameNode which DataNode in the cluster has the block of data requested. When writing data to HDFS, clients write a block of data to a DataNode determined by the NameNode. From there, that DataNode sets up a write pipeline to other DataNodes to complete the write based on the desired replication factor.

JournalNode

The JournalNode is a special type of component for HDFS. When HDFS is configured for *high availability (HA)*, JournalNodes take over the NameNode responsibility for writing HDFS metadata information. Clusters typically have an odd number of JournalNodes (usually three or five) to ensure majority. For example, if a new file is written to HDFS, the metadata about the file is written to every JournalNode. When the majority of the JournalNodes successfully write this information, the change is considered durable. HDFS clients and DataNodes do not interact with JournalNodes directly.

HttpFS

HttpFS is a component of HDFS that provides a proxy for clients to the NameNode and DataNodes. This proxy is a REST API and allows clients to communicate to the proxy to use HDFS without having direct connectivity to any of the other components in HDFS. HttpFS will be a key component in certain cluster architectures, as we will see later in the book.

NFS Gateway

The NFS gateway, as the name implies, allows for clients to use HDFS like an NFS-mounted filesystem. The NFS gateway is an actual daemon process that facilitates the NFS protocol communication between clients and the underlying HDFS cluster. Much like HttpFS, the NFS gateway sits between HDFS and clients and therefore affords a security boundary that can be useful in certain cluster architectures.

KMS

The *Hadoop Key Management Server*, or KMS, plays an important role in HDFS transparent encryption at rest. Its purpose is to act as the intermediary between HDFS clients, the NameNode, and a key server, handling encryption operations such as decrypting data encryption keys and managing encryption zone keys. This is covered in detail in Chapter 9.

Apache YARN

As Hadoop evolved, it became apparent that the MapReduce processing framework, while incredibly powerful, did not address the needs of additional use cases. Many problems are not easily solved, if at all, using the MapReduce programming paradigm. What was needed was a more generic framework that could better fit additional processing models. Apache YARN provides this capability. Other processing frameworks and applications, such as Impala and Spark, use YARN as the resource management framework. While YARN provides a more general resource management framework, MapReduce is still the canonical application that runs on it. MapReduce that runs on YARN is considered version 2, or MR2 for short. The YARN architecture consists of the following components:

ResourceManager

The ResourceManager daemon is responsible for application submission requests, assigning ApplicationMaster tasks, and enforcing resource management policies.

JobHistory Server

The JobHistory Server, as the name implies, keeps track of the history of all jobs that have run on the YARN framework. This includes job metrics like running time, number of tasks run, amount of data written to HDFS, and so on.

NodeManager

The NodeManager daemon is responsible for launching individual tasks for jobs within YARN *containers*, which consist of virtual cores (CPU resources) and RAM resources. Individual tasks can request some number of virtual cores and memory depending on its needs. The minimum, maximum, and increment ranges are defined by the ResourceManager. Tasks execute as separate processes with their own JVM. One important role of the NodeManager is to launch a special task called the *ApplicationMaster*. This task is responsible for managing the status of all tasks for the given application. YARN separates resource management from task management to better scale YARN applications in large clusters as each job executes its own ApplicationMaster.

Apache MapReduce

MapReduce is the processing counterpart to HDFS and provides the most basic mechanism to batch process data. When MapReduce is executed on top of YARN, it is often called MapReduce2, or MR2. This distinguishes the YARN-based verison of MapReduce from the standalone MapReduce framework, which has been retroactively named MR1. MapReduce *jobs* are submitted by clients to the MapReduce framework and operate over a subset of data in HDFS, usually a specified directory. MapReduce itself is a programming paradigm that allows chunks of data, or blocks in the case of HDFS, to be processed by multiple servers in parallel, independent of one another. While a Hadoop developer needs to know the intricacies of how MapReduce works, a security architect largely does not. What a security architect needs to know is that clients submit their jobs to the MapReduce framework and from that point on, the MapReduce framework handles the distribution and execution of the client code across the cluster. Clients do not interact with any of the nodes in the cluster to make their job run. Jobs themselves require some number of *tasks* to be run to complete the work. Each task is started on a given node by the MapReduce framework's scheduling algorithm.

Individual tasks started by the MapReduce framework on a given server are executed as different users depending on whether Kerberos is enabled. Without Kerberos enabled, individual tasks are run as the *mapred* system user. When Kerberos is enabled, the individual tasks are executed as the user that submitted the MapReduce job. However, even if Kerberos is enabled, it may not be immediately apparent which user is executing the underlying MapReduce tasks when another component or tool is submitting the MapReduce job. See "Impersonation" on page 82 for a relevant detailed discussion regarding Hive impersonation.

Similar to HDFS, MapReduce is also a head/worker architecture and is comprised of two primary components:

JobTracker (head)

When clients submit jobs to the MapReduce framework, they are communicating with the JobTracker. The JobTracker handles the submission of jobs by clients and determines how jobs are to be run by deciding things like how many tasks the job requires and which TaskTrackers will handle a given task. The JobTracker also handles security and operational features such as job queues, scheduling pools, and access control lists to determine authorization. Lastly, the JobTracker handles job metrics and other information about the job, which are communicated to it from the various TaskTrackers throughout the execution of a given job. The JobTracker includes both resource management and task management, which were split in MR2 between the ResourceManager and ApplicationMaster.

TaskTracker (worker)

TaskTrackers are responsible for executing a given task that is part of a MapReduce job. TaskTrackers receive tasks to run from the JobTracker, and spawn off separate JVM processes for each task they run. TaskTrackers execute both map and reduce tasks, and the amount of each that can be run concurrently is part of the MapReduce configuration. The important takeaway from a security standpoint is that the JobTracker decides what tasks to be run and on which TaskTrackers. Clients do not have control over how tasks are assigned, nor do they communicate with TaskTrackers as part of normal job execution.

A key point about MapReduce is that other Hadoop ecosystem components are frameworks and libraries on top of MapReduce, meaning that MapReduce handles the actual processing of data, but these frameworks and libraries abstract the MapReduce job execution from clients. Hive, Pig, and Sqoop are examples of components that use MapReduce in this fashion.

 Understanding how MapReduce jobs are submitted is an important part of user auditing in Hadoop, and is discussed in detail in "Block access tokens" on page 79. A user submitting her own Java MapReduce code is a much different activity from a security point of view than a user using Sqoop to import data from a RDBMS or executing a SQL query in Hive, even though all three of these activities use MapReduce.

Apache Hive

The Apache Hive project was started by Facebook. The company saw the utility of MapReduce to process data but found limitations in adoption of the framework due to the lack of Java programming skills in its analyst communities. Most of Facebook's analysts did have SQL skills, so the Hive project was started to serve as a SQL abstraction layer that uses MapReduce as the execution engine. The Hive architecture consists of the following components:

Metastore database

> The metastore database is a relational database that contains all the Hive metadata, such as information about databases, tables, columns, and data types. This information is used to apply structure to the underlying data in HDFS at the time of access, also known as *schema on read*.

Metastore server

> The Hive Metastore Server is a daemon that sits between Hive clients and the metastore database. This affords a layer of security by not allowing clients to have the database credentials to the Hive metastore.

HiveServer2

> HiveServer2 is the main access point for clients using Hive. HiveServer2 accepts JDBC and ODBC clients, and for this reason is leveraged by a variety of client tools and other third-party applications.

HCatalog

> HCatalog is a series of libraries that allow non-Hive frameworks to have access to Hive metadata. For example, users of Pig can use HCatalog to read schema information about a given directory of files in HDFS. The WebHCat server is a daemon process that exposes a REST interface to clients, which in turn access HCatalog APIs.

For more thorough coverage of Hive, have a look at *Programming Hive* by Edward Capriolo, Dean Wampler, and Jason Rutherglen (O'Reilly).

Cloudera Impala

Cloudera Impala is a massive parallel processing (MPP) framework that is purpose-built for analytic SQL. Impala reads data from HDFS and utilizes the Hive metastore for interpreting data structures and formats. The Impala architecture consists of the following components:

Impala daemon (impalad)
> The Impala daemon does all of the heavy lifting of data processing. These daemons are collocated with HDFS DataNodes to optimize for local reads.

StateStore
> The StateStore daemon process maintains state information about all of the Impala daemons running. It monitors whether Impala daemons are up or down, and broadcasts status to all of the daemons. The StateStore is not a required component in the Impala architecture, but it does provide for faster failure tolerance in the case where one or more daemons have gone down.

Catalog server
> The Catalog server is Impala's gateway into the Hive metastore. This process is responsible for pulling metadata from the Hive metastore and synchronizing metadata changes that have occurred by way of Impala clients. Having a separate Catalog server helps to reduce the load the Hive metastore server encounters, as well as to provide additional optimizations for Impala for speed.

> New users to the Hadoop ecosystem often ask what the difference is between Hive and Impala because they both offer SQL access to data in HDFS. Hive was created to allow users that are familiar with SQL to process data in HDFS without needing to know anything about MapReduce. It was designed to abstract the innards of MapReduce to make the data in HDFS more accessible. Hive is largely used for batch access and ETL work. Impala, on the other hand, was designed from the ground up to be a fast analytic processing engine to support ad hoc queries and business intelligence (BI) tools. There is utility in both Hive and Impala, and they should be treated as complementary components.

For more thorough coverage of all things Impala, check out *Getting Started with Impala* (O'Reilly).

Apache Sentry (Incubating)

Sentry is the component that provides fine-grained role-based access controls (RBAC) to several of the other ecosystem components, such as Hive and Impala. While individual components may have their own authorization mechanism, Sentry provides a unified authorization that allows centralized policy enforcement across components. It is a critical component of Hadoop security, which is why we have dedicated an entire chapter to the topic (Chapter 7). Sentry consists of the following components:

Sentry server
> The Sentry server is a daemon process that facilitates policy lookups made by other Hadoop ecosystem components. Client components of Sentry are configured to delegate authorization decisions based on the policies put in place by Sentry.

Policy database
> The Sentry policy database is the location where all authorization policies are stored. The Sentry server uses the policy database to determine if a user is allowed to perform a given action. Specifically, the Sentry server looks for a matching policy that grants access to a resource for the user. In earlier versions of Sentry, the policy database was a text file that contained all of the policies. The evolution of Sentry and the policy database is discussed in detail in Chapter 7.

Apache HBase

Apache HBase is a distributed key/value store inspired by Google's BigTable paper, "BigTable: A Distributed Storage System for Structured Data" (*http://research.google.com/archive/bigtable-osdi06.pdf*). HBase typically utilizes HDFS as the underlying storage layer for data, and for the purposes of this book we will assume that is the case. HBase *tables* are broken up into *regions*. These regions are partitioned by *row key*, which is the index portion of a given key. Row IDs are sorted, thus a given region has a range of sorted row keys. Regions are hosted by a *RegionServer*, where clients request data by a key. The key is comprised of several components: the row key, the *column family*, the *column qualifier*, and the *timestamp*. These components together uniquely identify a value stored in the table.

Clients accessing HBase first look up the RegionServers that are responsible for hosting a particular range of row keys. This lookup is done by scanning the hbase:meta table. When the right RegionServer is located, the client will make read/write requests directly to that RegionServer rather than through the master. The client caches the mapping of regions to RegionServers to avoid going through the lookup process. The location of the server hosting the hbase:meta table is looked up in ZooKeeper. HBase consists of the following components:

Master

> As stated, the HBase Master daemon is responsible for managing the regions that are hosted by which RegionServers. If a given RegionServer goes down, the HBase Master is responsible for reassigning the region to a different Region-Server. Multiple HBase Masters can be run simultaneously and the HBase Masters will use ZooKeeper to elect a single HBase Master to be active at any one time.

RegionServer

> RegionServers are responsible for serving regions of a given HBase table. Regions are sorted ranges of keys; they can either be defined manually using the HBase shell or automatically defined by HBase over time based upon the keys that are ingested into the table. One of HBase's goals is to evenly distribute the key-space, giving each RegionServer an equal responsibility in serving data. Each Region-Server typically hosts multiple regions.

REST server

> The HBase REST server provides a REST API to perform HBase operations. The default HBase API is provided by a Java API, just like many of the other Hadoop ecosystem projects. The REST API is commonly used as a language agnostic interface to allow clients to utilize any programming they wish.

Thrift server

> In addition to the REST server, HBase also has a Thrift server. This serves as yet another useful API interface for clients to leverage.

For more information on the architecture of HBase and the use cases it is best suited for, we recommend *HBase: The Definitive Guide* by Lars George (O'Reilly).

Apache Accumulo

Apache Accumulo (*http://accumulo.apache.org*) is a sorted and distributed key/value store designed to be a robust, scalable, high-performance storage and retrieval system. Like HBase, Accumulo was originally based on the Google BigTable design, but was built on top of the Apache Hadoop ecosystem of projects (in particular, HDFS, ZooKeeper, and Apache Thrift). Accumulo uses roughly the same data model as HBase. Each Accumulo table is split into one or more tablets that contains a roughly equal number of records distributed by the record's row ID. Each record also has a multipart column key that includes a column family, column qualifier, and visibility label. The visibility label was one of Accumulo's first major departures from the original BigTable design. Visibility labels added the ability to implement cell-level security (we'll discuss them in more detail in Chapter 6). Finally, each record also contains a timestamp that allows users to store multiple versions of records that otherwise share the same record key. Collectively, the row ID, column, and timestamp make up a record's key, which is associated with a particular value.

The tablets are distributed by splitting up the set of row IDs. The split points are calculated automatically as data is inserted into a table. Each tablet is hosted by a single TabletServer that is responsible for serving reads and writes to data in the given tablet. Each TabletServer can host multiple tablets from the same tables and/or different tables. This makes the tablet the unit of distribution in the system.

When clients first access Accumulo, they look up the location of the TabletServer hosting the accumulo.root table. The accumulo.root table stores the information for how the accumulo.meta table is split into tablets. The client will directly communicate with the TabletServer hosting accumulo.root and then again for TabletServers that are hosting the tablets of the accumulo.meta table. Because the data in these tables—especially accumulo.root—changes relatively less frequently than other data, the client will maintain a cache of tablet locations read from these tables to avoid bottlenecks in the read/write pipeline. Once the client has the location of the tablets for the row IDs that it is reading/writing, it will communicate directly with the required TabletServers. At no point does the client have to interact with the Master, and this greatly aids scalability. Overall, Accumulo consists of the following components:

Master

> The Accumulo Master is responsible for coordinating the assignment of tablets to TabletServers. It ensures that each tablet is hosted by exactly one TabletServer and responds to events such as a TabletServer failing. It also handles administrative changes to a table and coordinates startup, shutdown, and write-ahead log recovery. Multiple Masters can be run simultaneously and they will elect a leader so that only one Master is active at a time.

TabletServer

> The TabletServer handles all read/write requests for a subset of the tablets in the Accumulo cluster. For writes, it handles writing the records to the write-ahead log and flushing the in-memory records to disk periodically. During recovery, the TabletServer replays the records from the write-ahead log into the tablet being recovered.

GarbageCollector

> The GarbageCollector periodically deletes files that are no longer needed by any Accumulo process. Multiple GarbageCollectors can be run simultaneously and they will elect a leader so that only one GarbageCollector is active at a time.

Tracer

> The Tracer monitors the rest of the cluster using Accumulo's distributed timing API and writes the data into an Accumulo table for future reference. Multiple Tracers can be run simultaneously and they will distribute the load evenly among them.

Monitor

The Monitor is a web application for monitoring the state of the Accumulo cluster. It displays key metrics such as record count, cache hit/miss rates, and table information such as scan rate. The Monitor also acts as an endpoint for log forwarding so that errors and warnings can be diagnosed from a single interface.

Apache Solr

The Apache Solr project, and specifically *SolrCloud*, enables the search and retrieval of *documents* that are part of a larger *collection* that has been *sharded* across multiple physical servers. Search is one of the canonical use cases for big data and is one of the most common utilities used by anyone accessing the Internet. Solr is built on top of the Apache Lucene project, which actually handles the bulk of the indexing and search capabilities. Solr expands on these capabilities by providing enterprise search features such as faceted navigation, caching, hit highlighting, and an administration interface.

Solr has a single component, the server. There can be many Solr servers in a single deployment, which scale out linearly through the sharding provided by SolrCloud. SolrCloud also provides replication features to accommodate failures in a distributed environment.

Apache Oozie

Apache Oozie is a workflow management and orchestration system for Hadoop. It allows for setting up workflows that contain various *actions*, each of which can utilize a different component in the Hadoop ecosystem. For example, an Oozie workflow could start by executing a Sqoop import to move data into HDFS, then a Pig script to transform the data, followed by a Hive script to set up metadata structures. Oozie allows for more complex workflows, such as forks and joins that allow multiple steps to be executed in parallel, and other steps that rely on multiple steps to be completed before continuing. Oozie workflows can run on a repeatable schedule based on different types of input conditions such as running at a certain time or waiting until a certain path exists in HDFS.

Oozie consists of just a single server component, and this server is responsible for handling client workflow submissions, managing the execution of workflows, and reporting status.

Apache ZooKeeper

Apache ZooKeeper is a distributed coordination service that allows for distributed systems to store and read small amounts of data in a synchronized way. It is often used for storing common configuration information. Additionally, ZooKeeper is heavily used in the Hadoop ecosystem for synchronizing high availability (HA) services, such as NameNode HA and ResourceManager HA.

ZooKeeper itself is a distributed system that relies on an odd number of servers called a ZooKeeper *ensemble* to reach a *quorum*, or majority, to acknowledge a given transaction. ZooKeeper has only one component, the ZooKeeper server.

Apache Flume

Apache Flume is an event-based ingestion tool that is used primarily for ingestion into Hadoop, but can actually be used completely independent of it. Flume, as the name would imply, was initially created for the purpose of ingesting log events into HDFS. The Flume architecture consists of three main pieces: sources, sinks, and channels.

A Flume source defines how data is to be read from the upstream provider. This would include things like a syslog server, a JMS queue, or even polling a Linux directory. A Flume sink defines how data should be written downstream. Common Flume sinks include an HDFS sink and an HBase sink. Lastly, a Flume channel defines how data is stored between the source and sink. The two primary Flume channels are the memory channel and file channel. The memory channel affords speed at the cost of reliability, and the file channel provides reliability at the cost of speed.

Flume consists of a single component, a Flume *agent*. Agents contain the code for sources, sinks, and channels. An important part of the Flume architecture is that Flume agents can be connected to each other, where the sink of one agent connects to the source of another. A common interface in this case is using an Avro source and sink. Flume ingestion and security is covered in Chapter 10 and in Using Flume (*http://shop.oreilly.com/product/0636920030348.do*).

Apache Sqoop

Apache Sqoop provides the ability to do batch imports and exports of data to and from a traditional RDBMS, as well as other data sources such as FTP servers. Sqoop itself submits map-only MapReduce jobs that launch tasks to interact with the RDBMS in a parallel fashion. Sqoop is used both as an easy mechanism to initially seed a Hadoop cluster with data, as well as a tool used for regular ingestion and extraction routines. There are currently two different versions of Sqoop: Sqoop1 and Sqoop2. In this book, the focus is on Sqoop1. Sqoop2 is still not feature complete at the time of this writing, and is missing some fundamental security features, such as Kerberos authentication.

Sqoop1 is a set of client libraries that are invoked from the command line using the sqoop binary. These client libraries are responsible for the actual submission of the MapReduce job to the proper framework (e.g., traditional MapReduce or MapReduce2 on YARN). Sqoop is discussed in more detail in Chapter 10 and in Apache Sqoop Cookbook (*http://shop.oreilly.com/product/0636920029519.do*).

Cloudera Hue

Cloudera Hue is a web application that exposes many of the Hadoop ecosystem components in a user-friendly way. Hue allows for easy access into the Hadoop cluster without requiring users to be familiar with Linux or the various command-line interfaces the components have. Hue has several different security controls available, which we'll look at in Chapter 12. Hue is comprised of the following components:

Hue server
> This is the main component of Hue. It is effectively a web server that serves web content to users. Users are authenticated at first logon and from there, actions performed by the end user are actually done by Hue itself *on behalf of* the user. This concept is known as *impersonation* (covered in Chapter 5).

Kerberos Ticket Renewer
> As the name implies, this component is responsible for periodically renewing the *Kerberos ticket-granting ticket (TGT)*, which Hue uses to interact with the Hadoop cluster when the cluster has Kerberos enabled (Kerberos is discussed at length in Chapter 4).

Summary

This chapter introduced some common security terminology that builds the foundation of the topics covered throughout the rest of the book. A key takeaway from this chapter is to become comfortable with the fact that security for Hadoop is not a completely foreign discussion. Tried-and-true security principles such as CIA and AAA resonate in the Hadoop context and will be discussed at length in the chapters to come. Lastly, we took a look at many of the Hadoop ecosystem projects (and their individual components) to understand their purpose in the stack, and to get a sense at how security will apply.

In the next chapter, we will dive right into securing distributed systems. You will find that many of the security threats and mitigations that apply to Hadoop are generally applicable to distributed systems.

## PART I

Security Architecture

## CHAPTER 2

Securing Distributed Systems

In Chapter 1, we covered several key principles of secure computing. In this chapter, we will take a closer look at the interesting challenges that are present when considering the security of distributed systems. As we will see, being distributed considerably increases the potential threats to the system, thus also increasing the complexity of security measures needed to help mitigate those threats. A real-life example will help illustrate how security requirements increase when a system becomes more distributed.

Let's consider a bank as an example. Many years ago, everyday banking for the average person meant driving down to the local bank, visiting a bank teller, and conducting transactions in person. The bank's security measures would have included checking the person's identification, and account number, and verifying that the requested action could be performed, such as ensuring there was enough money in the account to cover a withdrawal.

Over the years, banks became larger. Your local hometown bank probably became a branch of a larger bank, thus giving you the ability to conduct banking not just at the bank's nearby location but also at any of its other locations. The security measures necessary to protect assets have grown because there is no longer just a single physical location to protect. Also, more bank tellers need to be properly trained.

Taking this a step further, banks eventually started making use of ATMs to allow customers to withdraw money without having to go to a branch location. As you might imagine, even more security controls are necessary to protect the bank beyond what was required when banking was a human interaction. Next, banks became interconnected with other banks, which allowed customers from one bank to use the ATMs of a different bank. Banks then needed to establish security controls between themselves to ensure that no security was lost as a result of this interconnectivity. Lastly, the Internet movement introduced the ability to do online banking through a website, or even from mobile devices. This dramatically increased potential threats and the security controls needed.

As you can see, what started as a straightforward security task to protect a small bank in your town has become orders of magnitude more difficult the more distributed and interconnected the bank became over decades of time. While this example might seem obvious, it starts to frame the problem of how to design a security architecture for a system that can be distributed across tens, hundreds, or even thousands of machines. It is no small task but it can be made less intimidating by breaking it down into pieces, starting with understanding threats.

Threat Categories

A key component to arriving at a robust security architecture for a distributed system is to understand the threats that are likely to be present, and to be able to categorize them to better understand what security mechanisms need to be in place to help mitigate those threats. In this section, we will review a few common threat categories that are important to be aware of. The threat categories will help you identify where the threats are coming from, what security features are needed to protect against them, and how to respond to an incident if and when it happens.

Unauthorized Access/Masquerade

One of the most common threat categories comes in the form of unauthorized access. This happens when someone successfully accesses a system when he should have otherwise been denied access. One common way for this to happen is from a *masquerade* attack. Masquerade is the notion that an invalid user presents himself as a valid user in order to gain access. You might wonder how the invalid user presented himself as a valid user. The most likely answer that the attacker obtained a valid username and associated password.

Masquerade attacks are especially prominent since the age of the Internet, and specifically for distributed systems. Attackers have a variety of ways to obtain valid usernames and passwords, such as trying common words and phrases as passwords, or knowing words that are related to the valid user that might be used as a password. For example, attackers looking to obtain valid login credentials for a social media website, might collect keywords from a person's public posts to come up with a password list to try (e.g., if the attackers were focusing on New York–based users who list "baseball" as a hobby, they might try the password *yankees*).

In the case of an invalid user executing a successful masquerade attack, how would a security administrator know? After all, if an attacker logged in with a valid user's credentials, wouldn't this appear as normal from the distributed system's perspective? Not necessarily. Typically, masquerade attacks can be profiled by looking at audit logs for login attempts. If an attacker is using a list of possible passwords to try against a user account, the unsuccessful attempts should show up in audit logfiles. Seeing a high number of failed login attempts for a user can usually be attributed to an attack. A valid user might mistype or forget her password, leading to a small number of failed login attempts, but 20 successive failed login attempts, for example, would be unusual.

Another common footprint for masquerade attacks is to look at where, from a network perspective, the login attempts are coming from. Profiling login attempts by IP addresses can be a good way to discover if a masquerade attack is attempted. Are the IP addresses shown as the client attempting to log in consistent with what is expected, such as coming from a known subnet of company IP addresses, or are they sourced from another country on the other side of the world? Also, what time of day did the login attempts occur? Did Alice try to login to the system at 3:00 a.m., or did she log in during normal business hours?

Another form of unauthorized access comes from an attacker exploiting a vulnerability in the system, thus gaining entry without needing to present valid credentials. Vulnerabilities are discussed in "Vulnerabilities" on page 28.

Insider Threat

Arguably the single most damaging threat category is the *insider threat*. As the name implies, the attacker comes from inside the business and is a regular user. Insider threats can include employees, consultants, and contractors. What makes the insider threat so scary is that the attacker already has internal access to the system. The attacker can log in with valid credentials, get authorized by the system to perform a certain function, and pass any number of security checks along the way because she is *supposed* to be granted access. This can result in a blatant attack on a system, or something much more subtle like the attacker leaking sensitive data to unauthorized users by leveraging her own accesses.

Throughout this book, you will find security features that ensure that the right users are accessing only the data and services they should be. Combating insider threats requires effective auditing practices (described in Chapter 8). In addition to the technical tools available to help combat the insider threat, business policies need to be established to enforce proper auditing, and procedures that respond to incidents must be outlined. The need for these policies is true for all of the threat categories described in this chapter, though best practices for setting such policies are not covered.

Denial of Service

Denial of service (DoS), is a situation where a service is unavailable to one or more clients. The term *service* in this case is an umbrella that includes access to data, processing capabilities, and the general usability of the system in question. How the denial of service happens can come from a variety of different attack vectors. In the age of the Internet, a common attack vector is to simply overwhelm the system in question with excessive network traffic. This is done by using many computers in parallel, thus making the attack a *distributed denial of service (DDoS)*. When the system is bombarded with too many requests for it to handle, it starts failing in some way, from dropping other valid requests to outright failure of the system.

While distributed systems typically benefit from having fault tolerance of some kind, DoS attacks are still possible. For example, if a distributed system contains 50 servers, it might be difficult for attackers to disrupt service to all 50 machines. What if the distributed system is behind just a few network devices, such as a network firewall and an access switch? Attackers can use this to their advantage by targeting the gateway into the distributed system rather than the distributed system itself. This point is important and will be covered in Chapter 3 when discuss about architecting a network perimeter around the cluster.

Threats to Data

Data is the single most important component of a distributed system. Without data, a distributed system is nothing more than an idle hum of servers that rack up the electric and cooling bills in a data center. Because data is so important, it is also the focus of security attacks. Threats to data are present in multiple places in a distributed system. First, data must be stored in a secure fashion to prevent unauthorized viewing, tampering, or deletion. Next, data must also be protected *in transit*, because distributed systems are, well, distributed. The passing of data across a network can be threatened by something disruptive like a DoS attack, or something more passive such as an attacker capturing the network traffic unbeknownst to the communicating parties. In Chapter 1, we discussed the CIA model and its components. Ultimately, the CIA model is all about mitigating threats to data.

Threat and Risk Assessment

The coverage of threat categories in the previous section probably was not the first time you have heard about these things. It's important that in addition to understanding these threat categories you also assess the *risk* to your particular distributed system. For example, while a denial-of-service attack may be highly likely to occur for systems that are directly connected to the Internet, systems that have no outside network access, such as those on a company intranet, have a much lower risk of this actually happening. Notice that the risk is *low* and not completely removed, an important distinction.

Assessing the threats to a distributed system involves taking a closer look at two key components: the users and the environment. Once you understand these components, assessing risk becomes more manageable.

User Assessment

It's important to understand what users your distributed system will be exposed to. This obviously includes users who will be accessing the system and directly interacting with the interfaces it provides. It also includes users who might be present elsewhere in the environment but won't directly access the system. Understanding users in this context leads to a better risk assessment. Users of a distributed system like Hadoop typically are first classified by their line of business. What do these users do? Are they business intelligence analysts? Developers? Risk analysts? Security auditors? Data quality analysts?

Once users are classified into groups by business function, you can start to identify access patterns and tools that these groups of users need in order to use the distributed system. For example, if the users of the distributed system are all developers, several assumptions can be made about the need for shell access to nodes in the system, logfiles to debug jobs, and developer tools. On the other hand, business intelligence analysts might not need any of those things and will instead require a suite of analytical tools that interact with the distributed system on the user's behalf.

There will also be users with indirect access to the system. These users won't need access to data or processing resources of the system. However, they'll still interact with it as a part of, for example, support functions such as system maintenance, health monitoring, and user auditing. These types of users need to be accounted for in the overall security model.

Environment Assessment

To assess the risk for our distributed system, we'll also need to understand the *environment* it resides in. Generally, this will mean assessing the operational environment both in relation to other logical systems and the physical world. We'll take a look at the specifics for Hadoop in Chapter 3.

One of the key criteria for assessing the environment, mentioned briefly, is to look at whether the distributed system is accessible to the Internet. If so, a whole host of threats are far more likely to be realized, such as DoS attacks, vulnerability exploits, and viruses. Distributed systems that are indeed connected to the Internet will require constant monitoring and alerting, as well as a regular cadence for applying software patches and updating various security software definitions.

Another criteria to evaluate the environment is to understand where the servers that comprise the distributed system are physically located. Are they located in your company data center? Are they in a third-party–managed data center? Are they in a public cloud infrastructure? Understanding the answer to these questions will start to frame the problem of providing a security assessment. For example, if the distributed system is hosted in a public cloud, a few threats are immediately apparent: the infrastructure is not owned by your company, so you do not definitively know who has direct access to the machines. This expands the scope of insider threat to include your hosting provider. Also, the usage of a public cloud begs the question of how your users are connecting to the distributed system and how data flows into and out of it. Again, threats to communications that occur across an open network to a shared public cloud have a much higher risk of happening than those that are within your own company data center.

The point is not to scare you into thinking that public clouds are bad and company data centers are good, but rather to impart that the existence of one versus another will vary the level of risk that a given threat may have against your distributed system. Regardless of the environment, the key to protecting your distributed system is to look at risk mitigation in a multitiered approach, as discussed in the next section.

Vulnerabilities

Vulnerabilities are a separate topic, but they are related to the discussion of threats and risk. Vulnerabilities exist in a variety of different forms in a distributed system. A common place for vulnerabilities is in the software itself. *All* software has vulnerabilities. This might seem like a harsh statement, but the truth of it is that no piece of software is 100% secure.

So what exactly is a software vulnerability? Put simply, it's a piece of code that is susceptible to some kind of error or failure condition that is not accounted for gracefully. For instance, consider the simple example of a piece of software with a password screen that allows users to change their password (we will assume that the intended logic for the software is to allow passwords up to 16 characters in length). What happens if the input field for a new password mistakenly has a maximum length of 8 characters, and thus truncates the chosen password? This could lead to users setting shorter passwords than they realized, and worse, less complex passwords that are easier for an attacker to guess.

Certainly, software vulnerabilities are not the only type of vulnerabilities that distributed systems are susceptible to. Other vulnerabilities include those related to the network infrastructure that a distributed system relies on. For example, many years ago there was a vulnerability that allowed an attacker to send a ping to a network broadcast address, causing every host in the network range to reply with a ping response. The attacker crafted the ping request so that the source IP address was set to a computer that was the intended target of the attack. The result was that the target host of the attack was overwhelmed with network communication to the point of failure. This attack was known as the *ping of death*. It has been mitigated, but the point is that until this was fixed by network hardware vendors, this was a vulnerability that had nothing to do with the software stack of machines on the network, yet an attacker could use it to disrupt the service of a particular machine on the network.

Software patches are regularly released to fix vulnerabilities as they are discovered, thus regular schedules for applying patches to a distributed system's software stack should be an integral part of every administrator's standard operating procedures. As the ping-of-death example shows, the scope of patches should also include firmware for switches, routers, other networking equipment, disk controllers, and the server BIOS.

Defense in Depth

One of the challenges that security administrators face is how to mitigate all of the threat categories and vulnerabilities discussed in this chapter. When looking at the variety of threat categories, it becomes immediately apparent that there is no single silver bullet that can effectively stop these threats. In order to have a fighting chance, many security controls must be in place—and must work together—in order to provide a comfortable level of security. This idea of deploying multiple security controls and protection methods is called *defense in depth*.

Looking back in history, defense in depth was not regularly followed. Security typically meant *perimeter security*, in that security controls existed only on the outside, or perimeter, of whatever was to be protected. A canonical example of this is imagining a thick, tall wall surrounding a castle. The mindset was that as long as the wall stood, the castle was safe. If the wall was breached, that was bad news for the castle dwellers. Today, things have gotten better.

Defense-in-depth security now exists in our everyday lives. Take the example of going to a grocery store. The grocery store has a door with a lock on it, and is only unlocked during normal business hours. There is also an alarm system that is triggered if an intruder illegally enters the building after hours. During regular hours, shoppers are monitored with security cameras throughout the store. Finally, store employees are trained to watch for patrons behaving suspiciously.

All of these security measures are in place to protect the grocery store from a variety of different threats, such as break-ins, shoplifters, and robberies. Had the grocery store only relied on the "castle wall" approach by only relying on strong door locks, most threats would not be addressed. Defense in depth is important here because any single security measure is not likely to mitigate all threats to the store. The same is true for distributed systems. There are many places where individual security measures can be deployed, such as setting up a network firewall around the perimeter, restrictive permissions on data, or access controls to the servers. But implementing all of these measures together helps to lower the chances that an attack will be successful.

Summary

In this chapter, we broke down distributed system security by analyzing threat categories and vulnerabilities, and demonstrating that applying a defense-in-depth security architecture will minimize security risks. We also discussed the insider threat and why it should not be overlooked when designing security architecture.

The next chapter focuses on protecting Hadoop in particular, and building a sound system architecture is the first step.

## CHAPTER 3

System Architecture

In Chapter 2, we took a look at how the security landscape changes when going from individual isolated systems to a fully distributed network of systems. It becomes immediately apparent just how daunting a task it is to secure hundreds if not thousands of servers in a single Hadoop cluster. In this chapter, we dive into the details of taking on this challenge by breaking the cluster down into several components that can independently be secured as part of an overall security strategy. At a high level, the Hadoop cluster can be divided into two major areas: the network and the hosts. But before we do this, let's explore the operating environment in which the Hadoop cluster resides.

Operating Environment

In the early days of Hadoop, a *cluster* likely meant a hodgepodge of repurposed machines used to try out the new technology. You might even have used old desktop-class machines and a couple of extra access switches to wire them up. Things have changed dramatically over the years. The days of stacking a few machines in the corner of a room has been replaced by the notion that Hadoop clusters are first-class citizens in real enterprises. Where Hadoop clusters physically and logically fit into the enterprise is called the *operating environment*.

Numerous factors that contribute to the choice of operating environment for Hadoop are out of scope of this book. We will focus on the typical operating environments in use today. As a result of rapid advances in server and network hardware (thank Moore's law), Hadoop can live in a few different environments:

In-house

This Hadoop environment consists of a collection of physical ("bare metal") machines that are owned and operated by the business, and live in data centers under the control of the business.

Managed

This Hadoop environment is a variation of in-house in that it consists of physical machines, but the business does not own and operate them. They are rented from a separate business that handles the full provisioning and maintenance of the servers, and the servers live in their own data centers.

Cloud

This Hadoop environment looks very different than the others. A cloud environment consists of virtual servers that may physically reside in many different locations. The most popular cloud provider for Hadoop environments is Amazon's Elastic Compute Cloud (EC2).

Network Security

Network security is a detailed topic and certainly cannot be covered exhaustively here. Instead, we will focus on a few important network security topics that are commonly used to secure a Hadoop cluster's network. The first of these is *network segmentation*.

Network Segmentation

Network segmentation is a common practice of isolating machines and services to a separate part of a larger network. This practice holds true no matter if we are talking about Hadoop clusters, web servers, department workstations, or some other system. Creating a network segment can be done in two different ways, often together.

The first option is *physical* network segmentation. This is achieved by sectioning off a portion of the network with devices such as routers, switches, and firewalls. While these devices operate at higher layers of the OSI model, from a physical-layer point of view the separation is just that all devices on one network segment are physically plugged into network devices that are separate from other devices on the larger network.

The second option is *logical* network segmentation. Logical segmentation operates at higher layers of the OSI model, most commonly at the network layer using *Internet Protocol* (IP) addressing. With logical separation, devices in the same network segment are grouped together in some way. The most common way this is achieved is through the use of network subnets. For example, if a Hadoop cluster has 150 nodes, it may be that these nodes are logically grouped on the same /24 subnet (e.g., an IP subnet mask of 255.255.255.0), which represents a maximum of 256 IP addresses (254 usable). Organizing hosts logically in this fashion makes it easy to administer and secure.

The most common method of network segmentation is a hybrid approach that uses aspects of both physical and logical network segmentation. The most common way of implementing the hybrid approach is through the use of *virtual local area networks* (VLANs). VLANs allow multiple network subnets to share physical switches. Each VLAN is a distinct broadcast domain even though all VLANs share a single layer-2 network. Depending on the capabilities of the network switches or routers, you might have to assign each physical port to a single VLAN or you may be able to take advantage of packet tagging to run multiple VLANs over the same port.

As briefly mentioned before, both physical and logical separation can be, and often are, used together. Physical and logical separation may be present in the in-house and managed environments where a Hadoop cluster has a logical subnet defined, and all machines are physically connected to the same group of dedicated network devices (e.g., top-of-rack switches and aggregation switches).

With the cloud operating environment, physical network segmentation is often more difficult. Cloud infrastructure design goals are such that the location of hardware is less important than the availability of services sized by operational need. Some cloud environments allow for users to choose machines to be in the same locality group. While this is certainly better from a performance point of view, such as in the case of network latencies, it does not usually help with security. Machines in the same locality group likely share the same physical network as other machines.

Now that we have a Hadoop cluster that resides on its own network segment, how is this segment protected? This is largely achieved with network firewalls, and intrusion detection and prevention systems.

Network Firewalls

Network firewalls are a great way to enforce separation of a Hadoop cluster from the rest of the network that it resides in. The basic premise of firewalls is that they are used as an added layer of security for network traffic that traverses from one network segment to another. For example, a network firewall is likely to exist between a segment of users inside a company and one that contains an Internet-facing website for the company. Likewise, a network firewall is not likely to exist between two desktop computers in the same department of an office building.

On the surface, it might seem that network firewalls are separate pieces of hardware in addition to other network hardware such as routers and switches, but this is not always true. Modern routers and (multilayer) switches often perform many of the same core functions as standalone firewalls. Several key points about firewalls that are important in the context of Hadoop are discussed in this section.

The fundamental feature of a network firewall is to allow or filter (drop) network packets based on network and transport layer properties. This typically boils down to making filtering decisions based on source and destination IP address; protocol type such as TCP, UDP, and ICMP; and source and destination ports, if applicable. These filtering decisions are easy to make by network devices because all of this information is contained in the header of a packet, meaning that deep packet inspection of the payload is not required.

The importance of basic filtering for Hadoop is often based on three general categories: data movement to and from the cluster; client access, which includes end users and third-party tools; and administration traffic. Each of these general categories carries a different perspective on how network firewalls will be used to ensure a secure network path between the Hadoop cluster and everything else.

Data movement

The first category, data movement, is how data is ingested into the cluster or served to downstream systems. A detailed discussion about securing these flows from a Hadoop ecosystem perspective takes place in Chapter 10. For now, the focus is on the network channel for these transfers and the type of data involved to determine the level of firewall inspection required.

Looking first at the network channel for data movement, the common options are general-purpose file transfer tools like FTP and SCP, RDBMS flows (via Sqoop), or streaming ingest flows such as those provided by Flume. Each of these common channels has associated IP addresses and ports that work well in classifying the network communication and creating firewall rules to allow it. It is important to understand what the intended flows look like. Which machines contain the source data? Is the data landing on a server on the edge of the cluster before being ingested into the cluster? Which machines are receiving extracted data from the cluster? Answers to these questions lead to network firewall rules that at a high level could:

- Permit FTP traffic from a limited set of FTP servers to one or more edge nodes (described later in this chapter)
- Permit worker nodes in the cluster to connect to one or more database servers to send and receive data over specified ports
- Permit data flowing from log events generated from a cluster of web servers to a set of Flume agents over a limited number of ports

A follow-up decision that needs to be made is determining where source data is coming from and if additional firewall inspection is needed. For example, if an upstream data source is coming from an internal business system, the firewall policies highlighted are sufficient. However, if an upstream data source comes from an untrusted source, such as data provided on the open Internet, it is likely that deep packet inspection is required to help protect the cluster from malicious content.

Client access

The second common category is all about client access. Again, this subject is covered in detail in Chapter 11, but what is important from a network firewall point of view is to understand, and thus classify, the methods clients will be using to interact with the cluster. Some clusters will operate in a fully "lights out" environment, meaning that there is no end-user activity permitted. These types of environments typically run continuous ETL jobs and generate result sets and reports to downstream systems in a fully automated fashion. In this environment, client access policies exist simply to block everything. The only policies necessary to keep the cluster up and running and secure are those of the data movement and administration variety.

A more typical environment is a mixed environment of users, tools, and applications accessing the cluster. In this case, organization is key. Where are the third-party tools running? Can they be isolated to a few known machines? Where are the users accessing the cluster from? Is it possible to require users to use an edge node? Where are custom applications running? Is the network firewall between the application and the cluster, or between the application and end users?

Administration traffic

The last common category is administration traffic. This includes things like administrative users logging into cluster machines, audit event traffic from the cluster to an external audit server, and backup traffic from the cluster to another network. Backups could be large data transfers using DistCp, or even backing up the Hive metastore database to a location outside the cluster's data center. The term *administration traffic* is not meant to give a sense of volume but rather to indicate that the traffic is not something that regular clients to the cluster generate.

Network firewalls serve as a good security boundary between the cluster and outside networks, but what about protecting against malicious traffic that might be actively targeting machines in the cluster? This is where intrusion detection and prevention come into the discussion.

Intrusion Detection and Prevention

In the previous section, network firewalls were introduced as a way to control flows into and out of the network that a Hadoop cluster lives in. While this works perfectly well when "normal" everyday traffic is flowing, what about when not-so-normal events are happening? What happens if a malicious attacker has bypassed the network firewall and is attempting exploits against machines in the cluster, such as buffer overflow attacks? How about distributed denial-of-service (DDoS) attacks?

Intrusion detection and prevention systems can help stop these types of attacks. Before we dive into where these devices fit into the system architecture for the cluster, let's cover a few basics about these systems.

Intrusion detection systems (IDS) and *intrusion prevention systems* (IPS) are often used interchangeably in the discussion of network security. However, these two systems are fundamentally different in the role they play in dealing with suspected intrusions. An IDS, as the name implies, *detects* an intrusion. It falls under the same category as monitoring and alerting systems. An IDS is typically connected to a switch listening in promiscuous mode, meaning that all traffic on the switch flows to the IDS in addition to the intended destination port(s). When an IDS finds a packet or stream of packets it suspects as an attack, it generates an alert. An alert might be an event that gets sent to a separate monitoring system, or even just an email alias that security administrators subscribe to. Figure 3-1 shows the network diagram when an IDS is in place; you will notice that the IDS is not in the network flow between the outside network and the cluster network.

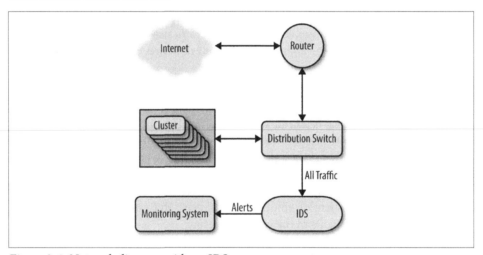

Figure 3-1. Network diagram with an IDS

An IPS, on the other hand, not only detects an intrusion, but actively tries to *prevent* or stop the intrusion as it is happening. This is made possible by the key difference between an IDS and IPS in that an IPS is not listening promiscuously on the network, but rather sitting *between* both sides of the network. Because of this fact, an IPS can actually stop the flow of intrusions to the other side of the network. A common feature of an IPS is to *fail close*. This means that upon failure of the IPS, such as being overwhelmed by an extensive DDoS attack to the point where it can no longer scan packets, it simply stops *all* packets from flowing through to the other side of the IPS. While this might seem like a successful DDoS attack, and in some ways it is, a fail close protects all the devices that are behind the IPS. Figure 3-2 shows the network diagram when an IPS is in place; you will notice that the IPS is actually in the network flow between the outside network and the cluster network.

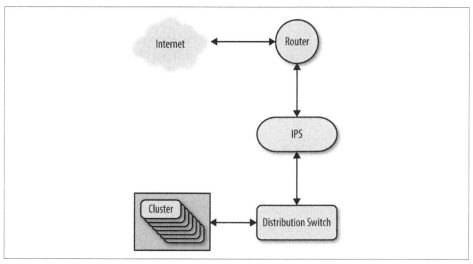

Figure 3-2. Network diagram with an IPS

Now that we have the 50,000-foot view of what these devices do, how does it help Hadoop? The answer is that it is another piece of the network security puzzle. Hadoop clusters inherently store massive amounts of data. Both detection and prevention of intrusion attempts to the cluster are critical to protecting the large swath of data. So where do these devices live relative to the rest of the network in which a Hadoop cluster lives? The answer: possibly several places.

In the discussion about network firewalls, it was mentioned that ingest pipelines that flow from the open Internet are likely to be treated differently from a security point of view. This is again the case with IDS and IPS devices. Intrusion attacks are largely sourced from malicious actors on the Internet. With that in mind, placing an IPS in the ingest path of an Internet data source is perfectly reasonable. The Internet might be a hotbed of malicious actors, but the insider threat to a business is also very real and should not be overlooked. Security architecture choices must always be made under the assumption that the malicious actor works inside the same building you do. Placing an IDS inside the trusted network can be a valuable tool to warn administrators against the insider threat.

An added bonus to the discussion of IDS and IPS is the fact that logging network traffic in high volumes is a fantastic Hadoop use case. Security companies often use Hadoop to collect IDS logs across many different customer networks in order to perform a variety of large-scale analytics and visualizations of the data, which can then feed into the advancement of rules engines used by firewalls and IDS/IPS devices.

Hadoop Roles and Separation Strategies

Earlier, we mentioned that nodes in the cluster can be classified into groups to aid in setting up an adequate security policy. In this section, we take a look at how to do that. Each node plays some kind of role in the cluster, and these roles will identify which security policies are necessary to protect it. First, let's review the common Hadoop ecosystem components and the service roles that each have (we assume that you already knows what these service roles do, but if that's not the case, refer back to Chapter 1 for a quick review):

HDFS
   NameNode (Active/Standby/Secondary), DataNode, JournalNode, FailoverController, HttpFS, NFSGateway

MapReduce
   JobTracker (Active/Standby), TaskTracker, FailoverController

YARN
   ResourceManager (Active/Standby), NodeManager, JobHistory Server

Hive
   Hive Metastore Server, HiveServer2, WebHCatServer

Impala
   Catalog Server, StateStore Server, Impalad

Hue
   HueServer, Beeswax, KerberosTicketRenewer

Oozie
   OozieServer

ZooKeeper
   ZooKeeper Server

HBase
   Master, RegionServer, ThriftServer, RESTServer

Accumulo
   Master, TabletServer, Tracer, GarbageCollector

Solr
   SolrServer

Management and monitoring services
   Cloudera Manager, Apache Ambari, Ganglia, Nagios, Puppet, Chef, etc.

Looking at this (nonexhaustive) list, you can see that many of the various ecosystem projects have a master/worker architecture. This lends itself well to organizing the service roles from a security architecture perspective. Additionally, some of the service roles are intended to be client-facing. Overall, the separation strategy is this: identify all of the master services to be run on *master nodes*, worker services on *worker nodes*, and management services on *management nodes*. Additionally, identify which components require client configuration files to be deployed such that users can access the services. These client configuration files, along with client-facing services, are placed on *edge nodes*. The classifications of nodes are explained in more detail in the following subsections.

Master Nodes

Master nodes are likely the most important of the node groups. They contain all of the primary services that are the backbone of Hadoop. Because of the importance of these roles to the components they represent, they carry an expectation of increased security policies to protect them. Following is a list of roles that should be run on dedicated master nodes:

- HDFS NameNode, Secondary NameNode (or Standby NameNode), Failover-Controller, JournalNode, and KMS
- MapReduce JobTracker and FailoverController
- YARN ResourceManager and JobHistory Server
- Hive Metastore Server
- Impala Catalog Server and StateStore Server
- Sentry Server
- ZooKeeper Server
- HBase Master
- Accumulo Master, Tracer, and GarbageCollector

Armed with this list of services, the first security question to ask is: Who needs access to a master node and for what purpose? The simple answer is administrators, to perform administrative functions (surprise, surprise). Clients to the cluster, be it actual end users or third-party tools, can access all of these services remotely using the standard interfaces that are exposed. For example, a user issuing the command `hdfs dfs -ls` can do so on any machine that has the proper client configuration for the HDFS service. The user does not need to execute this command on the master node that is running the HDFS NameNode for it to succeed. With that in mind, here are several important reasons for limiting access to master nodes to administrators:

Resource contention
> If regular end users are able to use master nodes to run arbitrary programs and thus use system resources, this takes away resources that may otherwise be needed by the master node roles. This can lead to a degradation of performance.

Security vulnerabilities
> Software has inherent vulnerabilities in it, and Hadoop is no different. Allowing users to have access to the same machines that have master node roles running can open the door for exploiting unpatched vulnerabilities in the Hadoop code (maliciously or accidentally). Restricting access to master nodes lowers the risk of exposing these security vulnerabilities.

Denial of service
> Users can do crazy things. There isn't really a nicer way to say it. If end users are sharing the same machines as master node roles, it inevitably sets the stage for a user to do something (for the sake of argument, accidentally) that will take down a master process. Going back to the resource contention argument, what happens if a user launches a runaway process that fills up the log directory? Will all of the master node roles handle it gracefully if they are unable to log anymore? Does an administrator want to find out? Another example would be a similar case where a runaway process maxed out CPU or RAM on the system, with the latter easily leading to out-of-memory errors.

Worker Nodes

Worker nodes handle the bulk of what a Hadoop cluster actually does, which is store and process data. The typical roles found on worker nodes are the following:

- HDFS DataNode
- MapReduce TaskTracker
- YARN NodeManager
- Impala Daemon
- HBase RegionServer
- Accumulo TabletServer
- SolrServer

On the surface, it might seem like all cluster users need access to these nodes because these roles handle user requests for data and processing. However, this is most often not true. Typically, only administrators need remote access to worker nodes for maintenance tasks. End users can ingest data, submit jobs, and retrieve records by utilizing the corresponding interfaces and APIs available. Most of the time, as will be elaborated on a bit later, services provide a proxy mechanism that allows administrators to channel user activity to a certain set of nodes different from the actual worker nodes. These proxies communicate with worker nodes on behalf of the user, eliminating the need for direct access.

As with master nodes, there are reasons why limiting access to worker nodes to administrators makes sense:

Resource contention

When regular end users are performing activities on a worker node outside the expected processes, it can create skew in resource management. For example, if YARN is configured to use a certain amount of system resources based on a calculation done by a Hadoop administrator taking into account the operating system needs and other software, what about end-user activity? It is often difficult to accurately profile user activity and account for it, so it is quite likely that heavily used worker nodes will not perform well or predictably compared to worker nodes that are not being used.

Worker role skew

If end users are using worker nodes for daily activities, it can create undesirable skew in how the roles on the worker nodes behave. For example, if end users regularly log into a particular worker node that is running the DataNode role, data ingestion from this node will create skew in disk utilization because HDFS writes will try to write the first block locally before choosing locations elsewhere in the cluster. This means that if a user is trying to upload a 10 GB file into her home directory in HDFS, all 10 GB will be written to the local DataNode they are ingesting from.

Management Nodes

Management nodes are the lifeblood for administrators. These nodes provide the mechanism to install, configure, monitor, and otherwise maintain the Hadoop cluster. The typical roles found on these nodes are:

- Configuration management
- Monitoring
- Alerting
- Software repositories
- Backend databases

These management nodes often contain the actual software repositories for the cluster. This is especially the case when the nodes in the Hadoop cluster do not have Internet access. The most critical role hosted on a management node is configuration management software. Whether it is Hadoop specific (e.g., Cloudera Manager,

Apache Ambari) or not (e.g., Puppet, Chef), this is the place where administrators will set up and configure the cluster. The corollary to configuration management is monitoring and alerting. These roles are provided by software packages like Ganglia, Nagios, and the Hadoop-specific management consoles.

It goes without saying but will be said anyway: these nodes are not for regular users. Management and maintenance of a Hadoop cluster is an administrative function and thus should be protected as such. That being said, there are exceptions to the rule. A common exception is for developers to have access to cluster monitoring dashboards to observe metrics while jobs are running so they can ascertain performance characteristics of their code.

Edge Nodes

Edge nodes are the nodes that all of the users of the Hadoop cluster care about. These nodes host web interfaces, proxies, and client configurations that ultimately provide the mechanism for users to take advantage of the combined storage and computing system that is Hadoop. The following roles are typically found on edge nodes:

- HDFS HttpFS and NFS gateway
- Hive HiveServer2 and WebHCatServer
- Network proxy/load balancer for Impala
- Hue server and Kerberos ticket renewer
- Oozie server
- HBase Thrift server and REST server
- Flume agent
- Client configuration files

When looking at the list of common roles found on edge nodes, it becomes apparent that this node class is a bit different than the others. Edge nodes in general might not be treated as equivalent to one another, as is often the case with the other node classes. For example, ingest pipelines using Flume agents will likely be on edge nodes not accessible by users, while edge nodes housing client configurations to facilitate command-line access would be accessible by users. How granular the classification of nodes within the edge node group will be dependent on a variety of factors, including cluster size and use cases. Here are some examples of further classifying edge nodes:

Data Gateway
    HDFS HttpFS and NFS gateway, HBase Thrift server and REST server, Flume agent

SQL Gateway
Hive HiveServer2 and WebHCatServer, Impala load-balancing proxy (e.g., HAProxy)

User Portal
Hue server and Kerberos ticket renewer, Oozie server, client configuration files

 While the Impala daemon does not have to be collocated with an HDFS DataNode, it is not recommended to use a standalone Impala daemon as a proxy. A better option is to use a load-balancing proxy, such as HAProxy (*http://www.haproxy.org*), to act as a load balancer. This is the recommended architecture in the case where clients cannot connect directly to an Impala daemon on a worker node because of a firewall or other restrictions.

Using the additional edge node classifications shown, it becomes easier to break down which nodes users are expected to have remote access to, and which nodes are only accessible remotely through the configured remote ports. While users need remote access to the user portal nodes to interact with the cluster from a shell, it is quite reasonable that both the data and SQL gateways are not accessible in this way. These nodes are accessible only via remote ports, which facilitates access to both command-line tools executed on the user portal, as well as additional business intelligence tools that might reside somewhere else in the network.

The groupings shown are just examples. It is important to understand not only the services installed in the cluster but also how the services are used and by whom. This circles back to earlier discussions about knowing the users and the operating environment.

Operating System Security

This section digs into how individual nodes should be protected at the operating-system level.

Remote Access Controls

In a typical server environment, remote access controls are pretty straightforward. For example, a server that hosts an RDBMS or web server is likely locked down to end users, allowing only privileged users and administrators to log into the machine. A Hadoop environment is not so simple. Because of the inherent complexity of the Hadoop ecosystem, a myriad of tools and access methods are available to interact with the cluster, in addition to the typical roles and responsibilities for basic administration.

While Hadoop clusters can span thousands of nodes, these nodes can be classified into groups, as we will see a bit later in this chapter. With that in mind, it is important to consider limiting remote access to machines by identifying which machines need to be accessed and why. Armed with this information, a remote access policy can be made to restrict remote access (typically SSH) to authorized users. On the surface, it might seem that authorized users are analogous to users of the Hadoop cluster, but this is typically not the case. For example, a developer writing Java MapReduce code or Pig scripts will likely require command-line access to one or more nodes in the cluster, whereas an analyst writing SQL queries for Hive and Impala might not need this access at all if they are using Hue or third-party business intelligence (BI) tools to interact with the cluster.

Host Firewalls

Remote access controls are a good way to limit which users are able to log into a given machine in the cluster. This is useful and necessary, but it is only a small component of protecting a given machine in the cluster. Host firewalls are an incredibly useful tool to limit the types of traffic going into and out of a node. In Linux systems, host firewalls are typically implemented using *iptables*. Certainly there are other third-party software packages that perform this function as well (e.g., commercial software), but we will focus on iptables, as it is largely available by default in most Linux distributions.

In order to leverage iptables, we must first understand and classify the network traffic in a Hadoop cluster. Table 3-1 shows common ports that are used by Hadoop ecosystem components. We will use this table to start building a host firewall policy for iptables.

Table 3-1. Common Hadoop service ports

Component	Service	Port(s)
Accumulo	Master	9999
	GarbageCollector	50091
	Tracer	12234
	ProxyServer	42424
	TabletServer	9997
	Monitor	4560, 50095
Cloudera Impala	Catalog Server	25020, 26000

Component	Service	Port(s)
	StateStore	24000, 25010
	Daemon	21000, 21050, 22000, 23000, 25000, 28000
	Llama ApplicationMaster	15000, 15001, 15002
Flume	Agent	41414
HBase	Master	60000, 60010
	REST Server	8085, 20550
	Thrift Server	9090, 9095
	RegionServer	60020, 60030
HDFS	NameNode	8020, 8022, 50070, 50470
	SecondaryNameNode	50090, 50495
	DataNode	1004, 1006, 50010, 50020, 50075, 50475
	JournalNode	8480, 8485
	HttpFS	14000, 14001
	NFS Gateway	111, 2049, 4242
	KMS	16000, 16001
Hive	Hive Metastore Server	9083
	HiveServer2	10000
	WebHCat Server	50111
Hue	Server	8888
MapReduce	JobTracker	8021, 8023, 9290, 50030
	FailoverController	8018
	TaskTracker	4867, 50060
Oozie	Server	11000, 11001, 11443

Component	Service	Port(s)
Sentry	Server	8038, 51000
Solr	Server	8983, 8984
YARN	ResourceManager	8030, 8031, 8032, 8033, 8088, 8090
	JobHistory Server	10020, 19888, 19890
	NodeManager	8040, 8041, 8042, 8044
ZooKeeper	Server	2181, 3181, 4181, 9010

Now that we have the common ports listed, we need to understand how strict of a policy needs to be enforced. Configuring iptables rules involves both ports and IP addresses, as well as the direction of communication. A typical basic firewall policy allows any host to reach the allowed ports, and all return (established) traffic is allowed. An example iptables policy for an HDFS NameNode might look like the one in Example 3-1.

Example 3-1. Basic NameNode iptables policy

```
iptables -N hdfs
iptables -A hdfs -p tcp -s 0.0.0.0/0 --dport 8020 -j ACCEPT
iptables -A hdfs -p tcp -s 0.0.0.0/0 --dport 8022 -j ACCEPT
iptables -A hdfs -p tcp -s 0.0.0.0/0 --dport 50070 -j ACCEPT
iptables -A hdfs -p tcp -s 0.0.0.0/0 --dport 50470 -j ACCEPT
iptables -A INPUT -j hdfs
```

This policy is more relaxed in that it allows all hosts (0.0.0.0/0) to connect to the machine over the common HDFS NameNode service ports. However, this might be too open a policy. Let us say that the Hadoop cluster nodes are all part of the 10.1.1.0/24 subnet. Furthermore, a dedicated edge node is set up on the host 10.1.1.254 for all communication to the cluster. Finally, SSL is enabled for web consoles. The adjusted iptables policy for the NameNode machine might instead look like the one in Example 3-2.

Example 3-2. Secure NameNode iptables policy

```
iptables -N hdfs
iptables -A hdfs -p tcp -s 10.1.1.254/32 --dport 8020 -j ACCEPT
iptables -A hdfs -p tcp -s 10.1.1.254/32 --dport 8022 -j DROP
iptables -A hdfs -p tcp -s 10.1.1.0/24 --dport 8022 -j ACCEPT
iptables -A hdfs -p tcp -s 0.0.0.0/0 --dport 50470 -j ACCEPT
iptables -A INPUT -j hdfs
```

The adjusted policy is now a lot more restrictive. It allows any user to get to the NameNode web console over SSL (port 50470), only cluster machines to connect to the NameNode over the dedicated DataNode RPC port (8022), and user traffic to the NameNode RPC port (8020) to occur only from the edge node.

 It might be necessary to insert the iptables jump target to a specific line number in the INPUT section of your policy for it to take effect. An append is shown for simplicity.

SELinux

Another often-discussed feature related to operating system security is *Security Enhanced Linux (SELinux)*, which was originally developed by the National Security Agency (NSA), an intelligence organization in the United States. The premise of SELinux is to provide Linux kernel enhancements that allow for the policies and enforcement of *mandatory access controls* (MAC). At a high level, SELinux can be configured in a few different ways:

Disabled
>   In this mode, SELinux is not active and does not provide any additional level of security to the operating system. This is far and away the most common configuration for Hadoop.

Permissive
>   In this mode, SELinux is enabled but does not protect the system. What it does instead is print warnings when a policy has been violated. This mode is very useful to profile the types of workloads on a system to begin building a customized policy.

Enforcing
>   In this mode, SELinux is enabled and protects the system based upon the specified SELinux policy in place.

In addition to the enabled modes of permissive and enforcing, SELinux has two different types of enforcement: targeted enforcement and *multilevel security* (MLS). With targeted enforcement, only certain processes are targeted, meaning they have an associated policy that governs the protection. Processes that do not have a policy are not protected by SELinux. This, of course, is a less stringent mode of protection. MLS, on the other hand, is much more in depth. The premise of MLS at a very high level is that all users and processes carry a security level, while files and other objects carry a security-level requirement. MLS is modeled after U.S. government classification levels, such as Top Secret, Secret, Confidential, and Unclassified. In the U.S. government classification system, these levels create a hierarchy where each user with a given level of access has permission to any information at a lower level. For example, if a user has a security level of Secret, then the user will be permitted to access objects in the operating system at the Secret, Confidential, and Unclassified security level because Confidential and Unclassified are both lower levels than Secret. However, they would not be able to access objects marked at the Top Secret security level.

All of this sounds great, but what does it have to do with Hadoop? Can SELinux be used as an additional level of protection to the operating system that is running the various Hadoop ecosystem components? The short answer: most likely not. This is not to say that it is not possible—rather, it is an admission that advancements in security integration with SELinux and the creation of associated policies that security administrators can deploy in the cluster are simply absent at this point. What compounds the problem is the nature of the Hadoop ecosystem. Today it is filled with hundreds of components, tools, and other widgets that integrate and/or enhance the platform in one way or another. The more tools that are added in the mix, the harder it is to come up with a set of SELinux policies to govern them all.

For those that push the limits of adoption, the likely choice is to set up systems in permissive mode and run what equates to "normal" workloads in the cluster, leveraging as many of the tools as deemed typical for the given environment. Once this has been done over a suitable period of time, the warnings generated by SELinux can be used to start building out a policy. The issue here is that this can quickly become a tedious process, and one that has to be revisited every time a new component or feature is introduced to the mix.

Summary

In this chapter, we analyzed the Hadoop environment with broad strokes, first identifying the operating environment that it resides in. Then we discussed protecting this environment from a network security perspective, taking advantage of common security practices such as network segmentation and introducing network security devices like firewalls and IDS/IPS. The next level of granularity was understanding how to break down a Hadoop cluster into different node groups based upon the types of services they run. Finally, we provided recommendations for securing the operating systems of individual nodes based on the node group.

In Chapter 4, we take a look at a fundamental component of Hadoop security architecture: Kerberos. Kerberos is a key player in enterprise systems, and Hadoop is no exception. The Kerberos chapter will close out the discussion on security architecture and set the stage for authentication, authorization, and accounting.

Kerberos

Kerberos often intimidates even experienced system administrators and developers at the first mention of it. Applications and systems that rely on Kerberos often have many support calls and trouble tickets filed to fix problems related to it. This chapter will introduce the basic Kerberos concepts that are necessary to understand how strong authentication works, and explain how it plays an important role with Hadoop authentication in Chapter 5.

So what exactly *is* Kerberos? From a mythological point of view, Kerberos is the Greek word for *Cerberus*, a multiheaded dog that guards the entrance to Hades to ensure that nobody who enters will ever leave. Kerberos from a technical (and more pleasant) point of view is the term given to an authentication mechanism developed at Massachusetts Institute of Technology (MIT). Kerberos evolved to become the de facto standard for strong authentication for computer systems large and small, with varying implementations ranging from MIT's Kerberos distribution to the authentication component of Microsoft's Active Directory.

Why Kerberos?

Playing devil's advocate here (pun intended), why does Hadoop need Kerberos at all? The reason becomes apparent when looking at the default model for Hadoop authentication. When presented with a username, Hadoop happily believes whatever you tell it, and ensures that every machine in the entire cluster believes it, too.

To use an analogy, if a person at a party approached you and introduced himself as "Bill," you naturally would believe that he is, in fact, Bill. How do you know that he really is Bill? Well, because he said so and you believed him without question. Hadoop without Kerberos behaves in much the same way, except that, to take the analogy a step further, Hadoop not only believes "Bill" is who he says he is but makes sure that everyone else believes it, too. This is a problem.

Hadoop by design is meant to store and process petabytes of data. As the old adage goes, with great power comes great responsibility. Hadoop in the enterprise can no longer get by with simplistic means for identifying (and trusting) users. Enter Kerberos. In the previous analogy, "Bill" introduces himself to you. Upon doing so, what if you responded by asking to see a valid passport and upon receiving it (naturally, because everyone brings a passport to a party…), checked the passport against a database to verify validity? This is the type of identify verification that Hadoop introduced by adding Kerberos authentication.

Kerberos Overview

The stage is now set and it is time to dig in and understand just how Kerberos works. Kerberos implementation is, as you might imagine, a client/server architecture. Before breaking down the components in detail, a bit of Kerberos terminology is needed.

First, identities in Kerberos are called *principals*. Every user and service that participates in the Kerberos authentication protocol requires a principal to uniquely identify itself. Principals are classified into two categories: *user* principals and *service* principals. *User principal names*, or UPNs, represent regular users. This closely resembles usernames or accounts in the operating system world. *Service principal names*, or SPNs, represent services that a user needs to access, such as a database on a specific server. The relationship between UPNs and SPNs will become more apparent when we work through an example later.

The next important Kerberos term is *realm*. A Kerberos realm is an authentication administrative domain. All principals are assigned to a specific Kerberos realm. A realm establishes a boundary, which makes administration easier.

Now that we have established what principals and realms are, the natural next step is to understand what stores and controls all of this information. The answer is a *key distribution center (KDC)*. The KDC is comprised of three components: the Kerberos database, the *authentication service (AS)*, and the *ticket-granting service (TGS)*. The Kerberos database stores all the information about the principals and the realm they belong to, among other things. Kerberos principals in the database are identified with a naming convention that looks like the following:

alice@EXAMPLE.COM

> A UPN that uniquely identifies the user (also called the *short name*): alice in the Kerberos realm EXAMPLE.COM. By convention, the realm name is always uppercase.

`bob/admin@EXAMPLE.COM`

A variation of a regular UPN in that it identifies an administrator bob for the realm `EXAMPLE.COM`. The slash (/) in a UPN separates the short name and the admin distinction. The `admin` component convention is regularly used, but it is configurable as we will see later.

`hdfs/node1.example.com@EXAMPLE.COM`

This principal represents an SPN for the `hdfs` service, on the host `node1.exam ple.com`, in the Kerberos realm `EXAMPLE.COM`. The slash (/) in an SPN separates the short name `hdfs` and the hostname `node1.example.com`.

> The entire principal name is case sensitive! For instance, `hdfs/ Node1.Hadoop.com@EXAMPLE.COM` is a different principal than the one in the third example. Typically, it is best practice to use all lowercase for the principal, except for the realm component, which is uppercase. The caveat here is, of course, that the underlying hostnames referred to in SPNs are also lowercase, which is also a best practice for host naming and DNS.

The second component of the KDC, the AS, is responsible for issuing a ticket-granting ticket (TGT) to a client when they initiate a request to the AS. The TGT is used to request access to other services.

The third component of the KDC, the TGS, is responsible for validating TGTs and granting *service tickets*. Service tickets allow an authenticated principal to use the service provided by the application server, identified by the SPN. The process flow of obtaining a TGT, presenting it to the TGS, and obtaining a service ticket is explained in the next section. For now, understand that the KDC has two components, the AS and TGS, which handle requests for authentication and access to services.

> There is a special principal of the form `krbtgt/<REALM>@<REALM>` within the Kerberos database, such as `krbtgt/EXAMPLE.COM@EXAM PLE.COM`. This principal is used internally by both the AS and the TGS. The key for this principal is actually used to encrypt the content of the TGT that is issued to clients, thus ensuring that the TGT issued by the AS can only be validated by the TGS.

Table 4-1 provides a summary of the Kerberos terms and abbreviations introduced in this chapter.

Table 4-1. Kerberos term abbreviations

Term	Name	Description
UPN	User principal name	A principal that identifies a user in a given realm, with the format *<short name><@REALM>* or *<shortname>/admin@<REALM>*
SPN	Service principal name	A principal that identifies a service on a specific host in a given realm, with the format *<shortname>/<hostname>@<REALM>*
TGT	Ticket-granting ticket	A special ticket type granted to a user after successfully authenticating to the AS
KDC	Key distribution center	A Kerberos server that contains three components: Kerberos database, AS, and TGS
AS	Authentication service	A KDC service that issues TGTs
TGS	Ticket-granting service	A KDC service that validates TGTs and grants service tickets

What has been presented thus far are a few of the basic Kerberos components needed to understand authentication at a high level. Kerberos in its own right is a very in-depth and complex topic that warrants an entire book on the subject. Thankfully, that has already been done. If you wish to dive far deeper than what is presented here, take a look at Jason Garman's excellent book, *Kerberos: The Definitive Guide* (O'Reilly).

Kerberos Workflow: A Simple Example

Now that the terminology and components have been introduced, we can now work through an example workflow showing how it all works at a high level. First, we will identify all of the components in play:

EXAMPLE.COM
> The Kerberos realm

Alice
> A user of the system, identified by the UPN alice@EXAMPLE.COM

myservice
> A service that will be hosted on server1.example.com, identified by the SPN myservice/server1.example.com@EXAMPLE.COM

kdc.example.com
> The KDC for the Kerberos realm EXAMPLE.COM

In order for Alice to use myservice, she needs to present a valid service ticket to myservice. The following list of steps shows how she does this (some details omitted for brevity):

1. Alice needs to obtain a TGT. To do this, she initiates a request to the AS at kdc.example.com, identifying herself as the principal alice@EXAMPLE.COM.

2. The AS responds by providing a TGT that is encrypted using the key (password) for the principal alice@EXAMPLE.COM.

3. Upon receipt of the encrypted message, Alice is prompted to enter the correct password for the principal alice@EXAMPLE.COM in order to decrypt the message.

4. After successfully decrypting the message containing the TGT, Alice now requests a service ticket from the TGS at kdc.example.com for the service identified by myservice/server1.example.com@EXAMPLE.COM, presenting the TGT along with the request.

5. The TGS validates the TGT and provides Alice a service ticket, encrypted with the myservice/server1.example.com@EXAMPLE.COM principal's key.

6. Alice now presents the service ticket to myservice, which can then decrypt it using the myservice/server1.example.com@EXAMPLE.COM key and validate the ticket.

7. The service myservice permits Alice to use the service because she has been properly authenticated.

This shows how Kerberos works at a high level. Obviously this is a greatly simplified example and many of the underlying details have not been presented. See Figure 4-1 for a sequence diagram of this example.

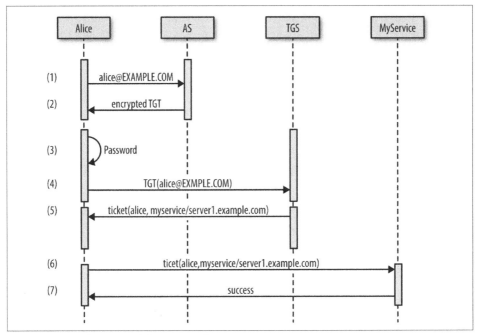

Figure 4-1. Kerberos workflow example

Kerberos Trusts

So far, Kerberos has been introduced under the implicit expectation that all users and services are contained within a single Kerberos realm. While this works well for introductory material, it is often not realistic given how large enterprises work. Over time, large enterprises end up with multiple Kerberos realms from things like mergers, acquisitions, or just simply wanting to segregate different parts of the enterprise. However, by default, a KDC only knows about its own realm and the principals in its own database. What if a user from one realm wants to use a service that is controlled by another realm? In order to make this happen, a Kerberos *trust* is needed between the two realms.

For example, suppose that Example is a very large corporation and has decided to create multiple realms to identify different lines of business, including `HR.EXAM` `PLE.COM` and `MARKETING.EXAMPLE.COM`. Because users in both realms might need to access services from both realms, the KDC for `HR.EXAMPLE.COM` needs to trust information from the `MARKETING.EXAMPLE.COM` realm and vice versa.

On the surface this seems pretty straightforward, except that there are actually two different types of trusts: *one-way trust* and *two-way trust* (sometimes called *bidirectional trust* or *full trust*). The example we just looked at represents a two-way trust.

What if there is also a `DEV.EXAMPLE.COM` realm where developers have principals that need to access the `DEV.EXAMPLE.COM` and `MARKETING.EXAMPLE.COM` realms, but marketing users should not be able to access the `DEV.EXAMPLE.COM` realm? This scenario requires a one-way trust. A one-way trust is very common in Hadoop deployments when a KDC is installed and configured to contain all the information about the SPNs for the cluster nodes, but all UPNs for end users exist in a different realm, such as Active Directory. Oftentimes, Active Directory administrators or corporate policies prohibit full trusts for a variety of reasons.

So how does a Kerberos trust actually get established? Earlier in the chapter it was noted that a special principal is used internally by the AS and TGS, and it is of the form `krbtgt/<REALM>@<REALM>`. This principal becomes increasingly important for establishing trusts. With trusts, the principal instead takes the form of `krbtgt/<TRUSTING_REALM>@<TRUSTED_REALM>`. A key concept of this principal is that it exists in *both* realms. For example, if the `HR.EXAMPLE.COM` realm needs to trust the `MARKETING.EXAMPLE.COM` realm, the principal `krbtgt/HR.EXAMPLE.COM@MARKETING.EXAMPLE.COM` needs to exist in both realms.

> The password for the `krbtgt/<TRUSTING_REALM>@<TRUSTED_REALM>` principal and the encryption types used *must* be the same in both realms in order for the trust to be established.

The previous example shows what is required for a one-way trust. In order to establish a full trust, the principal `krbtgt/MARKETING.EXAMPLE.COM@HR.EXAMPLE.COM` also needs to exist in both realms. To summarize, for the `HR.EXAMPLE.COM` realm to have a full trust with the `MARKETING.EXAMPLE.COM` realm, both realms need the principals `krbtgt/MARKETING.EXAMPLE.COM@HR.EXAMPLE.COM` and `krbtgt/HR.EXAMPLE.COM@MARKETING.EXAMPLE.COM`.

MIT Kerberos

As mentioned in the beginning of this chapter, Kerberos was first created at MIT. Over the years, it has undergone several revisions and the current version is *MIT Kerberos V5*, or *krb5* as it is often called. This section covers some of the components of the MIT Kerberos distribution to put some real examples into play with the conceptual examples introduced thus far.

> For the most up-to-date definitive resource on the MIT Kerberos distribution, consult the excellent documentation at the official project website (*http://web.mit.edu/~kerberos/*).

In the earlier example, we glossed over the fact that Alice initiated an authentication request. In practice, Alice does this by using the *kinit* tool (Example 4-1).

Example 4-1. kinit using the default user

```
[alice@server1 ~]$ kinit
Enter password for alice@EXAMPLE.COM:
[alice@server1 ~]$
```

This example pairs the current Linux username *alice* with the *default realm* to come up with the suggested principal `alice@EXAMPLE.COM`. The default realm is explained later when we dive into the configuration files. The `kinit` tool also allows the user to explicitly identify the principal to authenticate as (Example 4-2).

Example 4-2. kinit using a specified user

```
[alice@server1 ~]$ kinit alice/admin@EXAMPLE.COM
Enter password for alice/admin@EXAMPLE.COM:
[alice@server1 ~]$
```

Explicitly providing a principal name is often necessary to authenticate as an administrative user, as the preceding example depicts. Another option for authentication is by using a *keytab file*. A keytab file stores the actual encryption key that can be used in lieu of a password challenge for a given principal. Creating keytab files are useful for noninteractive principals, such as SPNs, which are often associated with long-running processes like Hadoop daemons. A keytab file does not have to be a 1:1 mapping to a single principal. Multiple different principal keys can be stored in a single keytab file. A user can use `kinit` with a keytab file by specifying the keytab file location, and the principal name to authenticate as (again, because multiple principal keys may exist in the keytab file), shown in Example 4-3.

Example 4-3. kinit using a keytab file

```
[alice@server1 ~]$ kinit -kt alice.keytab alice/admin@EXAMPLE.COM
[alice@server1 ~]$
```

The keytab file allows a user to authenticate without knowledge of the password. Because of this fact, keytabs should be protected with appropriate controls to prevent unauthorized users from authenticating with it. This is especially important when keytabs are created for administrative principals!

Another useful utility that is part of the MIT Kerberos distribution is called `klist`. This utility allows users to see what, if any, Kerberos credentials they have in their *credentials cache*. The credentials cache is the place on the local filesystem where, upon successful authentication to the AS, TGTs are stored. By default, this location is usually the file */tmp/krb5cc_<uid>* where *<uid>* is the numeric user ID on the local system. After a successful `kinit`, alice can view her credentials cache with `klist`, as shown in Example 4-4.

Example 4-4. Viewing the credentials cache with klist

```
[alice@server1 ~]$ kinit
Enter password for alice@EXAMPLE.COM:
[alice@server1 ~]$ klist
Ticket cache: FILE:/tmp/krb5cc_5000
Default principal: alice@EXAMPLE.COM

Valid starting     Expires            Service principal
02/13/14 12:00:27  02/14/14 12:00:27  krbtgt/EXAMPLE.COM@EXAMPLE.COM
        renew until 02/20/14 12:00:27
[alice@server1 ~]$
```

If a user tries to look at the credentials cache without having authenticated first, no credentials will be found (see Example 4-5).

Example 4-5. No credentials cache found

```
[alice@server1 ~]$ klist
No credentials cache found (ticket cache FILE:/tmp/krb5cc_5000
[alice@server1 ~]$
```

Another useful tool in the MIT Kerberos toolbox is `kdestroy`. As the name implies, this allows users to destroy credentials in their credentials cache. This is useful for switching users, or when trying out or debugging new configurations (see Example 4-6).

Example 4-6. Destroying the credentials cache with kdestroy

```
[alice@server1 ~]$ kinit
Enter password for alice@EXAMPLE.COM:
[alice@server1 ~]$ klist
Ticket cache: FILE:/tmp/krb5cc_5000
Default principal: alice@EXAMPLE.COM

Valid starting     Expires            Service principal
02/13/14 12:00:27  02/14/14 12:00:27  krbtgt/EXAMPLE.COM@EXAMPLE.COM
        renew until 02/20/14 12:00:27
[alice@server1 ~]$ kdestroy
[alice@server1 ~]$ klist
No credentials cache found (ticket cache FILE:/tmp/krb5cc_5000
[alice@server1 ~]$
```

So far, all of the MIT Kerberos examples shown "just work." Hidden away in these examples is the fact that there is a fair amount of configuration necessary to make it all work, both on the client and server side. The next two sections present basic configurations to tie together some of the concepts that have been presented thus far.

Server Configuration

Kerberos server configuration is primarily specified in the *kdc.conf* file, which is shown in Example 4-7. This file lives in */var/kerberos/krb5kdc/* on Red Hat/CentOS systems.

Example 4-7. kdc.conf

```
[kdcdefaults]
 kdc_ports = 88
 kdc_tcp_ports = 88

[realms]
 EXAMPLE.COM = {
  acl_file = /var/kerberos/krb5kdc/kadm5.acl
  dict_file = /usr/share/dict/words
  supported_enctypes = aes256-cts:normal aes128-cts:normal arcfour-hmac-md5:normal
  max_renewable_life = 7d
 }
```

The first section, kdcdefaults, contains configurations that apply to all the realms listed, unless the specific realm configuration has values for the same configuration items. The configurations kdc_ports and kdc_tcp_ports specify the UDP and TCP ports the KDC should listen on, respectively. The next section, realms, contains all of the realms that the KDC is the server for. A single KDC can support multiple realms. The realm configuration items from this example are as follows:

acl_file

> This specifies the file location to be used by the admin server for access controls (more on this later).

dict_file

> This specifies the file that contains words that are not allowed to be used as passwords because they are easily cracked/guessed.

supported_enctypes

> This specifies all of the encryption types supported by the KDC. When interacting with the KDC, clients must support at least one of the encryption types listed here. Be aware of using weak encryption types, such as DES, because they are easily exploitable.

`max_renewable_life`
> This specifies the maximum amount of time that a ticket can be renewable. Clients can request a renewable lifetime up to this length. A typical value is seven days, denoted by 7d.

> By default, encryption settings in MIT Kerberos are often set to a variety of encryption types, including weak choices such as DES. When possible, remove weak encryption types to ensure the best possible security. Weak encryption types are easily exploitable and well documented as such. When using AES-256, Java Cryptographic Extensions need to be installed on all nodes in the cluster to allow for unlimited strength encryption types. It is important to note that some countries prohibit the usage of these encryption types. Always follow the laws governing encryption strength for your country. A more detailed discussion of encryption is provided in Chapter 9.

The `acl_file` location (typically the file *kadm5.acl*) is used to control which users have privileged access to administer the Kerberos database. Administration of the Kerberos database is controlled by two different, but related, components: `kadmin.local` and `kadmin`. The first is a utility that allows the *root* user of the KDC server to modify the Kerberos database. As the name implies, it can *only* be run by the *root* user on the same machine where the Kerberos database resides. Administrators wishing to administer the Kerberos database remotely must use the `kadmin` server.

The `kadmin` server is a daemon process that allows remote connections to administer the Kerberos database. This is where the *kadm5.acl* file (shown in Example 4-8) comes into play. The `kadmin` utility uses Kerberos authentication, and the *kadm5.acl* file specifies which UPNs are allowed to perform privileged functions.

Example 4-8. kadm5.acl

```
*/admin@EXAMPLE.COM        *
cloudera-scm@EXAMPLE.COM *    hdfs/*@EXAMPLE.COM
cloudera-scm@EXAMPLE.COM *    mapred/*@EXAMPLE.COM
```

This allows any principal from the `EXAMPLE.COM` realm with the `/admin` distinction to perform any administrative action. While it is certainly acceptable to change the `admin` distinction to some other arbitrary name, it is recommended to follow the convention for simplicity and maintainability. Administrative users should only use their admin credentials for specific privileged actions, much in the same way administrators should not use the *root* user in Linux for everyday nonadministrative actions.

The example also shows how the ACL can be defined to restrict privileges to a *target* principal. It demonstrates that the user *cloudera-scm* can perform any action but only on SPNs that start with hdfs and mapred. This type of syntax is useful to grant access to a third-party tool to create and administer Hadoop principals, but not grant access to all of the admin functions.

As mentioned earlier, the kadmin tool allows for administration of the Kerberos database. This tool brings users to a shell-like interface where various commands can be entered to perform operations against the Kerberos database (see Examples 4-9 through 4-12.

Example 4-9. Adding a new principal to the Kerberos database

```
kadmin: addprinc alice@EXAMPLE.COM
WARNING: no policy specified for alice@EXAMPLE.COM; defaulting to no policy
Enter password for principal "alice@EXAMPLE.COM":
Re-enter password for principal "alice@EXAMPLE.COM":
Principal "alice@EXAMPLE.COM" created.
kadmin:
```

Example 4-10. Displaying the details of a principal in the Kerberos database

```
kadmin: getprinc alice@EXAMPLE.COM
Principal: alice@EXAMPLE.COM
Expiration date: [never]
Last password change: Tue Feb 18 20:48:15 EST 2014
Password expiration date: [none]
Maximum ticket life: 1 day 00:00:00
Maximum renewable life: 7 days 00:00:00
Last modified: Tue Feb 18 20:48:15 EST 2014 (root/admin@EXAMPLE.COM)
Last successful authentication: [never]
Last failed authentication: [never]
Failed password attempts: 0
Number of keys: 2
Key: vno 1, aes256-cts-hmac-sha1-96, no salt
Key: vno 1, aes128-cts-hmac-sha1-96, no salt
MKey: vno1
Attributes:
Policy: [none]
kadmin:
```

Example 4-11. Deleting a principal from the Kerberos database

```
kadmin: delprinc alice@EXAMPLE.COM
Are you sure you want to delete the principal "alice@EXAMPLE.COM"? (yes/no): yes
Principal "alice@EXAMPLE.COM" deleted.
Make sure that you have removed this principal from all ACLs before reusing.
kadmin:
```

Example 4-12. Listing all the principals in the Kerberos database

```
kadmin: listprincs
HTTP/server1.example.com@EXAMPLE.COM
K/M@EXAMPLE.COM
bob@EXAMPLE.COM
flume/server1.example.com@EXAMPLE.COM
hdfs/server1.example.com@EXAMPLE.COM
hdfs@EXAMPLE.COM
hive/server1.example.com@EXAMPLE.COM
hue/server1.example.com@EXAMPLE.COM
impala/server1.example.com@EXAMPLE.COM
kadmin/admin@EXAMPLE.COM
kadmin/server1.example.com@EXAMPLE.COM
kadmin/changepw@EXAMPLE.COM
krbtgt/EXAMPLE.COM@EXAMPLE.COM
mapred/server1.example.com@EXAMPLE.COM
oozie/server1.example.com@EXAMPLE.COM
yarn/server1.example.com@EXAMPLE.COM
zookeeper/server1.example.com@EXAMPLE.COM
kadmin:
```

Client Configuration

The default Kerberos client configuration file is typically named *krb5.conf*, and lives in the */etc/* directory on Unix/Linux systems. This configuration file is read whenever client applications need to use Kerberos, including the `kinit` utility. The *krb5.conf* shown in Example 4-13 configuration file is minimally configured from the default that comes with Red Hat/CentOS 6.4.

Example 4-13. krb5.conf

```
[logging]
 default = FILE:/var/log/krb5libs.log
 kdc = FILE:/var/log/krb5kdc.log
 admin_server = FILE:/var/log/kadmind.log

[libdefaults]
 default_realm = DEV.EXAMPLE.COM
 dns_lookup_realm = false
 dns_lookup_kdc = false
 ticket_lifetime = 24h
 renew_lifetime = 7d
 forwardable = true
 default_tkt_enctypes = aes256-cts aes128-cts
 default_tgs_enctypes = aes256-cts aes128-cts
 udp_preference_limit = 1

[realms]
 EXAMPLE.COM = {
```

```
  kdc = kdc.example.com
  admin_server = kdc.example.com
 }

 DEV.EXAMPLE.COM = {
   kdc = kdc.dev.example.com
   admin_server = kdc.dev.example.com
 }

[domain_realm]
 .example.com = EXAMPLE.COM
 example.com = EXAMPLE.COM
 .dev.example.com = DEV.EXAMPLE.COM
 dev.example.com = DEV.EXAMPLE.COM
```

In this example, there are several different sections. The first, logging, is self-explanatory. It defines where logfiles are stored for the various Kerberos components that generate log events. The second section, libdefaults, contains general default configuration information. Let's take a closer look at the individual configurations in this section:

default_realm
> This defines what Kerberos realm should be assumed if no realm is provided. This is right in line with the earlier kinit example when a realm was not provided.

dns_lookup_realm
> DNS can be used to determine what Kerberos realm to use.

dns_lookup_kdc
> DNS can be used to find the location of the KDC.

ticket_lifetime
> This specifies how long a ticket lasts for. This can be any length of time up to the maximum specified by the KDC. A typical value is 24 hours, denoted by 24h.

renew_lifetime
> This specifies how long a ticket can be *renewed* for. Tickets can be renewed by the KDC without having a client reauthenticate. This must be done prior to tickets expiring.

forwardable
> This specifies that tickets can be *forwardable*, which means that if a user has a TGT already but logs into a different remote system, the KDC can automatically reissue a new TGT without the client having to reauthenticate.

`default_tkt_enctypes`

This specifies the encryption types to use for session keys when making requests to the AS. Preference from highest to lowest is left to right.

`default_tgs_enctypes`

This specifies the encryption types to use for session keys when making requests to the TGS. Preference from highest to lowest is left to right.

`udp_preference_limit`

This specifies the maximum packet size to use before switching to TCP instead of UDP. Setting this to 1 forces TCP to always be used.

The next section, `realms`, lists all the Kerberos realms that the client is aware of. The `kdc` and `admin_server` configurations tell the client which server is running the KDC and kadmin processes, respectively. These configurations can specify the port along with the hostname. If no port is specified, it is assumed to use port 88 for the KDC and 749 for admin server. In this example, two realms are shown. This is a common configuration where a one-way trust exists between two realms, and clients need to know about both realms. In this example, perhaps the EXAMPLE.COM realm contains all of the end-user principals and DEV.EXAMPLE.COM contains all of the Hadoop service principals for a development cluster. Setting up Kerberos in this fashion allows users of this dev cluster to use their existing credentials in EXAMPLE.COM to access it.

The last section, `domain_realm`, maps DNS names to Kerberos realms. The first entry says all hosts under the `example.com` domain map to the EXAMPLE.COM realm, while the second entry says that `example.com` itself maps to the EXAMPLE.COM realm. This is similarly the case with `dev.example.com` and DEV.EXAMPLE.COM. If no matching entry is found in this section, the client will try to use the domain portion of the DNS name (converted to all uppercase) as the realm name.

Summary

The important takeaway from this chapter is that Kerberos authentication is a multi-step client/server process to provide strong authentication of both users *and* services. We took a look at the MIT Kerberos distribution, which is a popular implementation choice. While this chapter covered some of the details of configuring the MIT Kerberos distribution, we strongly encourage you to refer to the official MIT Kerberos documentation (*http://web.mit.edu/~kerberos/*), as it is the most up-to-date reference for the latest distribution; in addition, it serves as a more detailed guide about all of the configuration options available to a security administrator for setting up a Kerberos environment.

In the next chapter, the Kerberos concepts covered thus far will be taken a step further by putting them into the context of core Hadoop and the extended Hadoop ecosystem.

Authentication, Authorization, and Accounting

## CHAPTER 5

Identity and Authentication

The first step necessary for any system securing data is to provide each user with a unique identity and to authenticate a user's claim of a particular identity. The reason authentication and identity are so essential is that no authorization scheme can control access to data if the scheme can't trust that users are who they claim to be.

In this chapter, we'll take a detailed look at how authentication and identity are managed for core Hadoop services. We start by looking at identity and how Hadoop integrates information from Kerberos KDCs and from LDAP and Active Directory domains to provide an integrated view of distributed identity. We'll also look at how Hadoop represents users internally and the options for mapping external, global identities to those internal representations. Next, we revisit Kerberos and go into more details of how Hadoop uses Kerberos for strong authentication. From there, we'll take a look at how some core components use username/password–based authentication schemes and the role of distributed authentication tokens in the overall architecture. We finish the chapter with a discussion of user impersonation and a deep dive into the configuration of Hadoop authentication.

Identity

In the context of the Hadoop ecosystem, identity is a relatively complex topic. This is due to the fact that Hadoop goes to great lengths to be loosely coupled from authoritative identity sources. In Chapter 4, we introduced the Kerberos authentication protocol, a topic that will figure prominently in the following section, as it's the default secure authentication protocol used in Hadoop. While Kerberos provides support for robust authentication, it provides very little in the way of advanced identity features such as groups or roles. In particular, Kerberos exposes identity as a simple two-part string (or in the case of services, three-part string) consisting of a short name and a realm. While this is useful for giving every user a unique identifier, it is insufficient for the implementation of a robust authorization protocol.

In addition to users, most computing systems provide groups, which are typically defined as a collection of users. Because one of the goals of Hadoop is to integrate with existing enterprise systems, Hadoop took the pragmatic approach of using a pluggable system to provide the traditional group concept.

Mapping Kerberos Principals to Usernames

Before diving into more details on how Hadoop maps users to groups, we need to discuss how Hadoop translates Kerberos principal names to usernames. Recall from Chapter 4 that Kerberos uses a two-part string (e.g., `alice@EXAMPLE.COM`) or three-part string (e.g., `hdfs/namenode.example.com@EXAMPLE.COM`) that contains a short name, realm, and an optional instance name or hostname. To simplify working with usernames, Hadoop maps Kerberos principal names to local usernames. Hadoop can use the `auth_to_local` setting in the *krb5.conf* file, or Hadoop-specific rules can be configured in the `hadoop.security.auth_to_local` parameter in the *core-site.xml* file.

The value of `hadoop.security.auth_to_local` is set to one or more rules for mapping principal names to local usernames. A rule can either be the value `DEFAULT` or the string `RULE:` followed by three parts: the initial principal translation, the acceptance filter, and the substitution command. The special value `DEFAULT` maps names in Hadoop's local realm to just the first component (e.g., `alice/admin@EXAMPLE.COM` is mapped to `alice` by the `DEFAULT` rule).

The initial principal translation

The initial principal translation consists of a number followed by the substitution string. The number matches the number of components, not including the realm, of the principal. The substitution string defines how the principal will be initially translated. The variable `$0` will be substituted with the realm, `$1` will be substituted with the first component, and `$2` will be substituted with the second component. See Table 5-1 for some example initial principal translations. The format of the initial principal translation is [*<number>*:*<string>*] and the output is called the *initial local name*.

Table 5-1. Example principal translations

Principal translation	Initial local name for `alice@EXAMPLE.com`	Initial local name for `hdfs/namenode.example.com@EXAMPLE.COM`
`[1:$1.$0]`	`alice.EXAMPLE.COM`	*No match*

Principal translation	Initial local name for `alice@EXAMPLE.com`	Initial local name for `hdfs/namenode.example.com@EXAMPLE.COM`
`[1:$1]`	`alice`	*No match*
`[2:$1_$2@$0]`	No match	`hdfs_namenode.example.com@EXAMPLE.COM`
`[2:$1@$0]`	No match	`hdfs@EXAMPLE.COM`

The acceptance filter

The acceptance filter is a regular expression, and if the initial local name (i.e., the output from the first part of the rule) matches the regular expression, then the substitution command will be run over the string. The initial local name only matches if the entire string is matched by the regular expression. This is equivalent to having the regular expression start with a ^ and end with $. See Table 5-2 for some sample acceptance filters. The format of the acceptance filter is *(<regular expression>)*.

Table 5-2. Example acceptance filters

Acceptance filter	alice.EXAMPLE.COM	hdfs@EXAMPLE.COM
`(.*\.EXAMPLE\.COM)`	Match	No match
`(.*@EXAMPLE\.COM)`	No match	Match
`(.*EXAMPLE\.COM)`	Match	Match
`(EXAMPLE\.COM)`	No match	No match

The substitution command

The substitution command is a sed-style substitution with a regular expression pattern and a replacement string. Matching groups can be included by surrounding a portion of the regular expression in parentheses, and referenced in the replacement string by number (e.g., \1). The group number is determined by the order of the opening parentheses in the regular expression. See Table 5-3 for some sample substitution commands. The format of the substitution command is s/*<pattern>*/*<replacement>*/g. The g at the end is optional, and if it is present then the substitution will be global over the entire string. If the g is omitted, then only the first substring that matches the pattern will be substituted.

Table 5-3. Example substitution commands

Substitution Command	alice.EXAMPLE.COM	hdfs@EXAMPLE.COM
s/(.*)\.EXAMPLE.COM/\1/	alice	Not applicable
s/.EXAMPLE.COM//	alice	hdfs
s/E/Q/	alice.QXAMPLE.COM	hdfs@QXAMPLE.COM
s/E/Q/g	alice.QXAMPLQ.COM	hdfs@QXAMPLQ.COM

The complete format for a rule is RULE:[*<number>*:*<string>*](*<regular expres sion>*)s/*<pattern>*/*<replacement>*/. Multiple rules are separated by new lines and rules are evaluated in order. Once a principal fully matches a rule (i.e., the principal matches the number in the initial principal translation and the initial local name matches the acceptance filter), the username becomes the output of that rule and no other rules are evaluated. Due to this order constraint, it's common to list the DEFAULT rule last.

The most common use of the auth_to_local setting is to configure how to handle principals from other Kerberos realms. A common scenario is to have one or more trusted realms. For example, if your Hadoop realm is HADOOP.EXAMPLE.COM but your corporate realm is CORP.EXAMPLE.COM, then you'd add rules to translate principals in the corporate realm into local users. See Example 5-1 for a sample configuration that only accepts users in the HADOOP.EXAMPLE.COM and CORP.EXAMPLE.COM realms, and maps users to the first component for both realms.

Example 5-1. Example auth_to_local configuration for a trusted realm

```
<property>
  <name>hadoop.security.auth_to_local</name>
  <value>
    RULE:[1:$1@$0](.*@CORP.EXAMPLE.COM)s/@CORP.EXAMPLE.COM//
    RULE:[2:$1@$0](.*@CORP.EXAMPLE.COM)s/@CORP.EXAMPLE.COM//
    DEFAULT
  </value>
</property>
```

Hadoop User to Group Mapping

Hadoop exposes a configuration parameter called hadoop.security.group.mapping to control how users are mapped to groups. The default implementation uses either native calls or local shell commands to look up user-to-group mappings using the standard UNIX interfaces. This means that only the groups that are configured on the server where the mapping is called are visible to Hadoop. In practice, this is not a major concern because it is important for all of the servers in your Hadoop cluster to have a consistent view of the users and groups that will be accessing the cluster.

 In addition to knowing how the user-to-group mapping system works, it is important to know where the mapping takes place. As described in Chapter 6, it is important for user-to-group mappings to get resolved consistently and at the point where authorization decisions are made. For Hadoop, that means that the mappings occur in the NameNode, JobTracker (for MR1), and ResourceManager (for YARN/MR2) processes. This is a very important detail, as the default user-to-group mapping implementation determines group membership by using standard UNIX interfaces; for a group to exist from Hadoop's perspective, it must exist from the perspective of the servers running the NameNode, JobTracker, and ResourceManager.

The `hadoop.security.group.mapping` configuration parameter can be set to any Java class that implements the `org.apache.hadoop.security.GroupMappingServicePro` `vider` interface. In addition to the default described earlier, Hadoop ships with a number of useful implementations of this interface which are summarized here:

`JniBasedUnixGroupsMapping`
   A JNI-based implementation that invokes the `getpwnam_r()` and `getgroup` `list()` libc functions to determine group membership.

`JniBasedUnixGroupsNetgroupMapping`
   An extension of the `JniBasedUnixGroupsMapping` that invokes the `setnet` `grent()`, `getnetgrent()`, and `endnetgrent()` libc functions to determine members of netgroups. Only netgroups that are used in service-level authorization access control lists are included in the mappings.

`ShellBasedUnixGroupsMapping`
   A shell-based implementation that uses the `id -Gn` command.

`ShellBasedUnixGroupsNetgroupMapping`
   An extension of the `ShellBasedUnixGroupsMapping` that uses the `getent` `netgroup` shell command to determine members of netgroups. Only netgroups that are used in service-level authorization access control lists are included in the mappings.

`JniBasedUnixGroupsMappingWithFallback`
   A wrapper around the `JniBasedUnixGroupsMapping` class that falls back to the `ShellBasedUnixGroupsMapping` class if the native libraries cannot be loaded (this is the default implementation).

`JniBasedUnixGroupsNetgroupMappingWithFallback`
> A wrapper around the `JniBasedUnixGroupsNetgroupMapping` class that falls back to the `ShellBasedUnixGroupsNetgroupMapping` class if the native libraries cannot be loaded.

`LdapGroupsMapping`
> Connects directly to an LDAP or Active Directory server to determine group membership.

 Regardless of the group mapping configured, Hadoop will cache group mappings and only call the group mapping implementation when entries in the cache expire. By default, the group cache is configured to expire every 300 seconds (5 minutes). If you want updates to your underlying groups to appear in Hadoop more frequently, then set the `hadoop.security.groups.cache.secs` property in *core-site.xml* to the number of seconds you want entries cached. This should be set small enough for updates to be reflected quickly, but not so small as to require unnecessary calls to your LDAP server or other group provider.

Mapping users to groups using LDAP

Most deployments can use the default group mapping provider. However, for environments where groups are only available directly from an LDAP or Active Directory server and not on the cluster nodes, Hadoop provides the `LdapGroupsMapping` implementation. This method can be configured by setting several required parameters in the *core-site.xml* file on the NameNode, JobTracker, and/or ResourceManager:

`hadoop.security.group.mapping.ldap.url`
> The URL of the LDAP server to use for resolving groups. Must start with `ldap://` or `ldaps://` (if SSL is enabled).

`hadoop.security.group.mapping.ldap.bind.user`
> The distinguished name of the user to bind as when connecting to the LDAP server. This user needs read access to the directory and need not be an administrator.

`hadoop.security.group.mapping.ldap.bind.password`
> The password of the bind user. It is a best practice to not use this setting, but to put the password in a separate file and to configure the `hadoop.security.group.mapping.ldap.bind.password.file` property to point to that path.

If you're configuring Hadoop to directly use LDAP, you lose the local groups for Hadoop service accounts such as hdfs. This can lead to a large number of log messages similar to:

```
No groups available for user hdfs
```

For this reason, it's generally better to use the JNI or shell-based mappings and to integrate with LDAP/Active Directory at the operating system level. The System Security Services Daemon (SSSD) provides strong integration with a number of identity and authentication systems and handles common support for caching and offline access.

Using the parameters described earlier, Example 5-2 demonstrates how to implement LdapGroups Mapping in *coresite.xml*.

Example 5-2. Example LDAP mapping in core-site.xml

```
...
<property>
  <name>hadoop.security.group.mapping</name>
  <value>org.apache.hadoop.security.LdapGroupsMapping</value>
</property>
<property>
  <name>hadoop.security.group.mapping.ldap.url</name>
  <value>ldap://ad.example.com</value>
</property>
<property>
  <name>hadoop.security.group.mapping.ldap.bind.user</name>
  <value>Hadoop@ad.example.com</value>
</property>
<property>
  <name>hadoop.security.group.mapping.ldap.bind.password</name>
  <value>password</value>
</property>
...
```

In addition to the required parameters, there are several optional parameters that can be set to control how users and groups are mapped.

hadoop.security.group.mapping.ldap.bind.password.file
    The path to a file that contains the password of the bind user. This file should only be readable by the Unix users that run the daemons (typically hdfs, mapred, and yarn).

hadoop.security.group.mapping.ldap.ssl
    Set to true to enable the use of SSL when conntecting to the LDAP server. If this setting is enabled, the hadoop.security.group.mapping.ldap.url must start with ldaps://.

`hadoop.security.group.mapping.ldap.ssl.keystore`
> The path to a Java keystore that contains the client certificate required by the LDAP server when connecting with SSL enabled. The keystore must be in the Java keystore (JKS) format.

`hadoop.security.group.mapping.ldap.ssl.keystore.password`
> The password to the `hadoop.security.group.mapping.ldap.ssl.keystore` file. It is a best practice to not use this setting, but to put the password in a separate file and configure the `hadoop.security.group.mapping.ldap.ssl.key` `store.password.file` property to point to that path.

`hadoop.security.group.mapping.ldap.ssl.keystore.password.file`
> The path to a file that contains the password to the `hadoop.security.group.map` `ping.ldap.ssl.keystore` file. This file should only be readable by Unix users that run the daemons (typically `hdfs`, `mapred`, and `yarn`).

`hadoop.security.group.mapping.ldap.base`
> The search base for searching the LDAP directory. This is a distinguished name and will typically be configured as specifically as possible while still covering all users who access the cluster.

`hadoop.security.group.mapping.ldap.search.filter.user`
> A filter to use when searching the directory for LDAP users. The default setting, `(&(objectClass=user)(sAMAccountName={0}))`, is usually appropriate for Active Directory installations. For other LDAP servers, this setting must be changed. For OpenLDAP and compatible servers, the recommended setting is `(&(objectClass=inetOrgPerson)(uid={0}))`.

`hadoop.security.group.mapping.ldap.search.filter.group`
> A filter to use when searching the directory for LDAP groups. The default setting, `(objectClass=group)`, is usually appropriate for Active Directory installations.

`hadoop.security.group.mapping.ldap.search.attr.member`
> The attribute of the group object that identifies the users that are members of the group.

`hadoop.security.group.mapping.ldap.search.attr.group.name`
> The attribute of the group object that identifies the group's name.

`hadoop.security.group.mapping.ldap.directory.search.timeout`
> The maximum amount of time in milliseconds to wait for search results from the directory.

Provisioning of Hadoop Users

One of the most difficult requirements of Hadoop security to understand is that all users of a cluster must be provisioned on all servers in the cluster. This means they can either exist in the local */etc/passwd* password file or, more commonly, can be provisioned by having the servers access a network-based directory service, such as OpenLDAP or Active Directory. In order to understand this requirement, it's important to remember that Hadoop is effectively a service that lets you submit and execute arbitrary code across a cluster of machines. This means that if you don't trust your users, you need to restrict their access to any and all services running on those servers, including standard Linux services such as the local filesystem. Currently, the best way to enforce those restrictions is to execute individual tasks (the processes that make up a job) on the cluster using the username and UID of the user who submitted the job. In order to satisfy that requirement, it is necessary that every server in the cluster uses a consistent user database.

> While it is necessary for all users of the cluster to be provisioned on all of the servers in the cluster, it is not necessary to enable local or remote shell access to all of those users. A best practice is to provision the users with a default shell of */sbin/nologin* and to disable SSH access using the AllowUsers, DenyUsers, AllowGroups, and DenyGroups settings in the */etc/ssh/sshd_config* file.

Authentication

Early versions of Hadoop and the related ecosystem projects did not support strong authentication. Hadoop is a complex distributed system, but fortunately most components in the ecosystem have standardized on a relatively small number of authentication options, depending on the service and protocol. In particular, Kerberos is used across most components of the ecosystem because Hadoop standardized on it early on in its development of security features. A summary of the authentication methods by service and protocol is shown in Table 5-4. In this section, we focus on authentication for HDFS, MapReduce, YARN, HBase, Accumulo, and ZooKeeper. Authentication for Hive, Impala, Hue, Oozie, and Solr are deferred to Chapters 11 and 12 because those are commonly accessed directly by clients.

Table 5-4. Hadoop ecosystem authentication methods

Service	Protocol	Methods
HDFS	RPC	Kerberos, delegation token
HDFS	Web UI	SPNEGO (Kerberos), pluggable

Service	Protocol	Methods
HDFS	REST (WebHDFS)	SPNEGO (Kerberos), delegation token
HDFS	REST (HttpFS)	SPNEGO (Kerberos), delegation token
MapReduce	RPC	Kerberos, delegation token
MapReduce	Web UI	SPNEGO (Kerberos), pluggable
YARN	RPC	Kerberos, delegation token
YARN	Web UI	SPNEGO (Kerberos), pluggable
Hive Server 2	Thrift	Kerberos, LDAP (username/password)
Hive Metastore	Thrift	Kerberos, LDAP (username/password)
Impala	Thrift	Kerberos, LDAP (username/password)
HBase	RPC	Kerberos, delegation token
HBase	Thrift Proxy	None
HBase	REST Proxy	SPNEGO (Kerberos)
Accumulo	RPC	Username/password, pluggable
Accumulo	Thrift Proxy	Username/password, pluggable
Solr	HTTP	Based on HTTP container
Oozie	REST	SPNEGO (Kerberos, delegation token)
Hue	Web UI	Username/password (database, PAM, LDAP), SAML, OAuth, SPNEGO (Kerberos), remote user (HTTP proxy)
ZooKeeper	RPC	Digest (username/password), IP, SASL (Kerberos), pluggable

Kerberos

Out of the box, Hadoop supports two authentication mechanisms: `simple` and `ker beros`. The `simple` mechanism, which is the default, uses the effective UID of the client process to determine the username, which it passes to Hadoop with no additional credentials. In this mode, Hadoop servers fully trust their clients. This default is sufficient for deployments where any user that can gain access to the cluster is fully trusted with access to all data and administrative functions on said cluster. For proof-of-concept systems or lab environments, it is often permissible to run in this mode and rely on firewalls and limiting the set of users that can log on to any system with client-access to the cluster. However, this is rarely acceptable for a production system or any system with multiple tenants. Simple authentication is similarly supported by HBase as its default mechanism.

HDFS, MapReduce, YARN, HBase, Oozie, and ZooKeeper all support Kerberos as an authentication mechanism for clients, though the implementations differ somewhat by service and interface. For RPC-based protocols, the *Simple Authentication and Security Layer* (SASL) framework is used to add authentication to the underlying protocol. In theory, any SASL mechanism could be supported, but in practice, the only mechanisms that are supported are GSSAPI (specifically Kerberos V5) and DIGEST-MD5 (see "Tokens" on page 78 for details on DIGEST-MD5). Oozie does not have an RPC protocol and instead provides clients a REST interface. Oozie uses the *Simple and Protected GSSAPI Negotiation Mechanism* (SPNEGO), a protocol first implemented by Microsoft in Internet Explorer 5.0.1 and IIS 5.0 to do Kerberos authentication over HTTP. SPNEGO is also supported by the web interfaces for HDFS, MapReduce, YARN, Oozie, and Hue as well as the REST interfaces for HDFS (both WebHDFS and HttpFS) and HBase. For both SASL and SPNEGO, the authentication follows the standard Kerberos protocol and only the mechanism for presenting the service ticket changes.

Let's see how Alice would authenticate against the HDFS NameNode using Kerberos:

1. Alice requests a service ticket from the TGS at `kdc.example.com` for the HDFS service identified by `hdfs/namenode.example.com@EXAMPLE.COM`, presenting her TGT with the request.

2. The TGS validates the TGT and provides Alice a service ticket, encrypted with the `hdfs/namenode.example.com@EXAMPLE.COM` principal's key.

3. Alice presents the service ticket to the NameNode (over SASL), which can decrypt it using the `hdfs/namenode.example.com@EXAMPLE.COM` key and validate the ticket.

Username and Password Authentication

ZooKeeper supports authentication by username and password. Rather than using a database of usernames and passwords, ZooKeeper defers password checking to the authorization step (see "ZooKeeper ACLs" on page 123). When an ACL is attached to a ZNode, it includes the authentication scheme and a scheme-specific ID. The scheme-specific ID is verified using the authentication provider for the given scheme. Username and password authentication is implemented by the digest authentication provider, which generates a SHA-1 digest of the username and password. Because verification is deferred to the authorization check, the authentication step always succeeds. Users add their authentication details by calling the `addAuthInfo(String scheme, byte[] authData)` method with `"digest"` as the scheme and `"<user name>:<password>.getBytes()"` as the authData where *<username>* and *<password>* are replaced with their appropriate values.

Accumulo also supports username and password–based authentication. Unlike Zoo-Keeper, Accumulo uses the more common approach of storing usernames and passwords and having an explicit login step that verifies if the password is valid. Accumulo's authentication system is pluggable through different implementations of the `AuthenticationToken` interface. The most common implementation is the `Pass wordToken` class, which can be initialized from a `CharSequence` or a Java `Properties` file. Sample code for connecting to Accumulo using a username and password is shown in Example 5-3.

Example 5-3. Connecting to Accumulo with a username and password

```
// Create a handle to an Accumulo Instance
Instance instance = new ZooKeeperInstance("instance",
    "zk1.example.com,zk2.example.com,zk3.example.com");

// Create a token with the password
AuthenticationToken token = new PasswordToken("secret");

// Create the Connector; if the password is invalid, an
// AccumuloSecurityException will be thrown
Connector connector = instance.getConnector("alice", token);
```

Tokens

In any distributed system, it is necessary for all actions taken on behalf of a user to validate that user's identity. It is not sufficient to merely authenticate with the master of a service; authentication must happen at every interaction. Take the example of running a MapReduce job. Authentication happens between the client and the Name-Node in order to expand any wildcards in the command-line parameters, as well as between the client and the JobTracker, in order to submit the job.

The JobTracker then breaks the job into tasks that are subsequently launched by each TaskTracker in the cluster. Each task has to communicate with the NameNode in order to open the files that make up its input split. In order for the NameNode to enforce filesystem permissions, each task has to authenticate against the NameNode. If Kerberos was the only authentication mechanism, a user's TGT would have to be distributed to each task. The downside to that approach is it allows the tasks to authenticate against *any* Kerberos protected service, which is not desirable. Hadoop solves this problem by issuing authentication tokens that can be distributed to each task but are limited to a specific service.

Delegation tokens

Hadoop has multiple types of tokens that are used to allow subsequent authenticated access without a TGT or Kerberos service ticket. After authenticating against the NameNode using Kerberos, a client can obtain a *delegation token*. The delegation token is a shared secret between the client and the NameNode and can be used for RPC authentication using the DIGEST-MD5 mechanism.

Figure 5-1 shows two interactions between a client and the NameNode. First, the client requests a delegation token using the `getDelegationToken()` RPC call using a Kerberos service ticket for authentication (1). The NameNode replies with the delegation token (2). The client invokes the `getListing()` RPC call to request a directory listing, but this time it uses the delegation token for authentication. After validating the token, the NameNode responds with the requested `DirectoryListing` (4).

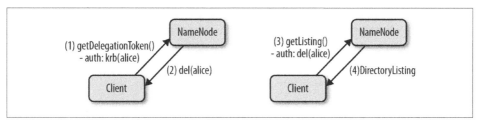

Figure 5-1. Retrieving and using a delegation token

The token has both an expiration date and a max issue date. The token will expire after the expiration date, but can be renewed even if expired up until the max issue date. A delegation token can be requested by the client after any initial Kerberos authentication to the NameNode. The token also has a designated *token renewer*. The token renewer authenticates using its Kerberos credentials when renewing a token on behalf of a user. The most common use of delegation tokens is for MapReduce jobs, in which case the client designates the JobTracker as the renewer. The delegation tokens are keyed by the NameNode's URL and stored in the JobTracker's system directory so they can be passed to the tasks. This allows the tasks to access HDFS without putting a user's TGT at risk.

Block access tokens

File permission checks are performed by the NameNode, not the DataNode. By default, any client can access any block given only its block ID. To solve this, Hadoop introduced the notion of *block access tokens*. Block access tokens are generated by the NameNode and given to a client after the client is authenticated and the NameNode has performed the necessary authorization check for access to a file/block. The token includes the ID of the client, the block ID, and the permitted access mode (READ, WRITE, COPY, REPLACE) and is signed using a shared secret between the Name-Node and DataNode. The shared secret is never shared with the client and when a block access token expires, the client has to request a new one from the NameNode.

Figure 5-2 shows how a client uses a block access token to read data. The client will first use Kerberos credentials to request the location of the block from the NameNode using the getBlockLocations() RPC call (1). The NameNode will respond with a LocatedBlock object which includes, among other details, a block access token for the requested block (2). The client will then request data from the DataNode using the readBlock() method in the data transfer protocol using the block access token for authentication (3). Finally, the DataNode will respond with the requested data (4).

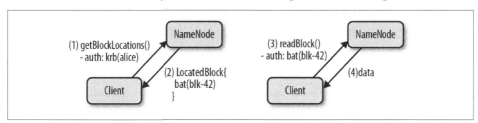

Figure 5-2. Accessing a block using a block access token

Job tokens

When submitting a MapReduce job, the JobTracker will create a secret key called a *job token* that is used by the tasks of the job to authenticate against the TaskTrackers. The JobTracker places the token in the JobTracker's system directory on HDFS and distributes it to the TaskTrackers over RPC. The TaskTrackers will place the token in the job directory on the local disk, which is only accessible to the job's user. The job token is used to authenticate RPC communication between the tasks and the Task-Trackers as well as to generate a hash, which ensures that intermediate outputs sent over HTTP in the shuffle phase are only accessible to the tasks of the job. Further-more, the TaskTracker returning shuffle data calculates a hash that each task can use to verify that it is talking to a true TaskTracker and not an impostor.

Figure 5-3 is a time sequence diagram showing which authentication methods are used during job setup. First, the client requests the creation of a new job using Ker-beros for authentication (1). The JobTracker responds with a job ID that's used to uniquely identify the job (2). The client then requests a delegation token from the NameNode with the JobTracker as the renewer (3). The NameNode responds with the delegation token (4). Delegation tokens will only be issued if the client authenti-cates with Kerberos. Finally, the client uses Kerberos to authenticate with the Job-Tracker sending the delegation token and other required job details.

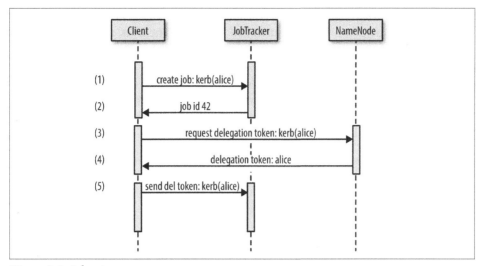

Figure 5-3. Job setup

Things get more interesting once the job starts executing, as Figure 5-4 shows.

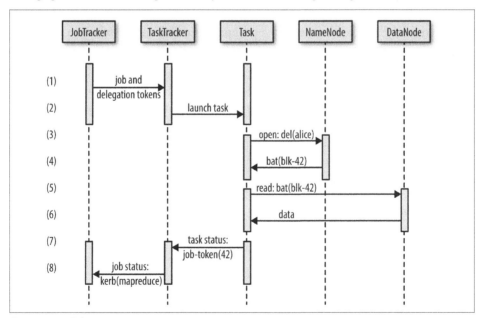

Figure 5-4. Job execution

The JobTracker will generate a job token for the job and then package up and send the job token, delegation token, and other required information to the TaskTracker (1). The JobTracker uses Kerberos authentication when talking to the TaskTracker.

The TaskTracker will then place the tokens into a directory only accessible by the user who submitted the job, and will launch the tasks (2). The Task uses the delegation token to open a file and request the block location for its input split (3). The Name-Node will respond with the block location including a block access token for the given block (4). The Task then uses the block access token to read data from the Data-Node (5) and the DataNode responds with the data (6). As the job progresses, the Task will report task status to the TaskTracker using the job token to authenticate (7). The TaskTracker will then report status back to the JobTracker using Kerberos authentication so that overall job status can be aggregated (8).

Impersonation

There are many services in the Hadoop ecosystem that perform actions on behalf of an end user. In order to maintain security, these services must authenticate their clients and be trusted to *impersonate* other users. Oozie, Hive (in HiveServer2), and Hue all support impersonating end users when accessing HDFS, MapReduce, YARN, or HBase. Secure impersonation works consistently across these services and is supported by designating which users are trusted to perform impersonation. When a trusted user needs to act on behalf of another user, she must authenticate as herself and supply the username of the user she is acting on behalf of. Trusted users can be limited to only impersonate specific groups of users, and only when accessing Hadoop from certain hosts to further constrain their privileges.

Impersonation is also sometimes called *proxying*. The user that can perform the impersonation (i.e., the user that can proxy other users) is called the *proxy*. The configuration parameters for enabling impersonation are `hadoop.prox yuser.<proxy>.hosts` and `hadoop.proxyuser.<proxy>.groups`, where `<proxy>` is the username of the user doing the impersonating. The values are comma-separated lists of hosts and groups, respectively, or * to mean all hosts/groups. If you want both Hue and Oozie to have proxy capabilities, but you want to limit the users that Oozie can proxy to members of the *oozie-users* group, then you'd use a configuration similar to that shown in Example 5-4.

Example 5-4. Example configuration for impersonation

```
<!-- Configure Hue impersonation from hue.example.com -->
<property>
  <name>hadoop.proxyuser.hue.hosts</name>
  <value>hue.example.com</value>
</property>
<property>
  <name>hadoop.proxyuser.hue.groups</name>
  <value>*</value>
</property>
```

```
<!--
    Configure Oozie impersonation from oozie01.example.com and
    oozie02.example.com for users in oozie-users
  -->
<property>
  <name>hadoop.proxyuser.oozie.hosts</name>
  <value>oozie01.example.com,oozie02.example.com</value>
</property>
<property>
  <name>hadoop.proxyuser.oozie.groups</name>
  <value>oozie-users</value>
</property>
```

Configuration

For production deployments, Hadoop supports the `kerberos` mechanism for authentication. When configured for Kerberos authentication, all users and daemons must provide valid credentials in order to access RPC interfaces. This means that you must create a Kerberos service principal for every server/daemon pair in the cluster. You'll recall that in Chapter 4 we described the concept of a service principal name (SPN), which consists of three parts: a service name, a hostname, and a realm. In Hadoop, each daemon that's part of a certain service uses that service's name (`hdfs` for HDFS, `mapred` for MapReduce, and `yarn` for YARN). Additionally, if you want to enable Kerberos authentication for the various web interfaces, then you also need to provision principals with the `HTTP` service name.

Let's see what needs to be done to configure a sample cluster with Kerberos authentication. For our example, we'll assume we have a cluster with hosts and services, as shown in Table 5-5.

The service layout in Table 5-5 is meant to serve as an example, but it isn't the best way to provision a cluster. For starters, we're showing our example with both YARN and MR1 services configured. This is only meant to show the full range of configuration settings needed for both services. In a real deployment, you would only deploy one or the other. Similarly, you would not need to deploy a SecondaryNameNode if you're running two NameNodes with HA as we're doing here. Again, this is just to make our example configuration comprehensive.

Table 5-5. Service layout

Hostname	Daemon
nn1.example.com	NameNode
	JournalNode
nn2.example.com	NameNode
	JournalNode
snn.example.com	SecondaryNameNode
	JournalNode
rm.example.com	ResourceManager
jt.example.com	JobTracker
	JobHistoryServer
dn1.example.com	DataNode
	TaskTracker
	NodeManager
dn2.example.com	DataNode
	TaskTracker
	NodeManager
dn3.example.com	DataNode
	TaskTracker
	NodeManager

The first step is to create all of the required SPNs in your Kerberos KDC and to export a keytab file for each daemon on each server. The list of SPNs required for each host/role is shown in Table 5-6 along with a recommended name for their respective keytab files. You need to create different keytab files per server. We recommend using consistent names per daemon in order to use the same configuration files on all hosts even though keytab files with the same name on different hosts will contain different keys.

Table 5-6. Required Kerberos principals

Hostname	Daemon	Keytab file	SPN
nn1.example.com	NameNode/JournalNode	hdfs.keytab	hdfs/nn1.example.com@EXAMPLE.COM
			HTTP/nn1.example.com@EXAMPLE.COM
nn2.example.com	NameNode/JournalNode	hdfs.keytab	hdfs/nn2.example.com@EXAMPLE.COM
			HTTP/nn2.example.com@EXAMPLE.COM
snn.example.com	SecondaryNameNode/JournalNode	hdfs.keytab	hdfs/snn.example.com@EXAMPLE.COM
			HTTP/snn.example.com@EXAMPLE.COM
rm.example.com	ResourceManager	yarn.keytab	yarn/rm.example.com@EXAMPLE.COM
jt.example.com	JobTracker	mapred.keytab	mapred/jt.example.com@EXAMPLE.COM
			HTTP/jt.example.com@EXAMPLE.COM
	JobHistoryServer	mapred.keytab	mapred/jt.example.com@EXAMPLE.COM
dn1.example.com	DataNode	hdfs.keytab	hdfs/dn1.example.com@EXAMPLE.COM
			HTTP/dn1.example.com@EXAMPLE.COM
	TaskTracker	mapred.keytab	mapred/dn1.example.com@EXAMPLE.COM
			HTTP/dn1.example.com@EXAMPLE.COM
	NodeManager	yarn.keytab	yarn/dn1.example.com@EXAMPLE.COM
			HTTP/dn1.example.com@EXAMPLE.COM
dn2.example.com	DataNode	hdfs.keytab	hdfs/dn2.example.com@EXAMPLE.COM
			HTTP/dn2.example.com@EXAMPLE.COM
	TaskTracker	mapred.keytab	mapred/dn2.example.com@EXAMPLE.COM
			HTTP/dn2.example.com@EXAMPLE.COM
	NodeManager	yarn.keytab	yarn/dn2.example.com@EXAMPLE.COM

Hostname	Daemon	Keytab file	SPN
			HTTP/dn2.example.com@EXAMPLE.COM
dn3.example.com	DataNode	hdfs.keytab	hdfs/dn3.example.com@EXAMPLE.COM
			HTTP/dn3.example.com@EXAMPLE.COM
	TaskTracker	mapred.keytab	mapred/dn3.example.com@EXAMPLE.COM
			HTTP/dn3.example.com@EXAMPLE.COM
	NodeManager	yarn.keytab	yarn/dn3.example.com@EXAMPLE.COM
			HTTP/dn3.example.com@EXAMPLE.COM

Take care when exporting keytab files, as the default is to random-
ize the Kerberos key each time a principal is exported. You can
export each principal once and then use the ktutil utility to combine the necessary keys into the keytab file for each daemon.

We recommend placing the appropriate keytab files into your
$HADOOP_CONF_DIR directory (typically */etc/hadoop/conf*).

Full Example Configuration Files

A complete set of example configuration files are available in the
example repository on GitHub (*http://bit.ly/1EAEmTr*) that accompanies this book.

After you've created all of the required SPNs and distributed the keytab files, you
need to configure Hadoop to use Kerberos for authentication. Start by setting
hadoop.security.authentication to kerberos in the *core-site.xml* file, as shown in
Example 5-5.

Example 5-5. Configuring the authentication type to Kerberos

```
<property>
  <name>hadoop.security.authentication</name>
  <value>kerberos</value>
</property>
```

HDFS

Next, we need to configure each daemon with its Kerberos principals and keytab files. For the NameNode, we also have to enable block access tokens by setting `dfs.block.access.token.enable` to `true`. The NameNode's configuration should be set in the *hdfs-site.xml* file, as shown in Example 5-6.

Example 5-6. Configuring the NameNode for Kerberos

```
<property>
  <name>dfs.block.access.token.enable</name>
  <value>true</value>
</property>
<property>
  <name>dfs.namenode.keytab.file</name>
  <value>hdfs.keytab</value>
</property>
<property>
  <name>dfs.namenode.kerberos.principal</name>
  <value>hdfs/_HOST@EXAMPLE.COM</value>
</property>
<property>
  <name>dfs.namenode.kerberos.internal.spnego.principal</name>
  <value>HTTP/_HOST@EXAMPLE.COM</value>
</property>
```

If you are not enabling high availability for HDFS, then you would next configure the SecondaryNameNode in the *hdfs-site.xml* file, as shown in Example 5-7.

Example 5-7. Configuring the SecondaryNameNode for Kerberos

```
<property>
  <name>dfs.secondary.namenode.keytab.file</name>
  <value>hdfs.keytab</value>
</property>
<property>
  <name>dfs.secondary.namenode.kerberos.principal</name>
  <value>hdfs/_HOST@EXAMPLE.COM</value>
</property>
<property>
  <name>dfs.secondary.namenode.kerberos.internal.spnego.principal</name>
  <value>HTTP/_HOST@EXAMPLE.COM</value>
</property>
```

If you are enabling high availability for HDFS, then you need to configure the JournalNodes with the following settings in the *hdfs-site.xml* file, as shown in Example 5-8.

Example 5-8. Configuring the JournalNode for Kerberos

```xml
<property>
  <name>dfs.journalnode.keytab.file</name>
  <value>hdfs.keytab</value>
</property>
<property>
  <name>dfs.journalnode.kerberos.principal</name>
  <value>hdfs/_HOST@EXAMPLE.COM</value>
</property>
<property>
  <name>dfs.journalnode.kerberos.internal.spnego.principal</name>
  <value>HTTP/_HOST@EXAMPLE.COM</value>
</property>
```

Next, we'll configure the DataNode's with the following settings in the *hdfs-site.xml* file. In addition to configuring the keytab and principal name, you must configure the DataNode to use a privileged port for its RPC and HTTP servers. These ports need to be privileged because the DataNode does not use Hadoop's RPC framework for the data transfer protocol. By using privileged ports, the DataNode is authenticating that it was started by *root* using `jsvc`, as shown in Example 5-9.

Example 5-9. Configuring the DataNode for Kerberos

```xml
<property>
  <name>dfs.datanode.address</name>
  <value>0.0.0.0:1004</value>
</property>
<property>
  <name>dfs.datanode.http.address</name>
  <value>0.0.0.0:1006</value>
</property>
<property>
  <name>dfs.datanode.keytab.file</name>
  <value>hdfs.keytab</value>
</property>
<property>
  <name>dfs.datanode.kerberos.principal</name>
  <value>hdfs/_HOST@EXAMPLE.COM</value>
</property>
```

WebHDFS is a REST-based protocol for accessing data in HDFS. WebHDFS scales by serving data over HTTP from the DataNode that stores the blocks being read. In order to secure access to WebHDFS, you need to set the following parameters in the *hdfs-site.xml* file of the NameNodes and DataNodes, as shown in Example 5-10.

Example 5-10. Configuring WebHDFS for Kerberos

```
<property>
  <name>dfs.web.authentication.kerberos.keytab</name>
  <value>hdfs.keytab</value>
</property>
<property>
  <name>dfs.web.authentication.kerberos.principal</name>
  <value>HTTP/_HOST@EXAMPLE.COM</value>
</property>
```

The configuration of HDFS is now complete!

YARN

Now we'll configure YARN, starting with the ResourceManager. You'll need to set the configuration parameters in the *yarn-site.xml* file, as shown in Example 5-11.

Example 5-11. Configuring the ResourceManager for Kerberos

```
<property>
  <name>yarn.resourcemanager.principal</name>
  <value>yarn/_HOST@EXAMPLE.COM</value>
</property>
<property>
  <name>yarn.resourcemanager.webapp.spnego-principal</name>
  <value>HTTP/_HOST@EXAMPLE.COM</value>
</property>
<property>
  <name>yarn.resourcemanager.keytab</name>
  <value>yarn.keytab</value>
</property>
<property>
  <name>yarn.resourcemanager.webapp.spnego-keytab-file</name>
  <value>yarn.keytab</value>
</property>
```

We configure the NodeManagers to use Kerberos by setting the configuration parameters in the *yarn-site.xml* file, as shown in Example 5-12.

Example 5-12. Configuring the NodeManager for Kerberos

```
<property>
  <name>yarn.nodemanager.principal</name>
  <value>yarn/_HOST@EXAMPLE.COM</value>
</property>
<property>
  <name>yarn.nodemanager.webapp.spnego-principal</name>
  <value>HTTP/_HOST@EXAMPLE.COM</value>
</property>
```

```
<property>
  <name>yarn.nodemanager.keytab</name>
  <value>yarn.keytab</value>
</property>
<property>
  <name>yarn.nodemanager.webapp.spnego-keytab-file</name>
  <value>yarn.keytab</value>
</property>
```

In addition to configuring the NodeMangaer to use Kerberos for authentication, we need to configure the NodeManager to use the LinuxContainerExecutor. The Linux ContainerExecutor uses a setuid binary to launch YARN containers. This allows the NodeManagers to run the containers using the UID of the user that submitted the job. This is required in a secure configuration to ensure that Alice can't access files created by a container launched by Bob. Without the LinuxContainerExecutor, all of the containers would run as the yarn user and containers could access each other's local files. First, set the configuration parameters in the *yarn-site.xml* file, as shown in Example 5-13.

Example 5-13. Configuring the NodeManager with the LinuxContainerExecutor

```
<property>
  <name>yarn.nodemanager.container-executor.class</name>
  <value>org.apache.hadoop.yarn.server.nodemanager.LinuxContainerExecutor</value>
</property>
<property>
  <name>yarn.nodemanager.linux-container-executor.group</name>
  <value>yarn</value>
</property>
```

We also have to configure the executor binary itself. That's done by setting the configuration parameters in the *container-executor.cfg* file, as shown in Example 5-14. The value for the yarn.nodemanager.linux-container-executor.group parameter should be set to the same value in the *yarn-site.xml* file and the *container-executor.cfg* file. Typically this is set to yarn.

Example 5-14. Configuring the LinuxContainerExecutor

```
yarn.nodemanager.linux-container-executor.group=yarn
min.user.id=1000
allowed.system.users=nobody,impala,hive,llama
banned.users=root,hdfs,yarn,mapred,bin
```

The min.user.id setting is used to prevent the LinuxContainerExecutor from running containers with UIDs below that value. This is typically set to 1000 or 500 depending on where regular user account UIDs start in your environment. In addition to this setting, you can set a list of explicitly allowed users and a list of explicitly banned users. The setting is used to allow, among other things, the *hive* user to run containers. This is needed when enabling Apache Sentry because Hive impersonation is turned off when Sentry is enabled.

The final step for configuring YARN to use Kerberos is to configure the JobHistoryServer. This can be done by setting the configuration parameters in the *mapred-site.xml* file, as shown in Example 5-15.

Example 5-15. Configuring the JobHistoryServer for Kerberos

```
<property>
  <name>mapreduce.jobhistory.principal</name>
  <value>mapred/_HOST@EXAMPLE.COM</value>
</property>
<property>
  <name>mapreduce.jobhistory.webapp.spnego-principal</name>
  <value>HTTP/_HOST@EXAMPLE.COM</value>
</property>
<property>
  <name>mapreduce.jobhistory.keytab</name>
  <value>mapred.keytab</value>
</property>
<property>
  <name>mapreduce.jobhistory.webapp.spnego-keytab-file</name>
  <value>mapred.keytab</value>
</property>
```

MapReduce (MR1)

If you're still using MR1, you will skip the preceding steps for YARN and configure the JobTracker and TaskTrackers. First, set the configuration parameters in the *mapred-site.xml* file, as shown in Example 5-16.

Example 5-16. Configuring the JobTracker for Kerberos

```
<property>
  <name>mapreduce.jobtracker.kerberos.principal</name>
  <value>mapred/_HOST@EXAMPLE.COM</value>
</property>
<property>
  <name>mapreduce.jobtracker.keytab.file</name>
  <value>mapred.keytab</value>
</property>
```

Configuring the TaskTrackers is also straightforward. Set the configuration parameters in the *mapred-site.xml* file, as shown in Example 5-17.

Example 5-17. Configuring the TaskTracker for Kerberos

```
<property>
  <name>mapreduce.tasktracker.kerberos.principal</name>
  <value>mapred/_HOST@EXAMPLE.COM</value>
</property>
<property>
  <name>mapreduce.tasktracker.keytab.file</name>
  <value>mapred.keytab</value>
</property>
```

When we configured the NodeManagers in Examples 5-12 and 5-13, we also had to enable the `LinuxContainerExecutor`. The `LinuxTaskController` is the equivalent in MR1. Start by setting the configuration parameters in the *mapred-site.xml* file, as shown in Example 5-18.

Example 5-18. Configuring the TaskTracker with the LinuxTaskController

```
<property>
  <name>mapred.task.tracker.task-controller</name>
  <value>org.apache.hadoop.mapred.LinuxTaskController</value>
</property>
<property>
  <name>mapreduce.tasktracker.group</name>
  <value>mapred</value>
</property>
```

We also have to configure the task controller itself. Set the configuration parameters in the *taskcontroller.cfg* file. Make sure that the values for `mapreduce.task tracker.group` match the value, typically `mapred`, used in the *mapred-site.xml* file. Unlike the `LinuxContainerExecutor`, the `LinuxTaskController` doesn't let you configure a list of allowed system users. That means that you might have to lower the `min.user.id` and increase the number of users explicitly banned in the `banned.users` list if you need to allow certain system users to run jobs, as shown in Example 5-19.

Example 5-19. Configuring the LinuxTaskController

```
mapred.local.dir=/mapred/local
hadoop.log.dir=/var/log/hadoop-0.20-mapreduce
mapreduce.tasktracker.group=mapred
banned.users=root,mapred,hdfs,bin
min.user.id=1000
```

Oozie

As already discussed, Oozie supports Kerberos for authentication. Before enabling authentication in Oozie, you first must configure Oozie to authenticate itself when accessing Hadoop. This is done by configuring the following parameters (a sample of the appropriate configuration parameters is shown in Example 5-20):

`oozie.service.HadoopAccessorService.kerberos.enabled`
    Set to `true` when Hadoop has `hadoop.security.authentication` set to `kerberos`.

`local.realm`
    Set this to the default realm of the Hadoop cluster. This should be the same realm as the `default_realm` setting in the *krb5.conf* file.

`oozie.service.HadoopAccessorService.kerberos.principal`
    The Kerberos principal that Oozie will use to authenticate. This is typically `oozie/<fqdn>@<REALM>` where *<fqdn>* is the fully qualified domain name of the server running Oozie and *<REALM>* is the local Kerberos realm.

`oozie.service.HadoopAccessorService.keytab.file`
    The path to the keytab file that has the key for the configured Kerberos principal.

Example 5-20. Configuring Oozie to work with a Kerberos-enabled Hadoop cluster

```
<property>
  <name>oozie.service.HadoopAccessorService.kerberos.enabled</name>
  <value>true</value>
</property>
<property>
  <name>local.realm</name>
  <value>EXAMPLE.COM</value>
</property>
<property>
  <name>oozie.service.HadoopAccessorService.keytab.file</name>
  <value>oozie.keytab</value>
</property>
<property>
  <name>oozie.service.HadoopAccessorService.kerberos.principal</name>
  <value>oozie/oozie01.example.com@EXAMPLE.COM</value>
</property>
```

After Oozie is configured to work with your Kerberos-enabled Hadoop cluster, you're ready to configure Oozie to use Kerberos for user authentication. The relevant settings are as follows (an example configuration is shown in Example 5-21):

`oozie.authentication.type`
    Set the type of authentication required by users. This can be set to `simple` (the default), `kerberos`, or the fully qualified class name of a class that implements the Hadoop `AuthenticationHandler` interface.

`oozie.authentication.token.validity`
> The amount of time, in seconds, that authentication tokens are valid. Authentication tokens are returned as a cookie following the initial authentication method (typically Kerberos/SPNEGO).

`oozie.authentication.signature.secret`
> A secret used to sign the authentication tokens. If left blank, a random secret will be generated on startup. If Oozie is configured in HA mode, then this must be the same secret on all Oozie servers.

`oozie.authentication.cookie.domain`
> The domain name used when generating the authentication cookie. This should be set to the domain name of the cluster.

`oozie.authentication.kerberos.principal`
> The Kerberos principal used for the Oozie service. Because Oozie uses SPNEGO over HTTP for authentication, this must be set to `HTTP/<fqdn>@<REALM>` where `<fqdn>` is the fully qualified domain name of the Oozie server and `<REALM>` is the local Kerberos realm.

`oozie.authentication.kerberos.keytab`
> The path to the keytab file that has the key for the Kerberos principal.

`oozie.authentication.kerberos.name.rules`
> Rules for translating from Kerberos principals to local usernames. This parameter uses the same format as the `hadoop.security.auth_to_local` parameter in Hadoop. See "Mapping Kerberos Principals to Usernames" on page 68 and Example 5-21 for how to configure.

Example 5-21. Configuring Oozie with Kerberos authentication

```
<property>
  <name>oozie.authentication.type</name>
  <value>kerberos</value>
</property>
<property>
  <name>oozie.authentication.token.validity</name>
  <value>36000</value>
</property>
<property>
  <name>oozie.authentication.signature.secret</name>
  <value>FiSEcve7lBsdGpvr</value>
</property>
<property>
  <name>oozie.authentication.cookie.domain</name>
  <value>example.com</value>
</property>
```

```
<property>
  <name>oozie.authentication.kerberos.principal</name>
  <value>HTTP/oozie01.example.com@EXAMPLE.COM</value>
</property>
<property>
  <name>oozie.authentication.kerberos.principal</name>
  <value>oozie.keytab</value>
</property>
<property>
  <name>oozie.authentication.kerberos.name.rules</name>
  <value>DEFAULT</value>
</property>
```

If you're running Oozie in high-availability mode, then you need some additional configuration. First, you should configure Oozie to use ZooKeeper ACLs by setting `oozie.zookeeper.secure` in the *oozie-site.xml* file, as shown in Example 5-22.

Example 5-22. Configuring ZooKeeper ACLs for Oozie in oozie-site.xml

```
<property>
  <name>oozie.zookeeper.secure</name>
  <value>true</value>
</property>
```

If you're using Oozie with a version of Hadoop prior to Hadoop 2.5.0, then you need to use the fully qualified domain of the load balancer in the HTTP principal name. For example, if you have Oozie servers running on `oozie01.example.com`, and `oozie02.example.com` and the load balancer runs on `oozie.example.com`, then you'd use a principal of `HTTP/oozie.example.com@EXAMPLE.COM` on all of the Oozie servers. In this mode, only access through the load balancer will work. Also, certain Oozie features such as log streaming won't work. In this setup, you'd set the following in your *oozie-site.xml* file, as shown in Example 5-23.

Example 5-23. Configuring the Oozie SPN in a load balancer environment

```
<property>
  <name>oozie.authentication.kerberos.principal</name>
  <value>HTTP/oozie.example.com@EXAMPLE.COM</value>
</property>
```

Starting with Hadoop 2.5.0 and later, you can include multiple Kerberos principals in Oozie's keytab file. In this case, you'll include the principal for the load balancer and the principal for the specific server in the keytab file (e.g., `HTTP/oozie.exam ple.com@EXAMPLE.COM` and `HTTP/oozie01.example.com@EXAMPLE.COM`). You then have to set `oozie.authentication.kerberos.principal` to *, as shown in Example 5-23.

Example 5-24. Configuring Oozie with multiple SPNs

```
<property>
  <name>oozie.authentication.kerberos.principal</name>
  <value>*</value>
</property>
```

HBase

Configuring HBase with Kerberos authentication is very similar to configuring core Hadoop. In the interest of space, we refer you to the "Securing Apache HBase" (*http://hbase.apache.org/book.html#security*) section of *The Apache HBase Reference Guide* (*http://hbase.apache.org/book.html*).

Summary

In this chapter, we introduced the concept of identity and showed how Hadoop leverages Kerberos principal names to map to usernames. We also saw that Hadoop retrieves group membership information about a user. This will become important in the next chapter, which covers authorization.

We also analyzed the different ways that authentication takes place in the cluster. While Kerberos is the canonical example and used frequently, we saw that there are other ways that authentication happens with the usage of delegation tokens. This is a key piece of the Hadoop authentication architecture because it reduces the number of Kerberos authentication paths that are necessary to complete a workflow—such as an Oozie workflow that executes a Hive query, which translates to a MapReduce job that ultimately processes files. Without delegation tokens, each of these steps would require Kerberos service tickets, adding strain on the Kerberos KDC.

Finally, we introduced the idea of impersonation. We discussed how system users can authenticate on behalf of other users. This is a frequently used concept because end users often use tools that sit between them and the services they are attempting to access. With impersonation, a system or service can then authenticate with a second remote service and be granted access privileges as if the end user authenticated directly.

From here, we will continue the AAA conversation by talking about authorization, as we get closer to users being able to access data and services.

## CHAPTER 6

Authorization

In "Authentication" on page 75, we saw how the various Hadoop ecosystem projects support strong authentication to ensure that users are who they claim to be. However, authentication is only part of the overall security story—you also need a way to model which actions or data an authenticated user can access. The protection of resources in this manner is called *authorization* and is probably one of the most complex topics related to Hadoop security. Each service is relatively unique in the services it provides, and thus the authorization model it supports. The sections in this chapter are divided into subsections based on how each service implements authorization.

We start by looking at HDFS and its support for POSIX-style file permissions, as well as its support for service-level authorization to restrict user access to specific HDFS functions. Next, we turn our attention to MapReduce and YARN, which support a similar style of service-level authorization as well as a queue-based model controlling access to system resources. In the case of MapReduce and YARN, authorization is useful for both security and resource management/multitenancy (for more information on resource management, we recommend *Hadoop Operations* by Eric Sammer [O'Reilly]). Finally, we cover the authorization features of the popular BigTable clones, Apache HBase and Apache Accumulo, including a discussion of the pros and cons of role-based and attribute-based security as well as a discussion of cell-level versus column-level security.

HDFS Authorization

Every attempt to access a file or directory in HDFS must first pass an authorization check. HDFS adopts the authorization scheme common to POSIX-compatible filesystems. Permissions are managed by three distinct classes of user: *owner*, *group*, and *others*. Each file or directory is owned by a specific user and that user makes up the object's *owner* class. Objects are also assigned a group and all of the members of that group make up the object's *group* class. All users that are not the owner and do not belong to the group assigned to the object make up the *others* class. Read, write, and execute permissions can be granted to each class independently.

These permissions are represented by a single octal integer that is calculated by summing the permission values (4 for read, 2 for write, and 1 for execute). For example, to represent that a class has read and execute permissions for a directory, an octal value of 5 (4+1) would be assigned. In HDFS, it is not meaningful, nor is it invalid, to assign the execute permission to a file. For directories, the execute bit gives permission to access a file's contents and metadata information if the name of the file is known. In order to list the names of files in a directory, you need read permission for the directory.

Regardless of the permissions on a file or a directory, the user that the NameNode runs as (typically *hdfs*) and any member of the group defined in `dfs.permis sions.superusergroup` (defaults to *supergroup*), can read, write, or delete any file and directory. As far as HDFS is concerned, they are the equivalent of *root* on a Linux system.

The permissions assigned to the owner, group, and others can be represented by concatenating the three octal values in that order. For example, take a file for which the owner has read and write permissions and all other users have only read permission. This file's permissions would be represented as 644; 6 is assigned to the owner because she has both read and write (4+2), and 4 is assigned to the group and other classes because they only have read permissions. For a file for which all permissions have been granted to all users, the permissions would be 777.

In addition to the standard permissions, HDFS supports three additional special permissions: *setuid*, *setgid*, and *sticky*. These permissions are also represented as an octal value with 4 for setuid, 2 for setgid, and 1 for sticky. These permissions are optional and are included to the *left* of the regular permission bits if they are specified. Because files in HDFS can't be executed, setuid has no effect. Setgid similarly has no effect on files, but for directories it forces the group of newly created immediate child files and directories to that of the parent. This is the default behavior in HDFS, so it is not necessary to enable setgid on directories. The final permission is often called the sticky bit and it means that files in a directory can only be deleted by the owner of that file. Without the sticky bit set, a file can be deleted by anyone that has write access to the directory. In HDFS, the owner of a directory and the HDFS superuser can also delete files regardless of whether the sticky bit is set. The sticky bit is useful for directories, such as */tmp*, where you want all users to have write access to the directory but only the owner of the data should be able to delete data.

HDFS Extended ACLs

Using the basic POSIX permissions of owner, group, and world to allow access to a given file or directory is not always easy. What happens if two or more different groups of users need access to the same HDFS directory? With basic POSIX permissions, an administrator is left with two options: (1) make the directory world-accessible, or (2) create a group that encompasses all of the users that need access to the directory and assign group permissions to it. This is not ideal because option #1 risks making the data available to more than the intended users, and option #2 can quickly become a headache from a group management perspective. This problem becomes further compounded when one group of users requires read access and another group of users requires both read and write access.

With the release of Hadoop 2.4, HDFS is now equipped with extended ACLs. These ACLs work very much the same way as extended ACLs in a Unix environment. This allows files and directories in HDFS to have more permissions than the basic POSIX permissions.

To use HDFS extended ACLs, they must first be enabled on the NameNode. To do this, set the configuration property `dfs.namenode.acls.enabled` to `true` in *hdfs-site.xml*. Example 6-1 shows how HDFS extended ACLs are used.

Example 6-1. HDFS extended ACLs example

```
[alice@hadoop01 ~]$ hdfs dfs -ls /data
Found 1 items
drwxr-xr-x   - alice analysts        0 2014-10-25 19:03 /data/alice
[alice@hadoop01 ~]$ hdfs dfs -getfacl /data/alice
# file: /data/alice
# owner: alice
# group: analysts
user::rwx
group::r-x
other::r-x
[alice@hadoop01 ~]$ hdfs dfs -setfacl -m user:bob:r-x /data/alice
[alice@hadoop01 ~]$ hdfs dfs -setfacl -m group:developers:rwx /data/alice
[alice@hadoop01 ~]$ hdfs dfs -ls /data
Found 1 items
drwxr-xr-x+   - alice analysts        0 2014-10-25 19:03 /data/alice
[alice@hadoop01 ~]$ hdfs dfs -getfacl /data/alice
# file: /data/alice
# owner: alice
# group: analysts
user::rwx
user:bob:r-x
group::r-x
group:developers:rwx
mask::rwx
other::r-x
```

```
[alice@hadoop01 ~]$ hdfs dfs -chmod 750 /data/alice
[alice@hadoop01 ~]$ hdfs dfs -getfacl /data/alice
# file: /data/alice
# owner: alice
# group: analysts
user::rwx
group::r-x
group:developers:rwx    #effective:r-x
mask::r-x
other::---
[alice@hadoop01 ~]$ hdfs dfs -setfacl -b /data/alice
[alice@hadoop01 ~]$ hdfs dfs -getfacl /data/alice
# file: /data/alice
# owner: alice
# group: analysts
user::rwx
group::r-x
other::---
```

There are a few points worth highlighting. First, by default, files and directories do not have any ACLs. After adding an ACL entry to an object, the HDFS listing now appends a + to the permissions listing, such as in drwxr-xr-x+. Also, after adding an ACL entry, a new property is listed in the ACL called mask. The mask defines what the most restrictive permissions will be. For example, if user bob has rwx permissions, but the mask is r-x, bob's effective permissions are r-x and are noted as such in the output of getfacl, as shown in the example.

Another important part about the mask is that it gets adjusted to the least restrictive permissions that are set on an ACL. For example, if a mask is currently set to be r-x and a new ACL entry is added for a group to grant rwx permissions, the mask is adjusted to rwx.

> Setting standard POSIX permissions on a file or directory that contains an extended ACL might immediately impact all entries because hdfs dfs -chmod will effectively set the mask, regardless of what ACL entries are present. For example, setting 700 permissions on a file or directory yields effective permissions of *no access* to all ACL entries defined, except the owner!

The last part of the example demonstrates how to completely remove all ACL entries for a directory, leaving just the basic POSIX permissions in place. One final point about extended ACLs is that they are limited to 32 entries per object (i.e., file or directory). That being said, four of the entries are taken up by user, group, other, and mask, so the net is 28 entries, which can be added before the NameNode throws an error: setfacl: Invalid ACL: ACL has 33 entries, which exceeds maximum of 32.

Another useful feature of extended ACLs is the usage of a *default ACL*. A default ACL applies only to a directory, and the effect is that all subdirectories and files created in that directory inherit the default ACL of the parent directory. For example, if a directory has a default ACL entry of `default:group:analysts:rwx`, then all files created in the directory will get a `group:analysts:rwx` entry, and subdirectories will get *both* the default ACL and the access ACL copied over. To set a default ACL, simply prepend `default:` to the user or group entry in the `setfacl` command. Remember that default ACLs *do not* themselves grant authorization. They simply define the inheritance behavior of newly created subdirectories and files.

Service-Level Authorization

Hadoop also supports authorization at the service level. This can be used to control which users or groups of users can access certain protocols, as well as prevent rogue processes from masquerading as daemons. Service-level authorization is enabled by setting the `hadoop.security.authorization` variable to `true` in *core-site.xml*. The actual polices are configured in a file called *hadoop-policy.xml*. This file is structured similarly to the standard configuration files where each property is defined in a `property` tag with one sub-tag for the `name` of the property and another for the `value` of the property. Each service-level authorization property defines an access control list (ACL) with a comma-delimited list of users and groups that can access that protocol. The two lists are separated by a space. A leading space implies an empty list of users and a trailing space implies an empty list of groups. A special value of * can be used to signify that all users are granted access to that protocol (this is the default setting). Example ACLs are provided in Table 6-1.

Table 6-1. Hadoop access control lists

ACL	Meaning
`"*"`	All users are permitted
`" "`	No users are permitted
`"alice,bob hdusers"`	*alice*, *bob*, and anyone in the *hdusers* group are permitted
`"alice,bob "` (trailing space)	*alice* and *bob* are permitted, but no groups
`" hdusers"` (leading space)	Anyone in the *hdusers* group is permitted, but no other users

Before we look at the available ACLs, let's define some users and groups to help guide the configuration. Assume that we have a small cluster with a handful of users and a Hadoop administrator. The users of our cluster have Linux workstations and we want to make sure that they are able to do as much development from their workstations as possible, so we aren't planning to put a firewall between the workstation network and the cluster. Furthermore, assume that we have a central Active Directory that defines users and groups for the entire corporate network. The cluster's KDC is configured with a one-way trust to allow AD users to log into the cluster without needing new credentials. Now we want our Hadoop developers to have access to the cluster, but we don't want the entire enterprise browsing HDFS or launching MapReduce jobs. To help in our setup, we've configured two groups, one called *hadoop-users* and one called *hadoop-admins*. Because this is a new environment, we initially populate the *hadoop-users* group with just three users: Alice, Bob, and Joey. Joey is a certified Hadoop administrator so he's also added to the *hadoop-admins* group.

Service-level authorizations are supported by HDFS, MapReduce (MR1), and YARN (MR2). The list of protocol ACLs and suggested configuration values for our example are defined for HDFS, MapReduce (MR1), and YARN (MR2) in Tables 6-2, 6-3, and 6-4, respectively. Some of the properties are shared among the services, such as protocols for refreshing the policy configuration, so they will appear in multiple tables. Because MR1 is not included in Hadoop 2.3, some of the property names are different for the MR1 policies. The MR1 property names are used when deploying Hadoop 1.2 or a distribution that includes MR1 for use with HDFS from Hadoop 2.x.

Table 6-2. HDFS service-level authorization properties

Property name	Description	Suggested value
`security.client.protocol.acl`	Client to NameNode protocol; used by user code via the `DistributedFileSystem` class	`"yarn,mapred hadoop-users"`
`security.client.datanode.protocol.acl`	Client to DataNode protocol	`"yarn,mapred hadoop-users"`
`security.get.user.mappings.protocol.acl`	Protocol to retrieve the groups that a user maps to	`"yarn,mapred hadoop-users"`
`security.datanode.protocol.acl`	DataNode to NameNode protocol	`"hdfs"`
`security.inter.datanode.protocol.acl`	DataNode to DataNode protocol	`"hdfs"`
`security.namenode.protocol.acl`	SecondaryNameNode to NameNode protocol	`"hdfs"`
`security.qjournal.service.protocol.acl`	NameNode to JournalNode protocol	`"hdfs"`

Property name	Description	Suggested value
`security.zkfc.protocol.acl`	Protocol exposed by the `ZKFailoverControl ler`	`"hdfs"`
`security.ha.service.proto col.acl`	Protocol used by the `hdfs hadmin` command to manage the HA states of the NameNodes	`"hdfs,yarn hadoop-admins"`
`security.refresh.policy.proto col.acl`	Used by the `hdfs dfsadmin` command to load the latest *hadoop-policy.xml* file	`"hadoop-admins"`
`security.refresh.user.map pings.protocol.acl`	Protocol to refresh the user to group mappings	`"hadoop-admins"`

Table 6-3. MapReduce (MR1) Service Level Authorization Properties

Property Name	Description	Suggested Value
`security.task.umbilical.pro tocol.acl`	Protocol used by MR tasks to report task progress. **Note: must be set to ***	`"*"`
`security.job.submission.pro tocol.acl`	Protocol for clients to submit jobs to the JobTracker	`"hadoop- users"`
`security.inter.tracker.pro tocol.acl`	Protocol used by TaskTrackers to communicate with the JobTracker	`"mapred"`
`security.refresh.policy.pro tocol.acl`	Used by `hadoop mradmin` command to load the latest *hadoop-policy.xml* file	`"hadoop- admins"`
`security.refresh.user togroups.mappings.proto col.acl`	Protocol to refresh the user to group mappings **Note: property name changed in Hadoop 2.0**	`"hadoop- admins"`
`security.admin.opera tions.protocol.acl`	Used by the `hadoop mradmin` command to refresh queues and nodes at the JobTracker	`"hadoop- admins"`

Table 6-4. YARN and MR2 service-level authorization properties

Property name	Description	Suggested value
`security.job.task.proto col.acl`	Protocol used by MR tasks to report task progress **Note: must be set to ***	`"*"`

Property name	Description	Suggested value
`security.containermanage ment.protocol.acl`	Protocol used by ApplicationMasters to communicate with the NodeManager **Note: must be set to ***	`"*"`
`security.applicationmas ter.protocol.acl`	Protocol used by ApplicationMasters to communicate with the ResourceManager **Note: must be set to ***	`"*"`
`security.get.user.map pings.protocol.acl`	Protocol to retrieve the groups that a user maps to	`"yarn,mapred hadoop-users"`
`security.application client.protocol.acl`	Protocol for clients to submit applications to the ResourceManager	`"hadoop-users"`
`security.job.client.proto col.acl`	Protocol used by job clients to communicate with the MR ApplicationMaster	`"hadoop-users"`
`security.mrhs.client.proto col.acl`	Protocol used by job clients to communicate with the MapReduce JobHistory server	`"hadoop-users"`
`security.resourcetracker.pro tocol.acl`	ResourceManager to NodeManager protocol	`"yarn"`
`security.resourcemanager- administration.protocol.acl`	Protocol used by the `yarn rmadmin` command to administer the ResourceManager	`"yarn"`
`security.resourcelocal izer.protocol.acl`	Protocol used by ResourceLocalizationService and NodeManager to communicate	`"testing"`
`security.ha.service.proto col.acl`	Protocol used by the `yarn rmadmin` command to manage the HA states of the ResourceManager	`"hdfs,yarn hadoop-admins"`
`security.refresh.policy.pro tocol.acl`	Used by the `yarn rmadmin` command to load the latest *hadoop-policy.xml* file	`"hadoop- admins"`
`security.refresh.user.map pings.protocol.acl`	Protocol to refresh the user to group mappings	`"hadoop- admins"`

You'll notice that even though we want to keep the cluster fairly locked down, we had to configure four protocols with permissions to allow any user to connect. The reason for this is that these protocols are accessed by running tasks that assume the identity of the application or task attempt. The identity used will vary with every run and is not related to the username that launched the job. Because these identities cannot be enumerated in advance, they can't be listed in the ACLs or added to a group that could be used to limit access to those protocols. This is not a major concern, as those interfaces are further protected by a job token (see "Tokens" on page 78) that must be presented in order to gain access.

Most of the protocols fall into one of two categories: protocols that need to be accessed by clients, and administration protocols. You can use a more restrictive value for the client protocols if you want to limit which users can use Hadoop to a whitelist of users or groups. Note, however, that security.job.task.protocol.acl (for YARN/MR2) and security.task.umbilical.protocol.acl (for MR1) *must* always be set to *. This is required because the user that uses those protocols is always set to the job ID of the MapReduce job. The job ID changes per job and is not likely to appear in any groups provisioned for your cluster. Therefore, any setting other than * for these properties would cause your jobs to fail. Let's look at two user sessions, first with the default settings in *hadoop-policy.xml* (Example 6-2) and then again with the suggested values from the tables (Example 6-3).

Example 6-2. Using the default service-level authorization policies

```
[alice@hadoop01 ~]$ hdfs dfs -ls .
Found 2 items
drwx------   - alice alice          0 2014-03-29 18:59 .Trash
drwx------   - alice alice          0 2014-03-29 18:59 .staging

[alice@hadoop01 ~]$ hdfs dfs -put file.txt .

[alice@hadoop01 ~]$ hdfs dfs -rm file.txt
14/03/29 21:26:07 INFO fs.TrashPolicyDefault: Namenode trash configuration:
  Deletion interval = 1440 minutes, Emptier interval = 0 minutes.
Moved: 'hdfs://hadoop02:8020/user/alice/file.txt' to trash at:
  hdfs://hadoop02:8020/user/alice/.Trash/Current

[alice@hadoop01 ~]$ hdfs dfs -expunge
14/03/29 21:26:08 INFO fs.TrashPolicyDefault: Namenode trash configuration:
  Deletion interval = 1 minutes, Emptier interval = 0 minutes.
14/03/29 21:26:09 INFO fs.TrashPolicyDefault: Deleted trash checkpoint:
  /user/alice/.Trash/140329185911
14/03/29 21:26:09 INFO fs.TrashPolicyDefault: Created trash checkpoint:
  /user/alice/.Trash/140329212609

[alice@hadoop01 ~]$ hdfs groups
alice@CLOUDERA : alice production-etl hadoop-users

[alice@hadoop01 ~]$ hdfs dfsadmin -refreshNodes
refreshNodes: Access denied for user alice. Superuser privilege is required

[alice@hadoop01 ~]$ hdfs dfsadmin -refreshServiceAcl

[alice@hadoop01 ~]$ hdfs dfsadmin -refreshUserToGroupsMappings

[alice@hadoop01 ~]$ hdfs dfsadmin -refreshSuperUserGroupsConfiguration
```

```
[alice@hadoop01 ~]$ yarn rmadmin -refreshQueues
14/03/29 21:26:16 INFO client.RMProxy: Connecting to ResourceManager at
  hadoop02/172.25.2.223:8033

[alice@hadoop01 ~]$ yarn rmadmin -refreshNodes
14/03/29 21:26:18 INFO client.RMProxy: Connecting to ResourceManager at
  hadoop02/172.25.2.223:8033

[alice@hadoop01 ~]$ yarn rmadmin -refreshSuperUserGroupsConfiguration
14/03/29 21:26:19 INFO client.RMProxy: Connecting to ResourceManager at
  hadoop02/172.25.2.223:8033

[alice@hadoop01 ~]$ yarn rmadmin -refreshUserToGroupsMappings
14/03/29 21:26:21 INFO client.RMProxy: Connecting to ResourceManager at
  hadoop02/172.25.2.223:8033

[alice@hadoop01 ~]$ yarn rmadmin -refreshAdminAcls
14/03/29 21:26:22 INFO client.RMProxy: Connecting to ResourceManager at
  hadoop02/172.25.2.223:8033

[alice@hadoop01 ~]$ yarn rmadmin -refreshServiceAcl
14/03/29 21:26:23 INFO client.RMProxy: Connecting to ResourceManager at
  hadoop02/172.25.2.223:8033

[alice@hadoop01 ~]$ yarn rmadmin -getGroups alice
14/03/29 21:26:25 INFO client.RMProxy: Connecting to ResourceManager at
  hadoop02/172.25.2.223:8033
alice : alice production-etl hadoop-users

[alice@hadoop01 ~]$ yarn jar /opt/cloudera/parcels/CDH/lib/
  hadoop-mapreduce/hadoop-mapreduce-examples.jar randomtextwriter random-text
14/03/29 21:26:26 INFO client.RMProxy: Connecting to ResourceManager at
  hadoop02/172.25.2.223:8032
Running 30 maps.
Job started: Sat Mar 29 21:26:27 EDT 2014
14/03/29 21:26:27 INFO client.RMProxy: Connecting to ResourceManager at
  hadoop02/172.25.2.223:8032
14/03/29 21:26:27 INFO hdfs.DFSClient: Created HDFS_DELEGATION_TOKEN
  token 10 for alice on 172.25.2.223:8020
14/03/29 21:26:27 INFO security.TokenCache: Got dt for hdfs://hadoop02:8020;
  Kind: HDFS_DELEGATION_TOKEN, Service: 172.25.2.223:8020, Ident:
  (HDFS_DELEGATION_TOKEN token 10 for alice)
14/03/29 21:26:28 INFO mapreduce.JobSubmitter: number of splits:30
14/03/29 21:26:28 INFO mapreduce.JobSubmitter: Submitting tokens for job:
  job_1396142628007_0001
14/03/29 21:26:28 INFO mapreduce.JobSubmitter: Kind: HDFS_DELEGATION_TOKEN,
  Service: 172.25.2.223:8020, Ident: (HDFS_DELEGATION_TOKEN token 10 for alice)
14/03/29 21:26:29 INFO impl.YarnClientImpl: Submitted application
  application_1396142628007_0001
14/03/29 21:26:29 INFO mapreduce.Job: The url to track the job:
  http://hadoop02:8088/proxy/application_1396142628007_0001/
```

```
14/03/29 21:26:29 INFO mapreduce.Job: Running job: job_1396142628007_0001
14/03/29 21:26:38 INFO mapreduce.Job: Job job_1396142628007_0001 running
  in uber mode : false
14/03/29 21:26:38 INFO mapreduce.Job:  map 0% reduce 0%
14/03/29 21:28:37 INFO mapreduce.Job:  map 3% reduce 0%
14/03/29 21:28:47 INFO mapreduce.Job:  map 7% reduce 0%
14/03/29 21:28:53 INFO mapreduce.Job:  map 10% reduce 0%
14/03/29 21:29:09 INFO mapreduce.Job:  map 17% reduce 0%
14/03/29 21:29:16 INFO mapreduce.Job:  map 23% reduce 0%
14/03/29 21:29:17 INFO mapreduce.Job:  map 27% reduce 0%
14/03/29 21:29:18 INFO mapreduce.Job:  map 30% reduce 0%
14/03/29 21:29:19 INFO mapreduce.Job:  map 33% reduce 0%
14/03/29 21:29:22 INFO mapreduce.Job:  map 50% reduce 0%
14/03/29 21:29:23 INFO mapreduce.Job:  map 60% reduce 0%
14/03/29 21:29:25 INFO mapreduce.Job:  map 70% reduce 0%
14/03/29 21:29:31 INFO mapreduce.Job:  map 77% reduce 0%
14/03/29 21:30:05 INFO mapreduce.Job:  map 83% reduce 0%
14/03/29 21:30:10 INFO mapreduce.Job:  map 90% reduce 0%
14/03/29 21:30:12 INFO mapreduce.Job:  map 93% reduce 0%
14/03/29 21:30:14 INFO mapreduce.Job:  map 97% reduce 0%
14/03/29 21:30:15 INFO mapreduce.Job:  map 100% reduce 0%
14/03/29 21:30:15 INFO mapreduce.Job: Job job_1396142628007_0001
  completed successfully
14/03/29 21:30:15 INFO mapreduce.Job: Counters: 29
        File System Counters
                FILE: Number of bytes read=0
                FILE: Number of bytes written=2679890
                FILE: Number of read operations=0
                FILE: Number of large read operations=0
                FILE: Number of write operations=0
                HDFS: Number of bytes read=4550
                HDFS: Number of bytes written=33067041057
                HDFS: Number of read operations=120
                HDFS: Number of large read operations=0
                HDFS: Number of write operations=60
        Job Counters
                Launched map tasks=30
                Other local map tasks=30
                Total time spent by all maps in occupied slots (ms)=4015333
                Total time spent by all reduces in occupied slots (ms)=0
        Map-Reduce Framework
                Map input records=30
                Map output records=49159093
                Input split bytes=4550
                Spilled Records=0
                Failed Shuffles=0
                Merged Map outputs=0
                GC time elapsed (ms)=22565
                CPU time spent (ms)=808110
                Physical memory (bytes) snapshot=12234526720
                Virtual memory (bytes) snapshot=40489713664
                Total committed heap usage (bytes)=12699172864
```

```
            org.apache.hadoop.examples.RandomTextWriter$Counters
                    BYTES_WRITTEN=32212265105
                    RECORDS_WRITTEN=49159093
            File Input Format Counters
                    Bytes Read=0
            File Output Format Counters
                    Bytes Written=33067041057
    Job ended: Sat Mar 29 21:30:15 EDT 2014
    The job took 227 seconds.

    [alice@hadoop01 ~]$ hdfs dfs -rm -r random-text
    14/03/29 21:30:17 INFO fs.TrashPolicyDefault: Namenode trash configuration:
      Deletion interval = 1440 minutes, Emptier interval = 0 minutes.
    Moved: 'hdfs://hadoop02:8020/user/alice/random-text' to trash at:
      hdfs://hadoop02:8020/user/alice/.Trash/Current

    [alice@hadoop01 ~]$ hdfs dfs -expunge
    14/03/29 21:30:18 INFO fs.TrashPolicyDefault: Namenode trash configuration:
      Deletion interval = 1 minutes, Emptier interval = 0 minutes.
    14/03/29 21:30:19 INFO fs.TrashPolicyDefault: Deleted trash checkpoint:
      /user/alice/.Trash/140329212609
    14/03/29 21:30:19 INFO fs.TrashPolicyDefault: Created trash checkpoint:
      /user/alice/.Trash/140329213019
```

The listing in Example 6-2 shows Alice using a number of user and administrative commands. While some commands, such as hdfs dfsadmin -refreshNodes, require superuser permissions, many don't require any special privileges when using the default service-level authorization policies. Example 6-3 runs through the exact same set of commands using the previously recommended policies.

Example 6-3. Using the recommended service-level authorization policies

```
    [alice@hadoop01 ~]$ hdfs dfs -ls .
    Found 2 items
    drwx------   - alice alice          0 2014-03-29 18:52 .Trash
    drwx------   - alice alice          0 2014-03-29 18:45 .staging

    [alice@hadoop01 ~]$ hdfs dfs -put file.txt .

    [alice@hadoop01 ~]$ hdfs dfs -rm file.txt
    14/03/29 18:54:11 INFO fs.TrashPolicyDefault: Namenode trash configuration:
      Deletion interval = 1440 minutes, Emptier interval = 0 minutes.
    Moved: 'hdfs://hadoop02:8020/user/alice/file.txt' to trash at:
      hdfs://hadoop02:8020/user/alice/.Trash/Current

    [alice@hadoop01 ~]$ hdfs dfs -expunge
    14/03/29 18:54:13 INFO fs.TrashPolicyDefault: Namenode trash configuration:
      Deletion interval = 1 minutes, Emptier interval = 0 minutes.
    14/03/29 18:54:13 INFO fs.TrashPolicyDefault: Deleted trash checkpoint:
      /user/alice/.Trash/140329185237
    14/03/29 18:54:13 INFO fs.TrashPolicyDefault: Created trash checkpoint:
```

```
/user/alice/.Trash/140329185413

[alice@hadoop01 ~]$ hdfs groups
alice@CLOUDERA : alice production-etl hadoop-users

[alice@hadoop01 ~]$ hdfs dfsadmin -refreshNodes
refreshNodes: Access denied for user alice. Superuser privilege is required

[alice@hadoop01 ~]$ hdfs dfsadmin -refreshServiceAcl
refreshServiceAcl: User alice@CLOUDERA (auth:KERBEROS) is not authorized for
  protocol interface
  org.apache.hadoop.security.authorize.RefreshAuthorizationPolicyProtocol,
  expected client Kerberos principal is null

[alice@hadoop01 ~]$ hdfs dfsadmin -refreshUserToGroupsMappings
refreshUserToGroupsMappings: User alice@CLOUDERA (auth:KERBEROS) is not
  authorized for protocol interface
  org.apache.hadoop.security.RefreshUserMappingsProtocol, expected client
  Kerberos principal is null

[alice@hadoop01 ~]$ hdfs dfsadmin -refreshSuperUserGroupsConfiguration
refreshSuperUserGroupsConfiguration: User alice@CLOUDERA (auth:KERBEROS) is
  not authorized for protocol interface
  org.apache.hadoop.security.RefreshUserMappingsProtocol, expected client
  Kerberos principal is null

[alice@hadoop01 ~]$ yarn rmadmin -refreshQueues
14/03/29 18:54:21 INFO client.RMProxy: Connecting to ResourceManager at
  hadoop02/172.25.2.223:8033
refreshQueues: User alice@CLOUDERA (auth:KERBEROS) is not authorized
  for protocol interface
  org.apache.hadoop.yarn.server.api.ResourceManagerAdministrationProtocolPB,
  expected client Kerberos principal is null

[alice@hadoop01 ~]$ yarn rmadmin -refreshNodes
14/03/29 18:54:22 INFO client.RMProxy: Connecting to ResourceManager at
  hadoop02/172.25.2.223:8033
refreshNodes: User alice@CLOUDERA (auth:KERBEROS) is not authorized
  for protocol interface
  org.apache.hadoop.yarn.server.api.ResourceManagerAdministrationProtocolPB,
  expected client Kerberos principal is null

[alice@hadoop01 ~]$ yarn rmadmin -refreshSuperUserGroupsConfiguration
14/03/29 18:54:24 INFO client.RMProxy: Connecting to ResourceManager at
  hadoop02/172.25.2.223:8033
refreshSuperUserGroupsConfiguration: User alice@CLOUDERA (auth:KERBEROS)
  is not authorized for protocol interface
  org.apache.hadoop.yarn.server.api.ResourceManagerAdministrationProtocolPB,
  expected client Kerberos principal is null

[alice@hadoop01 ~]$ yarn rmadmin -refreshUserToGroupsMappings
14/03/29 18:54:25 INFO client.RMProxy: Connecting to ResourceManager at
```

```
  hadoop02/172.25.2.223:8033
refreshUserToGroupsMappings: User alice@CLOUDERA (auth:KERBEROS)
  is not authorized for protocol interface
  org.apache.hadoop.yarn.server.api.ResourceManagerAdministrationProtocolPB,
  expected client Kerberos principal is null

[alice@hadoop01 ~]$ yarn rmadmin -refreshAdminAcls
14/03/29 18:54:26 INFO client.RMProxy: Connecting to ResourceManager at
  hadoop02/172.25.2.223:8033
refreshAdminAcls: User alice@CLOUDERA (auth:KERBEROS)
  is not authorized for protocol interface
  org.apache.hadoop.yarn.server.api.ResourceManagerAdministrationProtocolPB,
  expected client Kerberos principal is null

[alice@hadoop01 ~]$ yarn rmadmin -refreshServiceAcl
14/03/29 18:54:28 INFO client.RMProxy: Connecting to ResourceManager at
  hadoop02/172.25.2.223:8033
refreshServiceAcl: User alice@CLOUDERA (auth:KERBEROS)
  is not authorized for protocol interface
  org.apache.hadoop.yarn.server.api.ResourceManagerAdministrationProtocolPB,
  expected client Kerberos principal is null

[alice@hadoop01 ~]$ yarn rmadmin -getGroups alice
14/03/29 18:54:29 INFO client.RMProxy: Connecting to ResourceManager at
  hadoop02/172.25.2.223:8033
getGroups: User alice@CLOUDERA (auth:KERBEROS)
  is not authorized for protocol interface
  org.apache.hadoop.yarn.server.api.ResourceManagerAdministrationProtocolPB,
  expected client Kerberos principal is null

[alice@hadoop01 ~]$ yarn jar /opt/cloudera/parcels/CDH/lib/hadoop-mapreduce/
  hadoop-mapreduce-examples.jar randomtextwriter random-text
14/03/29 18:54:31 INFO client.RMProxy: Connecting to ResourceManager at
  hadoop02/172.25.2.223:8032
Running 30 maps.
Job started: Sat Mar 29 18:54:32 EDT 2014
14/03/29 18:54:32 INFO client.RMProxy: Connecting to ResourceManager at
  hadoop02/172.25.2.223:8032
14/03/29 18:54:32 INFO hdfs.DFSClient: Created HDFS_DELEGATION_TOKEN
  token 9 for alice on 172.25.2.223:8020
14/03/29 18:54:32 INFO security.TokenCache: Got dt for hdfs://hadoop02:8020;
  Kind: HDFS_DELEGATION_TOKEN, Service: 172.25.2.223:8020, Ident:
  (HDFS_DELEGATION_TOKEN token 9 for alice)
14/03/29 18:54:32 INFO mapreduce.JobSubmitter: number of splits:30
14/03/29 18:54:32 INFO mapreduce.JobSubmitter: Submitting tokens for job:
  job_1396131817617_0003
14/03/29 18:54:32 INFO mapreduce.JobSubmitter: Kind: HDFS_DELEGATION_TOKEN,
  Service: 172.25.2.223:8020, Ident: (HDFS_DELEGATION_TOKEN token 9 for alice)
14/03/29 18:54:33 INFO impl.YarnClientImpl: Submitted application
  application_1396131817617_0003
14/03/29 18:54:33 INFO mapreduce.Job: The url to track the job:
  http://hadoop02:8088/proxy/application_1396131817617_0003/
```

```
14/03/29 18:54:33 INFO mapreduce.Job: Running job: job_1396131817617_0003
14/03/29 18:54:40 INFO mapreduce.Job: Job job_1396131817617_0003
  running in uber mode : false
14/03/29 18:54:40 INFO mapreduce.Job:  map 0% reduce 0%
14/03/29 18:56:20 INFO mapreduce.Job:  map 3% reduce 0%
14/03/29 18:56:53 INFO mapreduce.Job:  map 7% reduce 0%
14/03/29 18:56:57 INFO mapreduce.Job:  map 10% reduce 0%
14/03/29 18:56:59 INFO mapreduce.Job:  map 13% reduce 0%
14/03/29 18:57:02 INFO mapreduce.Job:  map 17% reduce 0%
14/03/29 18:57:15 INFO mapreduce.Job:  map 20% reduce 0%
14/03/29 18:57:36 INFO mapreduce.Job:  map 27% reduce 0%
14/03/29 18:57:44 INFO mapreduce.Job:  map 30% reduce 0%
14/03/29 18:57:59 INFO mapreduce.Job:  map 33% reduce 0%
14/03/29 18:58:09 INFO mapreduce.Job:  map 37% reduce 0%
14/03/29 18:58:19 INFO mapreduce.Job:  map 40% reduce 0%
14/03/29 18:58:23 INFO mapreduce.Job:  map 43% reduce 0%
14/03/29 18:58:25 INFO mapreduce.Job:  map 47% reduce 0%
14/03/29 18:58:35 INFO mapreduce.Job:  map 50% reduce 0%
14/03/29 18:58:36 INFO mapreduce.Job:  map 53% reduce 0%
14/03/29 18:58:39 INFO mapreduce.Job:  map 57% reduce 0%
14/03/29 18:58:40 INFO mapreduce.Job:  map 60% reduce 0%
14/03/29 18:58:44 INFO mapreduce.Job:  map 63% reduce 0%
14/03/29 18:58:45 INFO mapreduce.Job:  map 67% reduce 0%
14/03/29 18:58:47 INFO mapreduce.Job:  map 70% reduce 0%
14/03/29 18:58:53 INFO mapreduce.Job:  map 73% reduce 0%
14/03/29 18:58:55 INFO mapreduce.Job:  map 80% reduce 0%
14/03/29 18:58:57 INFO mapreduce.Job:  map 83% reduce 0%
14/03/29 18:59:01 INFO mapreduce.Job:  map 90% reduce 0%
14/03/29 18:59:05 INFO mapreduce.Job:  map 93% reduce 0%
14/03/29 18:59:07 INFO mapreduce.Job:  map 100% reduce 0%
14/03/29 18:59:07 INFO mapreduce.Job: Job job_1396131817617_0003
  completed successfully
14/03/29 18:59:07 INFO mapreduce.Job: Counters: 29
        File System Counters
                FILE: Number of bytes read=0
                FILE: Number of bytes written=2679890
                FILE: Number of read operations=0
                FILE: Number of large read operations=0
                FILE: Number of write operations=0
                HDFS: Number of bytes read=4550
                HDFS: Number of bytes written=33067034387
                HDFS: Number of read operations=120
                HDFS: Number of large read operations=0
                HDFS: Number of write operations=60
        Job Counters
                Launched map tasks=30
                Other local map tasks=30
                Total time spent by all maps in occupied slots (ms)=5319195
                Total time spent by all reduces in occupied slots (ms)=0
        Map-Reduce Framework
                Map input records=30
                Map output records=49157281
```

```
                Input split bytes=4550
                Spilled Records=0
                Failed Shuffles=0
                Merged Map outputs=0
                GC time elapsed (ms)=13711
                CPU time spent (ms)=741910
                Physical memory (bytes) snapshot=10065694720
                Virtual memory (bytes) snapshot=40491339776
                Total committed heap usage (bytes)=14946533376
        org.apache.hadoop.examples.RandomTextWriter$Counters
                BYTES_WRITTEN=32212267432
                RECORDS_WRITTEN=49157281
        File Input Format Counters
                Bytes Read=0
        File Output Format Counters
                Bytes Written=33067034387
Job ended: Sat Mar 29 18:59:07 EDT 2014
The job took 275 seconds.

[alice@hadoop01 ~]$ hdfs dfs -rm -r random-text
14/03/29 18:59:09 INFO fs.TrashPolicyDefault: Namenode trash
  configuration: Deletion interval = 1440 minutes, Emptier
  interval = 0 minutes.
Moved: 'hdfs://hadoop02:8020/user/alice/random-text' to trash
  at: hdfs://hadoop02:8020/user/alice/.Trash/Current

[alice@hadoop01 ~]$ hdfs dfs -expunge
14/03/29 18:59:10 INFO fs.TrashPolicyDefault: Namenode trash
  configuration: Deletion interval = 1 minutes, Emptier
  interval = 0 minutes.
14/03/29 18:59:11 INFO fs.TrashPolicyDefault: Deleted trash checkpoint:
  /user/alice/.Trash/140329185413
14/03/29 18:59:11 INFO fs.TrashPolicyDefault: Created trash checkpoint:
  /user/alice/.Trash/140329185911
```

This time Alice was still able to access all of the user functions, but administrative functions are denied and report the error User alice@CLOUDERA (auth:KERBEROS) is not authorized for protocol interface <protocol>. This indicates that the user is not listed in the ACL for that protocol and also doesn't belong to a group listed in the ACL. Service-level authorizations are a very powerful, although complex, tool for controlling access to a Hadoop cluster. For example, with the policies we configured, the *hdfs* user no longer has access to view or modify files in HDFS unless it is added to the *hadoop-users* group. This is very useful for organizations that need to track any administrative action back to the administrator who performed it. If we combine the recommended service-level authorizations by setting dfs.permissions.superusergroup to hadoop-admins, we can tie admin actions back to a specific account. Example 6-4 shows what happens when the *hdfs* user attempts to list the files in Alice's home directory and delete a file that she uploaded.

Example 6-4. User hdfs is denied access to the ClientProtocol

```
[hdfs@hadoop01 ~]$ hdfs dfs -ls /user/alice/
ls: User hdfs@CLOUDERA (auth:KERBEROS) is not authorized for protocol interface
  org.apache.hadoop.hdfs.protocol.ClientProtocol, expected client Kerberos principal
is null
[hdfs@hadoop01 ~]$ hdfs dfs -rm /user/alice/file.txt
rm: User hdfs@CLOUDERA (auth:KERBEROS) is not authorized for protocol interface
  org.apache.hadoop.hdfs.protocol.ClientProtocol, expected client Kerberos principal
is null
```

Notice that the *hdfs* user is denied access at the protocol level before any permission checks can be performed at the HDFS level. Even though *hdfs* is a superuser from the filesystem's perspective, no data can be viewed or modified due to the service-level check which happens first. Example 6-5 shows what happens when Joey, a member of the *hadoop-admins* group, tries to perform the same actions.

Example 6-5. A member of the hadoop-admins group deleting user files

```
[joey@hadoop01 ~]$ hdfs dfs -ls /user/alice/
Found 3 items
drwx------   - alice alice          0 2014-03-29 21:30 /user/alice/.Trash
drwx------   - alice alice          0 2014-03-29 21:30 /user/alice/.staging
-rw-------   3 alice alice          5 2014-03-29 21:48 /user/alice/file.txt
[joey@hadoop01 ~]$ hdfs dfs -rm /user/alice/file.txt
14/03/29 21:49:26 INFO fs.TrashPolicyDefault: Namenode trash configuration: Deletion
  interval = 1440 minutes, Emptier interval = 0 minutes.
Moved: 'hdfs://hadoop02:8020/user/alice/file.txt' to trash at:
  hdfs://hadoop02:8020/user/joey/.Trash/Current
[joey@hadoop01 ~]$ hdfs groups joey
joey : joey hadoop-admins hadoop-users
[joey@hadoop01 ~]$ hdfs groups hdfs
hdfs : hdfs hadoop
```

You'll notice that this time the actions were allowed. That is because Joey is a member of both the *hadoop-admins* group (which is configured as the superuser group in HDFS) and the *hadoop-users* group (which gives him access to the HDFS client protocols).

In addition to configuring ACLs in *hadoop-policy.xml*, certain HDFS administrative actions, such as forcing an HA failover, are only available to HDFS cluster administrators. The administrators are configured by setting dfs.cluster.administrators in *hdfs-site.xml* to a comma-delimited list of users and a comma-delimited list of groups that can administer HDFS. The two lists are separated by a space. A leading space implies an empty list of users and a trailing space implies an empty list of groups. A special value of * can be used to signify that all users have administrative access to HDFS; a value of " " (without the quotes) signifies that no users have access (this is the default setting). See Example 6-6 for the recommended setting based on our example environment.

Example 6-6. The dfs.cluster.administrators setting in hdfs-site.xml

```
<property>
  <name>dfs.cluster.administrators</name>
  <value>hdfs hadoop-admins</value>
</property>
```

The ACL for administration of the MapReduce Job History server is not configured in the *hadoop-policy.xml* file. The ACL is configured by setting `mapreduce.jobhis tory.admin.acl` in *mapred-site.xml* to a comma-delimited list of users and a comma-delimited list of groups, identical in format to those described in "Service-Level Authorization" on page 101 and depicted in Table 6-1. A special value of * can be used to signify that all users have administrative access to the JobHistory server (this is the default setting). See Example 6-7 for the recommended setting.

Example 6-7. The mapreduce.jobhistory.admin.acl setting in mapred-site.xml

```
<property>
  <name>mapreduce.jobhistory.admin.acl</name>
  <value>mapred hadoop-admins</value>
</property>
```

MapReduce and YARN Authorization

Neither MapReduce nor YARN control access to data, but both provide access to cluster resources such as CPU, memory, disk I/O, and network I/O. Because these resources are finite, it is common for administrators to allocate resources to specific users or groups, especially in multitenant environments. The service-level authorizations described in the previous section control access to specific protocols, such as who can and cannot submit a job to the cluster, but they are not granular enough to control access to cluster resources. Both MapReduce (MR1) and YARN support job queues as a way of putting limits on how jobs are allocated resources. In order to securely control those resources, Hadoop supports access control lists (ACLs) on the job queues. These ACLs control which users can submit to certain queues as well as which users can administer a queue. MapReduce defines different classes of users, which affect the way that ACLs are interpreted:

MapReduce/YARN cluster owner

The user that starts the JobTracker process (MR1) or the ResourceManager process (YARN) is defined as the cluster owner. That user has permissions to submit jobs to any queue and can administer any queue or job. In most cases, the cluster owner is *mapred* for MapReduce (MR1) and *yarn* for YARN. Because it is dangerous to run jobs as the cluster owner, the LinuxTaskController defaults to blacklisting the *mapred* and *yarn* user accounts so they can't submit jobs.

MapReduce administrator

There is a setting to create global MapReduce administrators that have the same privileges as the cluster owner. The advantage to defining specific users or groups as administrators is that you can still audit the individual actions of each administrator. This also lets you avoid having to distribute the password to a shared account, thus increasing the likelihood that the password could be compromised.

Job owner

The owner of a job is the user that submitted it. Job owners can always administer their own jobs but can only submit jobs to queues for which they've been granted the submit permission.

Queue administrator

Users or groups can be given administrative permissions over all of the jobs in a queue. Queue administrators can also submit jobs to the queues they administer.

MapReduce (MR1)

For MR1, ACLs are administered globally and apply to any job scheduler that supports ACLs. Both the CapacityScheduler and FairScheduler support ACLs; the FIFO (default) scheduler does not. Before configuring per-queue ACLs, you must enable MapReduce ACLs, configure the MapReduce administrators, and define the queue names in *mapred-site.xml*:

`mapred.acls.enabled`

When set to `true`, ACLs will be checked when submitting or administering jobs. ACLs are also checked for authorizing the viewing and modification of jobs in the JobTracker interface.

`mapreduce.cluster.administrators`

Configure administrators for the MapReduce cluster. Cluster administrators can always administer any job or queue regardless of the configuration of job- or queue-specific ACLs. The format for this setting is a comma-delimited list of users and a comma-delimited list of groups that can access that protocol. The two lists are separated by a space. A leading space implies an empty list of users and a trailing space implies an empty list of groups. A special value of * can be used to signify that all users are granted access to that protocol (this is the default setting). See Table 6-1 for examples.

`mapred.queue.names`

A comma-delimited list of queue names. In order to configure ACLs for a queue, that queue must be listed in this property. MapReduce always supports at least one queue named *default*, so this parameter should always include *default* among the list of defined queues.

The configuration for per-queue ACLs is stored in *mapred-queue-acls.xml*. There are two types of ACLs that can be configured for each queue, a submit ACL and an administer ACL:

mapred.queue.*<queue_name>*.acl-submit-job

> The access control list for users that can submit jobs to the queue named *queue_name*. The format for the submit job ACL is a comma-delimited list of users and a comma-delimited list of groups that are allowed to submit jobs to this queue, identical in format to hose described in "Service-Level Authorization" on page 101 and depicted in Table 6-1. A special value of * can be used to signify that all users are granted access to that protocol (this is the default setting). Regardless of the value of this setting, the cluster owner and MapReduce administrators can submit jobs.

mapred.queue.*<queue_name>*.acl-administer-jobs

> The access control list for users that are allowed to view job details, kill jobs, or modify a job's priority for all jobs in the queue named *queue_name*. The format for the administer-jobs ACL is a comma-delimited list of users and a comma delimited list of groups that are allowed to administer jobs in this queue, identical in format to those described in "Service-Level Authorization" on page 101 and depicted in Table 6-1. A special value of * can be used to signify that all users are granted access to that protocol (this is the default setting). Regardless of the value of this setting, the cluster owner and MapReduce administrators can administer all the jobs in all the queues. The job owner can also administer jobs.

In addition to the per-queue ACLs, there are two types of ACLs that can be configured on a per-job basis. Defaults for these settings can be placed in the *mapred-site.xml* file used by clients and can be overridden by individual jobs:

mapreduce.job.acl-view-job

> The access control list for users that are allowed to view job details. The format for the view-job ACL is a comma-delimited list of users and a comma-delimited list of groups that are allowed to view job details, identical in format to those described in "Service-Level Authorization" on page 101 and depicted in Table 6-1. A special value of * can be used to signify that all users are granted access to that protocol (this is the default setting). Regardless of the value of this setting, the job owner, the cluster owner, MapReduce administrators, and administrators of the queue to which the job was submitted always have access to view a job. This ACL controls access to job-level counters, task-level counters, a task's diagnostic information, task logs displayed on the TaskTracker web UI, and the *job.xml* shown by the JobTracker's web UI.

`mapreduce.job.acl-modify-job`

The access control list for users that are allowed to kill a job, kill a task, fail a task, and set the priority of a job. The format for the modify-job ACL is a comma-delimited list of users and a comma-delimited list of groups that are allowed to modify the job, identical in format to those described in "Service-Level Authorization" on page 101 and depicted in Table 6-1. A special value of * can be used to signify that all users are granted access to that protocol (this is the default setting). Regardless of the value of this setting, the job owner, the cluster owner, MapReduce administrators, and administrators of the queue to which the job was submitted always have access to modify a job.

For deployments where you want a default deny policy for access to job details, a sensible default value for both settings is a single space, " " (without the quotes). This will deny access to job details to all users except the job owner, queue administrators, cluster administrators, and cluster owner.

> In order to control access to job details in the JobTracker web UI, you must configure MapReduce ACLs as described earlier, as well as enable web UI authentication as described in Chapter 11.

YARN (MR2)

With YARN/MR2, queue ACLs are no longer defined globally and each scheduler provides its own method of defining ACLs. ACLs are still enabled globally and there is a global ACL that defines YARN administrators. The settings to enable YARN ACLs and to define the admins are configured in the *yarn-site.xml*. Example values are provided in Example 6-8.

Example 6-8. YARN ACL configuration in yarn-site.xml

```
<property>
  <name>yarn.acl.enable</name>
  <value>true</value>
</property>
<property>
  <name>yarn.admin.acl</name>
  <value>yarn hadoop-admins</value>
</property>
```

Because each scheduler is configured differently, we will walk through setting up queue ACLs one scheduler at a time. For both examples, we will implement the same use case. Our cluster is primarily used for running production ETL pipelines, as well as production queries that generate regular reports. There is some ad hoc reporting as well, but production jobs should always take priority. In order to control access, we define two additional groups of users that contain only a subset of the *hadoop-users* we defined earlier. The *production-etl* group contains users that run production ETL jobs and the *production-queries* group contains users that run production queries. For this example, Alice is a member of the *production-etl* group while Bob is a member of the *production-queries* group. Let's start by configuring the FairScheduler.

FairScheduler

In order to guarantee the resources needed by the production jobs, we must first disable the default behavior of the FairScheduler, which is to place each user into their own queue that matches their username. This is done by setting two parameters, `yarn.scheduler.fair.user-as-default_queue` and `yarn.scheduler.fair.allow-undeclared-pools`, to `false`. The first parameter changes the default queue to `default` and the second ensures that users can't submit jobs to queues that have not be predefined. These settings, as well as the setting to enable the FairScheduler, are found in Example 6-9.

Example 6-9. FairScheduler configuration in yarn-site.xml

```
<property>
  <name>yarn.resourcemanager.scheduler.class</name>
  <value>
    org.apache.hadoop.yarn.server.resourcemanager.scheduler.fair.FairScheduler
  </value>
</property>
<property>
  <name>yarn.scheduler.fair.user-as-default-queue</name>
  <value>false</value>
</property>
<property>
  <name>yarn.scheduler.fair.allow-undeclared-pools</name>
  <value>false</value>
</property>
```

Next, we must define the queues and their ACLs within the *fair-scheduler.xml* file. The FairScheduler uses a hierarchical queue system and each queue is a descendant of the *root* queue. In our example, we want to provide 90% of the cluster resources to production jobs and 10% to ad hoc jobs. To achieve this, we define two direct children of the root queue: `prod` for production jobs and `default` for ad hoc jobs. We use the name "default" for the ad hoc queue because that is the queue jobs are submitted to if a queue is not specified. Resource management is a complex topic and we could tweak a lot of different settings to control the resources just so. Because our focus is on security, we'll use a simplified scheme and just control the resources with the weight of the queues. All that you need to understand is that for all queues that share a common parent, their resource allocation is defined as their weight divided by the weight of all of their siblings. In this case, we can assign `prod` a weight of 9.0 and `default` a weight of 1.0 to get the desired 90/10 split.

We also want to break up the production queue into two subqueues: one for ETL jobs and one for queries. For this example, we'll leave the two queues equally weighted by setting both queues to a weight of 1.0. It is important to note that the calculation of fair share happens in the context of your parent queue. In this example, that means that because we're giving both the `etl` and `queries` queues 50% of the resources of the `prod` queue, they'll end up with a global fair share of 45% each (50% × 90% = 45%).

Just as resources are inherited, so too are ACLs. With the FairScheduler, any user that has permission to submit jobs to a queue also has permission to submit jobs to any descendant queues. The same applies to users with administrative privileges to a queue. In keeping with earlier examples, we want any member of the *hadoop-admins* group to be able to administer any job/queue, so we add them to the `aclAdminister Apps` ACL of the root queue. It's also worth noting that you must set the `aclSubmi tApps` ACL to " " (without the quotes), otherwise any user could submit to any queue, as the default ACL when one is not defined is to allow all. For the default queue, we want to allow any member of the *hadoop-users* group permission to submit jobs, so we set `aclSubmitApps` to " hadoop-users" (without the quotes, and note the leading space). The `prod.etl` and `prod.queries` queues have `aclSubmitApps` set to " production-etl" and " production-queries" (without the quotes), respectively, as these are the groups we defined earlier. The complete configuration for the Fair-Scheduler is shown in Example 6-10.

Example 6-10. fair-scheduler.xml

```xml
<?xml version="1.0" encoding="UTF-8" standalone="yes"?>
<allocations>
    <queue name="root">
        <weight>1.0</weight>
        <aclSubmitApps> </aclSubmitApps>
        <aclAdministerApps> hadoop-admins</aclAdministerApps>
        <queue name="prod">
            <weight>9.0</weight>
            <aclSubmitApps> </aclSubmitApps>
            <aclAdministerApps> </aclAdministerApps>
            <queue name="etl">
                <weight>1.0</weight>
                <aclSubmitApps> production-etl</aclSubmitApps>
                <aclAdministerApps>alice </aclAdministerApps>
            </queue>
            <queue name="queries">
                <weight>1.0</weight>
                <aclSubmitApps> production-queries</aclSubmitApps>
                <aclAdministerApps>bob </aclAdministerApps>
```

```
              </queue>
          </queue>
          <queue name="default">
              <weight>1.0</weight>
              <aclSubmitApps> hadoop-users</aclSubmitApps>
              <aclAdministerApps> </aclAdministerApps>
          </queue>
      </queue>
</allocations>
```

Now let's see what happens when Bob tries to kill one of Alice's job's without having queue ACLs defined. First, Bob gets a list of running jobs to find the JobId for Alice's job. Then he requests that the job be killed. Because there are no controls over who is and isn't allowed to administer jobs, YARN will happily oblige his request. See Example 6-11 for the complete listing of Bob's user session.

Example 6-11. Killing another user's job when no ACLs are defined

```
[bob@hadoop01 ~]$ mapred job -list
Total jobs:1
                  JobId        State          StartTime       UserName
 job_1396200012809_0002      RUNNING       1396201153018        alice
[bob@hadoop01 ~]$ mapred job -kill job_1396200012809_0002
Killed job job_1396200012809_0002
```

This is less than ideal, as users can interfere with one another's production jobs. More importantly, a simple copy/paste error could result in a user *accidentally* killing another user's job. If we try the same exact process after configuring ACLs in the Fair-Scheduler, we instead get the result shown in Example 6-12.

Example 6-12. Bob is denied administrative permissions by the queue ACLs

```
[bob@hadoop01 ~]$ mapred job -list
Total jobs:1
                  JobId        State          StartTime       UserName
 job_1396192703139_0001      RUNNING       1396192707596        alice
[bob@hadoop01 ~]$ mapred job -kill job_1396192703139_0001
...
Exception in thread "main" java.io.IOException: org.apache.hadoop.yarn.exceptions.Yar
nException: java.security.AccessControlException: User bob cannot perform operation M
ODIFY_APP on application_1396192703139_0001
        at org.apache.hadoop.yarn.ipc.RPCUtil.getRemoteException(RPCUtil.java:38)
...
[bob@hadoop01 ~]$
```

There are almost always times when some admin must be able to kill another user's jobs, which is why we configured admin access to the *hadoop-admins* group on the root queue. So if Joey, one of the Hadoop administrators, attempts to kill a job, it will proceed as shown in Example 6-13.

Example 6-13. Successfully killing a MapReduce job

```
[joey@hadoop01 ~]$ mapred job -list
Total jobs:1
                 JobId     State        StartTime      UserName
 job_1396192703139_0002   RUNNING      1396193202565     alice
[joey@hadoop01 ~]$ mapred job -kill job_1396192703139_0002
Killed job job_1396192703139_0002
```

Controlling administrative access is obviously useful, but it's also helpful to prevent users from submitting jobs to the wrong queue. In our example, Alice has permission to submit jobs to the prod.etl queue because she is a member of the *production-etl* group. However, she is not a member of the *production-queries* group, so if she tries to submit a job there, she will be denied, as shown in Example 6-14.

Example 6-14. Alice is not allowed to submit jobs to the prod.queries queue

```
[alice@hadoop01 ~]$ yarn jar \
  /opt/cloudera/parcels/CDH/lib/hadoop-mapreduce/hadoop-mapreduce-examples.jar \
  randomtextwriter -Dmapreduce.job.queuename=prod.queries random-text
...
Job started: Sun Mar 30 13:20:57 EDT 2014
14/03/30 13:20:59 ERROR security.UserGroupInformation: PriviledgedActionException
as:alice@CLOUDERA (auth:KERBEROS) cause:java.io.IOException: Failed to run job :
User alice cannot submit applications to queue root.prod.queries
...
```

CapacityScheduler

The CapacityScheduler supports hierarchical queues just like the FairScheduler. It also supports the same per-queue ACLs and the same ACL inheritance policy of the FairScheduler. In fact, from a security perspective, the two schedulers are identical and only differ in the format of their configuration files. In order to implement the same polices described earlier, you must first enable the CapacityScheduler in the *yarn-site.xml* file, as shown in Example 6-15.

Example 6-15. CapacityScheduler configuraiton in yarn-site.xml

```
<property>
 <name>
  yarn.resourcemanager.scheduler.class
 </name>
 <value>
  org.apache.hadoop.yarn.server.resourcemanager.scheduler.capacity.CapacityScheduler
```

```
    </value>
</property>
```

Once enabled, the CapacityScheduler reads its configuration from a file called *capacity-scheduler.xml*. A sample configuration that implements the same queues and ACLs is shown in Example 6-16. For the FairScheduler, the ACLs are configured as child elements of the queue definition using the `aclSubmitApps` tag to control who can submit applications to a queue and the `aclAdministerApps` tag to control who can administer the jobs in a queue. The equivalent settings for the CapacityScheduler are these properties, respectively, with the *<path-to-queue>* replaced with a queue's hierarchy:

- `yarn.scheduler.capacity.root.<path-to-queue>.acl_submit_applications`
- `yarn.scheduler.capacity.root.<path-to-queue>.acl_administer_applications`

For example, the name of the property that defines the *prod.etl* queue's ACL is `yarn.scheduler.capacity.root.prod.etl.acl_submit_applications`, as shown in Example 6-16.

Example 6-16. capacity-scheduler.xml

```
<!-- Define ACLs and subqueues for the root queue -->
<property>
  <name>yarn.scheduler.capacity.root.acl_submit_applications</name>
  <value> </value>
</property>
<property>
  <name>yarn.scheduler.capacity.root.acl_administer_applications</name>
  <value> hadoop-admins</value>
</property>
<property>
  <name>yarn.scheduler.capacity.root.queues</name>
  <value>prod,default</value>
</property>

<!-- Define capacity and ACLs for the root.default queue -->
<property>
  <name>yarn.scheduler.capacity.root.default.capacity</name>
  <value>10.0</value>
</property>
<property>
  <name>yarn.scheduler.capacity.root.acl_submit_applications</name>
  <value> hadoop-users</value>
</property>

<!-- Define capacity, ACLs, and subqueues for the root.prod queue -->
<property>
```

```
      <name>yarn.scheduler.capacity.root.prod.capacity</name>
      <value>90.0</value>
  </property>
  <property>
      <name>yarn.scheduler.capacity.root.prod.queues</name>
      <value>etl,queries</value>
  </property>
  <property>
      <name>yarn.scheduler.capacity.root.prod.acl_submit_applications</name>
      <value> </value>
  </property>
  <property>
      <name>yarn.scheduler.capacity.root.prod.acl_administer_applications</name>
      <value> </value>
  </property>

  <!-- Define capacity and ACLs for the root.prod.etl queue -->
  <property>
      <name>yarn.scheduler.capacity.root.prod.etl.capacity</name>
      <value>50.0</value>
  </property>
  <property>
      <name>yarn.scheduler.capacity.root.prod.etl.acl_submit_applications</name>
      <value> production-etl</value>
  </property>
  <property>
      <name>yarn.scheduler.capacity.root.prod.etl.acl_administer_applications</name>
      <value>alice </value>
  </property>

  <!-- Define capacity and ACLs for the root.prod.queries queue -->
  <property>
      <name>yarn.scheduler.capacity.root.prod.queries.capacity</name>
      <value>50.0</value>
  </property>
  <property>
      <name>yarn.scheduler.capacity.root.prod.queries.acl_submit_applications</name>
      <value> production-queries</value>
  </property>
  <property>
      <name>yarn.scheduler.capacity.root.prod.queries.acl_administer_applications</name>
      <value>bob </value>
  </property>
```

ZooKeeper ACLs

Apache ZooKeeper controls access to ZNodes (paths) through the use of access con‐
trol lists (ACLs). ZooKeeper's ACLs are similar to POSIX permission bits, but are
more flexible because permissions are set on a per-user basis rather than based on
owner and primary group. In fact, ZooKeeper doesn't have the notion of owners or

groups. As described in "Username and Password Authentication" on page 77, users are specified by an authentication scheme and a scheme-specific ID. The format for the IDs varies by the scheme.

An individual ACL has a scheme, ID, and the permissions. The list of available permissions is shown in Table 6-5. It's important to note that in ZooKeeper, permissions are not recursive; they apply only the ZNode that they are attached to, not to any of its children. Because ZooKeeper doesn't have the notion of owners for ZNodes, a user must have the ADMIN permission on a ZNode to be able to set the ACLs.

Table 6-5. ZooKeeper ACL permissions

Permission	Description
CREATE	Permission to create a child ZNode
READ	Permission to get data from a ZNode and to list its children
WRITE	Permission to set the data for a ZNode
DELETE	Permission to delete children ZNodes
ADMIN	Permission to set ACLs

The CREATE and DELETE permissions are used to control who can create children of a ZNode. The use case that motivates granting CREATE but not DELETE is when you want a path in which users can create children but only an administrator can delete children.

If you're adding ACLs using the Java API, you'll first create an Id object with the scheme and ID, and then create an ACL oject with the Id and the permissions as an integer. You can manually calculate a permission value or use the constants in the ZooDefs.Perms class to get the combined permission integer for the permissions you want to set. See Example 6-17 for sample Java code for setting the ACL on a path.

Example 6-17. Setting ZooKeeper ACLs with the Java API

```
// Connect to ZooKeeper
ZooKeeper zk = new ZooKeeper("zk.example.com:2181", 60000, watcher);

// Create the Id for alice using the password 'secret'
Id id = new Id("digest", "alice:secret");

// Create the ACL grantin Alice READ and CREATE permissions
ACL acl = new ACL(ZooDefs.Perms.READ | ZooDefs.Perms.CREATE, id);

zk.setAcl("/test", Arrays.asList(new ACL[] {acl}), -1);
```

The `digest` scheme was described in "Username and Password Authentication" on page 77, but ZooKeeper supports a number of other built-in schemes. Table 6-6 describes the available schemes and the format of an ID when used in an ACL. For the scheme `world`, the only ID is the literal string `anyone`. The `digest` scheme uses the base64 encoding of the sha1 digest of the *<username>*:*<password>* string. The `ip` scheme lets you set ACLs based on an IP address or a range using CIDR notation. Finally, the `sasl` scheme uses the *<principal>* as the ID. By default, the principal is the full UPN of the user. You can control how to canonicalize the principal by setting the `kerberos.removeRealmFromPrincipal` and/or `kerberos.removeHostFromPrincipal` to remove the realm and second component, respectively, before comparing the IDs.

Table 6-6. ZooKeeper schemes

Scheme	Description	ACL ID format
world	Represents any user	anyone
digest	Represents a user that is authenticated with a password	*<username>*:base64(sha1sum(*<username>*:*<password>*))
ip	Uses the client IP address as an identity	*<ip>*[/*<cidr>*]
sasl	Represents a SASL authenticated user (e.g., a Kerberos user)	*<principal>*

Oozie Authorization

Apache Oozie has a very simple authorization model with two levels of accounts: *users* and *admin users*. Users have the following permissions:

- Read access to all jobs
- Write access to their own jobs
- Write access to jobs based on a per-job access control list (list of users and groups)
- Read access to admin operations

Admin users have the following permissions:

- Write access to all jobs
- Writes access to admin operations

You can enable Oozie authorization by setting the following parameters in the *oozie-site.xml* file:

```
<property>
  <name>oozie.service.AuthorizationService.security.enabled</name>
  <value>true</value>
</property>
<property>
  <name>oozie.service.AuthorizationService.admin.groups</name>
  <value>oozie-admins</value>
</property>
```

If you don't set the `oozie.service.AuthorizationService.admin.groups` parameter, then you can specify a list of admin users, one per line, in the *adminusers.txt* file:

```
oozie
alice
```

In addition to owners and admin users having write access to a job, users can be granted write privileges through the use of a job-specific access control list. An Oozie ACL uses the same syntax as Hadoop ACLs (see Table 6-1) and is set in the `oozie.job.acl` property of a workflow, coordinator, or bundle *job.properties* file when submitting a job.

HBase and Accumulo Authorization

Apache HBase and Apache Accumulo are sorted, distributed key/value stores based on the design of Google's BigTable and built on top of HDFS and ZooKeeper. Both systems share a similar data model and are designed to enable random access and update workloads on top of HDFS which is a write-once filesystem. Data is stored in *rows* that contain one or more *columns*. Unlike a relational database, the columns in each row can differ. This makes it easier to implement complex data models where not every record shares the same schema. Each row is indexed with a primary key called a *row id* or *row key*; and within a row, each value is further indexed by a *column key* and *timestamp*. The intersection of a row key, column key and timestamp, along with the value they point to, is often called a *cell*. Internally, HBase and Accumulo store data as a sorted sequence of key/value pairs with the key consisting of the row ID, column key, and timestamp. Column keys are further split into two components; a *column family* and a *column qualifier*. In HBase, all of the columns in the same column family are stored in separate files on disk whereas in Accumulo multiple column families can be grouped together into *locality groups*.

A collection of sorted rows is called a *table*. In HBase, the set of column families is predefined per table while Accumulo lets users create new column families on the fly. In both systems, column qualifiers do not need to be predefined and arbitrary qualifiers can be inserted into any row. A logical grouping of tables, similar to a database or schema in a relational database system, is called a *namespace*. Both HBase and Accumulo support permissions at the system, namespace, and table level. The available permissions and their semantics differ between Accumulo and HBase, so let's start by taking a look at Accumulo's permission model.

System, Namespace, and Table-Level Authorization

At the highest level, Accumulo supports system permissions. Generally, system permissions are reserved for the Accumulo root user or Accumulo administrators. Permissions set at a higher level are inherited by objects at a lower level. For example, if you have the system permission `CREATE_TABLE`, you can create a table in any namespace even if you don't have explicit permissions to create tables in that namespace. See Table 6-7 for a list of system-level permissions, their descriptions, and the equivalent namespace-level permission.

 Throughout this section, you'll see many references to the Accumulo root user. This is not the same as the root system account. The Accumulo root user is automatically created when Accumulo is initialized, and that user is granted all of the system-level permissions. The root user can never have these permissions revoked, which prevents leaving Accumulo in a state where no one can administer it.

Table 6-7. System-level permissions in Accumulo

Permission	Description	Equivalent namespace permission
`System.GRANT`	Permission to grant permissions to other users; reserved for the Accumulo root user	`Namespace.ALTER_NAME SPACE`
`System.CREATE_TABLE`	Permission to create tables	`Namespace.CREATE_TABLE`
`System.DROP_TABLE`	Permission to delete tables	`Namespace.DROP_TABLE`
`System.ALTER_TABLE`	Permission to modify tables	`Namespace.ALTER_TABLE`
`System.DROP_NAMESPACE`	Permission to drop namespaces	`Namespace.DROP_NAME SPACE`
`System.ALTER_NAME SPACE`	Permission to modify namespaces	`Namespace.ALTER_NAME SPACE`
`System.CREATE_USER`	Permission to create new users	N/A
`System.DROP_USER`	Permission to delete users	N/A

Permission	Description	Equivalent namespace permission
System.ALTER_USER	Permission to change user passwords, permissions, and authorizations	N/A
System.SYSTEM	Permission to perform administrative actions on tables or users	N/A
System.CREATE_NAME SPACE	Permission to create new namespaces	N/A

Namespaces are a logical collection of tables and are useful for organizing tables and delegating administrative functions to smaller groups. Suppose the marketing department needs to host a number of Accumulo tables to power some of its applications. In order to reduce the burden on the Accumulo administrator, we can create a marketing namespace and give GRANT, CREATE_TABLE, DROP_TABLE, and ALTER_TABLE permissions to an administrator in marketing. This will allow the department to create and manage its own tables without having to grant system-level permissions or wait for the Accumulo administrator. A number of namespace-level permissions are inherited by tables in the namespace. See Table 6-8 for the list of namespace-level permissions, their descriptions, and the equivalent table-level permission.

Table 6-8. Namespace-level permissions in Accumulo

Permission	Description	Equivalent table permission
Namespace.READ	Permission to read (scan) tables in the namespace	Table.READ
Namespace.WRITE	Permission to write (put/delete) to tables in the namespace	Table.WRITE
Namespace.GRANT	Permission to grant permissions to tables in the namespace	Table.GRANT
Namespace.BULK_IMPORT	Permission to bulk import data into tables in the namespace	Table.BULK_IMPORT
Namespace.ALTER_TABLE	Permission to set properties on tables in the namespace	Table.ALTER_TABLE
Namespace.DROP_TABLE	Permission to delete tables in the namespace	Table.DROP_TABLE
Namespace.CREATE_TABLE	Permission to create tables in the namespace	N/A
Namespace.ALTER_NAME SPACE	Permission to set properties on the namespace	N/A

Permission	Description	Equivalent table permission
Namespace.DROP_NAME SPACE	Permission to delete the namespace	N/A

Table-level permissions are used to control coarse-grained access to individual tables. Table 6-9 contains a list of table-level permissions and their descriptions.

Table 6-9. Table-level permissions in Accumulo

Permission	Description
Table.READ	Permission to read (scan) the table
Table.WRITE	Permission to write (put/delete) to the table
Table.BULK_IMPORT	Permission to bulk import data into the table
Table.ALTER_TABLE	Permission to set properties on the table
Table.GRANT	Permission to grant permissions to the table
Table.DROP_TABLE	Permission to delete the table

System, namespace, and table-level permissions can be managed using the Accumulo shell. In particular, permissions are granted using the grant command and can be revoked using the revoke command. See Example 6-18 for an example of using the Accumulo shell to administer permissions.

Example 6-18. Administering permissions using the Accumulo shell

```
root@cloudcat> userpermissions -u alice
System permissions:

Namespace permissions (accumulo): Namespace.READ

Table permissions (accumulo.metadata): Table.READ
Table permissions (accumulo.root): Table.READ
root@cloudcat> user alice
Enter password for user alice: *****
alice@cloudcat> table super_secret_squirrel
alice@cloudcat super_secret_squirrel> scan
2014-03-31 16:11:06,828 [shell.Shell] ERROR: java.lang.RuntimeException:
  org.apache.accumulo.core.client.AccumuloSecurityException: Error PERMISSION_DENIED
  for user alice on table super_secret_squirrel(ID:a) - User does not have permission
  to perform this action
alice@cloudcat super_secret_squirrel> user root
Enter password for user root: ******
```

```
root@cloudcat super_secret_squirrel> grant Namespace.READ -ns "" -u alice
root@cloudcat super_secret_squirrel> user alice
Enter password for user alice: *****
alice@cloudcat super_secret_squirrel> scan
r f:c []    value
alice@cloudcat super_secret_squirrel>
```

HBase uses the same set of permissions (Table 6-10) for ACLs at the system, namespace, and table level. Permissions granted at a higher level are inherited by objects at
the lower level. For example, if you grant system-level READ permissions to a user,
that user can read all tables in the cluster. HBase supports assigning permissions to
groups as well as individual users. Group permissions are assigned by prefixing the
group name with an @ when using the grant shell command. HBase uses the same
user-to-group mapping classes that come with Hadoop. Group mapping defaults to
loading the Linux groups on the HBase Master and supports using LDAP groups or a
custom mapping.

Table 6-10. Permissions in HBase

Permission	Description
READ (R)	Permission to read (get/scan) data
WRITE (W)	Permission to write (put/delete)
EXEC (X)	Permission to execute coprocessor endpoints
CREATE (C)	Permission to drop the table; alter table attributes; and add, alter, or drop column families
ADMIN (A)	Permission to enable and disable the table, trigger region reassignment or relocation, and the permissions granted by CREATE

Example 6-19 takes a look at using system-level permissions to grant read access to all
tables. First, Alice brings up the HBase shell, gets a list of tables, and attempts to scan
the super_secret_squirrel table.

Example 6-19. Alice is denied access to an HBase table

```
[alice@cdh5-hbase ~]$ hbase shell
HBase Shell; enter 'help<RETURN>' for list of supported commands.
Type "exit<RETURN>" to leave the HBase Shell
Version 0.98.0, rUnknown, Fri Feb  7 12:26:17 PST 2014

hbase(main):001:0> list
TABLE
super_secret_squirrel
1 row(s) in 2.2110 seconds
```

```
hbase(main):002:0> scan 'super_secret_squirrel'
ROW                                        COLUMN+CELL

ERROR: org.apache.hadoop.hbase.security.AccessDeniedException: Insufficient
  permissions for user 'alice' for scanner open on table super_secret_squirrel

hbase(main):003:0> user_permission
User                                       Table,Family,Qualifier:Permission
0 row(s) in 0.7350 seconds
```

Notice that when Alice executes the user_permission command, she is nowhere to be found. Alice asks the HBase administrator to grant her access to all the tables in HBase. The admin logs into the HBase shell as the hbase user and uses the grant command to give Alice READ permissions at the system level.

Example 6-20. HBase admin grants Alice system-level READ permissions

```
[hbase@cdh5-hbase ~]$ hbase shell
HBase Shell; enter 'help<RETURN>' for list of supported commands.
Type "exit<RETURN>" to leave the HBase Shell
Version 0.96.1.1-cdh5.0.0-beta-2, rUnknown, Fri Feb  7 12:26:17 PST 2014

hbase(main):001:0> grant 'alice', 'R'
0 row(s) in 2.6990 seconds

hbase(main):002:0> user_permission 'super_secret_squirrel'
User                                       Table,Family,Qualifier:Permission
 hbase                                     super_secret_squirrel,,: [Permission:
 actions=READ,WRITE,EXEC,CREATE,ADMIN]
1 row(s) in 0.2140 seconds
```

Notice that Alice still doesn't have permissions specific to the super_secret_squir rel table as she was granted access at the system level. Permissions at the system level are displayed in the shell as applying to the hbase:acl table, as shown in Example 6-21. Now when Alice executes a scan, she gets back the rows from the table.

Example 6-21. Alice can now scan any HBase table

```
hbase(main):004:0> user_permission
User                                       Table,Family,Qualifier:Permission
 alice                                     hbase:acl,,: [Permission: actions=REA
D]
1 row(s) in 0.1540 seconds

hbase(main):005:0> scan 'super_secret_squirrel'
ROW                                        COLUMN+CELL
 r                                         column=f:q, timestamp=1396369612376,
```

```
value=value
1 row(s) in 0.1310 seconds
```

Column- and Cell-Level Authorization

HBase and Accumulo also support fine-grained authorization at the data level. In HBase, you can specify permissions down to the column level. Only the READ and WRITE permissions are applicable to column-level ACLs. Because HBase supports assigning permissions to groups, this is a form of role-based access control (roles are mapped one-to-one to groups). The HBase model is similar to Sentry, which also uses RBAC, in that access permissions are stored at the metadata layer and are applied when a user attempts to access a table or column. Rather than an RBAC approach, Accumulo supports a form of attribute-based security. Attribute-based security works by labeling data with tags that are compared with a user's authorizations to determine whether the user has permission to read the value.

In Accumulo, security labels are stored at the cell level and each key/value pair has its own label. Accumulo stores the security labels as part of the key by extending the BigTable data model with a *visibility* element between the column qualifier and timestamp. Like all of the elements of Accumulo's keys, security labels do not need to be predefined and can be created when data is inserted. In order to support more complex combinations of permissions, security labels consist of a set of user-defined tokens that are combined using the boolean | and & operators. Parentheses can also be used to specify precedence of the boolean operators.

In addition to the labels stored with data, each Accumulo user has a set of security labels. These labels are compared with the boolean expressions as data is scanned, and any cells that a user is not authorized to see are filtered from the results. Because the labels are stored at the cell level and form part of the key, it is very easy to implement multilevel security; the same row and column key can refer to data at different authorization levels. This is a very powerful capability for organizations that collect related data with multiple compartments, where part of a record is open to all users but more sensitive parts are restricted.

Summary

In this chapter, we covered authorization for permitting or denying access to data and services in the cluster. Setting permissions and ACLs to control access to data and resources is fundamental in Hadoop administration. We saw that authorization controls look a bit different from component to component, especially the differences between those that authorize access to data (HDFS, HBase, Accumulo) and those that authorize access to processing and resources (MapReduce, YARN).

So far, we've dealt with authorization in terms of independent controls that are applied on a per-component basis. While this is effective in locking down access to the individual component, it increases the complexity and burden placed on an administrator having to learn these different controls. In the next chapter, we will look at how authorization controls are converging with the introduction of Apache Sentry (Incubating).

## CHAPTER 7

Apache Sentry (Incubating)

Over the lifetime of the various Hadoop ecosystem projects, secure authorization has been added in a variety of different ways. It has become increasingly challenging for administrators to implement and maintain a common system of authorization across multiple components. To compound the problem, the various components have different levels of granularity and enforcement of authorization controls, which often leave an administrator confused as to what a given user can actually do (or not do) in the Hadoop environment. These issues, and many others, were the driving force behind the proposal for Apache Sentry (Incubating).

The Sentry proposal (*http://wiki.apache.org/incubator/SentryProposal*) identified a need for fine-grained *role-based access controls (RBAC)* to give administrators more flexibility to control what users can access. Traditionally, and covered already, HDFS authorization controls are limited to simple POXIS-style permissions and extended ACLs. What about frameworks that work on top of HDFS, such as Hive, Cloudera Impala, Solr, HBase, and others? Sentry's goals are to implement authorization for Hadoop ecosystem components in a unified way so that security administrators can easily control what users and groups have access to without needing to know the ins and outs of every single component in the Hadoop stack.

Sentry Concepts

Each component that leverages Sentry for authorization must have a Sentry *binding*. The binding is a plug-in that the component uses to delegate authorization decisions to Sentry. This binding applies the relevant *model* to use for authorization decisions. For example, a SQL model would apply for the components Hive and Impala, a Search model would apply to Solr, and a BigTable model would apply to HBase and Accumulo. Sentry privilege models are discussed in detail a bit later.

With the appropriate model in place, Sentry uses a *policy engine* to determine if the requested action is authorized by checking the *policy provider*. The policy provider is the storage mechanism for the policies, such as a database or text file. Figure 7-1 shows how this looks conceptually.

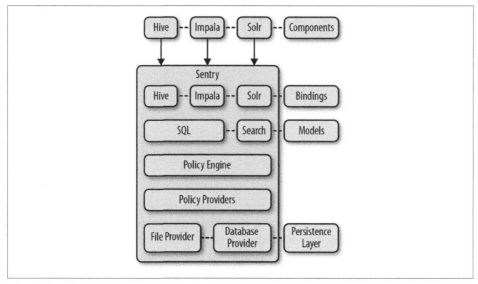

Figure 7-1. Sentry components

This flow makes sense for how components leverage Sentry at a high level, but what about the actual decision-making process for authorization by the policy engine? Regardless of the model in place for a given component, there are several key concepts that are common. *Users* are what you expect them to be. They are identities performing a specific action, such as executing a SQL query, searching a collection, reading a file, or retrieving a key/value pair. Users also belong to *groups*. In the Sentry context, groups are a collection of users that have the same needs and privileges. A *privilege* in Sentry is a unit of data access and is represented by a tuple of an object and an action to be performed on the object. For example, an object could be a DATA BASE, TABLE, or COLLECTION, and the action could be CREATE, READ, WRITE.

 Sentry privileges are always defined in the positive case because, by default, Sentry denies access to every object. This is not to be confused with REVOKE syntax covered later, which simply removes the positive case privileges.

Lastly, a *role* is a collection of privileges and is the basic unit of grant within Sentry. A role typically aligns with a business function, such as a marketing analyst or database administrator. The relationship between users, groups, privileges, and roles is important in Sentry, and adheres to the following logic:

- A group contains multiple users
- A role is assigned a group
- A role is granted privileges

This is illustrated in Figure 7-2.

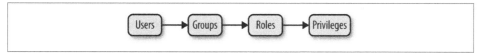

Figure 7-2. Sentry entity relationships

This relationship is strictly enforced in Sentry. It is not possible to assign a role to a user or grant privileges to a group, for example. While this relationship is strict, there are several many-to-many relationships in play here. A user can belong to many groups and a group can contain many users. For example, Alice could belong to both the Marketing and Developer groups, and the Developer group could contain both Alice and Bob.

Also, a role can be assigned to many groups and a group can have many roles. For example, the SQL Analyst role could be assigned to both the Marketing and Developer groups, and the Developer group could have both the SQL Analyst role and Database Administrator role.

Lastly, a role can be granted many privileges and a given privilege can be a part of many roles. For example, the SQL Analyst role could have SELECT privileges on the clickstream TABLE and CREATE privileges on the marketing DATABASE, and the same CREATE privilege on the marketing DATABASE could also be granted to the Database Administrator role.

Now that the high-level Sentry concepts have been covered, we can take a closer look at implementation, starting with the latest and greatest: the Sentry service.

The Sentry Service

When the Sentry project first made its way into the Apache incubator, the first release available to the public was one that utilized a plug-in–based approach. Services that leveraged Sentry were configured with a Sentry plug-in (the binding), and this plug-in ran inside the service in question and directly read the policy file. There was no daemon process for Sentry, like many of the other Hadoop ecosystem components. Furthermore, Sentry policies were configured in a plain text file that enumerated every policy. Whenever a policy was added, modified, or removed, it required a modification to the file. As you might imagine, this approach is rather simplistic, cumbersome to maintain, and prone to errors. To compound the problem, mistakes made in the policy file invalidated the *entire* file!

Thankfully, Sentry has largely moved beyond this early beginning and has grown into a first-class citizen in the Hadoop ecosystem. Starting with version 1.4, Sentry comes with a service that can be leveraged by Hive and Impala. This service utilizes a database backend instead of a text file for policy storage. Additionally, services that use Sentry are now configured with a binding that points to the Sentry service instead of a binding to handle all of the authorization decisions locally. Because of advancements in Sentry's architecture, it is not recommended to use the policy file–based configuration for Hive and Impala except on legacy systems. That being said, this chapter will include information about both configuration options. Figure 7-3 depicts how the Sentry service fits in with SQL access.

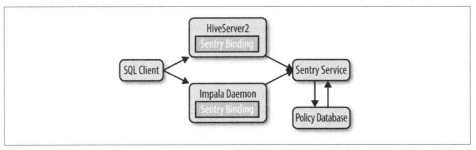

Figure 7-3. Sentry service architecture

At the time of this writing, Solr still utilizes policy files. It is expected that Solr as well as any other new Sentry-enabled services will move away from using policy file–based configurations.

Sentry Service Configuration

The first part of getting Sentry up and running in the cluster is to configure the Sentry service. The master configuration file for Sentry is called *sentry-site.xml*. Example 7-1 shows a typical configuration for the Sentry server in a Kerberos-enabled cluster, and Table 7-1 explains the configuration parameters. Later on in the chapter, we will take a look at how Hadoop ecosystem components utilize this Sentry service for authorization.

Example 7-1. Sentry service sentry-site.xml

```
<?xml version="1.0" encoding="UTF-8"?>

<configuration>
  <property>
```

```
    <name>sentry.service.server.rpc-address</name>
    <value>server1.example.com</value>
  </property>
  <property>
    <name>sentry.service.server.rpc-port</name>
    <value>8038</value>
  </property>
  <property>
    <name>sentry.service.admin.group</name>
    <value>hive,impala,hue</value>
  </property>
  <property>
    <name>sentry.service.allow.connect</name>
    <value>hive,impala,hue</value>
  </property>
  <property>
    <name>sentry.store.group.mapping</name>
    <value>org.apache.sentry.provider.common.HadoopGroupMappingService</value>
  </property>
  <property>
    <name>sentry.service.server.principal</name>
    <value>sentry/_HOST@EXAMPLE.COM</value>
  </property>
  <property>
    <name>sentry.service.security.mode</name>
    <value>kerberos</value>
  </property>
  <property>
    <name>sentry.service.server.keytab</name>
    <value>sentry.keytab</value>
  </property>
  <property>
    <name>sentry.store.jdbc.url</name>
    <value>jdbc:mysql://server2.example.com:3306/</value>
  </property>
  <property>
    <name>sentry.store.jdbc.driver</name>
    <value>com.mysql.jdbc.Driver</value>
  </property>
  <property>
    <name>sentry.store.jdbc.user</name>
    <value>sentry</value>
  </property>
  <property>
    <name>sentry.store.jdbc.password</name>
    <value>sentry_password</value>
  </property>
</configuration>
```

Table 7-1 shows all of the relevant configuration parameters for *sentry-site.xml*. This
includes parameters that are used for configuring the Sentry service, as well as config-

urations for policy file–based implementations and component-specific configurations.

Table 7-1. sentry-site.xml configurations

Configuration	Description
`hive.sentry.provider`	Typically `org.apache.sentry.provider.file.HadoopGroupRe sourceAuthorizationProvider` for Hadoop groups; local groups can be defined only in a policy-file deployment and use `org.apache.sen try.provider.file.LocalGroupResourceAuthorization Provider`
`hive.sentry.provider.resource`	The location of the policy file; can be both `file://` and `hdfs://` URIs
hive.sentry.server	The name of the Sentry server; can be anything
`sentry.hive.provider.backend`	Type of Sentry service: `org.apache.sentry.provider.file.Sim pleFileProviderBackend` or `org.apache.sentry.pro vider.db.SimpleDBProviderBackend`
`sentry.metastore.service.users`	List of users allowed to bypass Sentry policies for the Hive metastore; only applies to Sentry service deployments
`sentry.provider`	Same options as `hive.sentry.provider`; used by Solr
`sentry.service.admin.group`	List of comma-separated groups that are administrators of the Sentry server
`sentry.service.allow.connect`	List of comma-separated users that are allowed to connect; typically only service users, not end users
`sentry.service.client.server.rpc-address`	Client configuration of the Sentry service endpoint
`sentry.service.client.server.rpc-port`	Client configuration of the Sentry service port
`sentry.service.security.mode`	The security mode the Sentry server is operating under; kerberos or none
`sentry.service.server.keytab`	Keytab filename that contains the credentials for `sentry.ser vice.server.principal`
`sentry.service.server.principal`	Service principal name contained in `sentry.service.server.key tab` that the Sentry server identifies itself as
`sentry.service.server.rpc-address`	The hostname to start the Sentry server on

Configuration	Description
`sentry.service.server.rpc-port`	The port to listen on
`sentry.solr.provider.resource`	The location of the policy file for Solr; can be both `file://` and `hdfs://` URIs
`sentry.store.jdbc.driver`	The JDBC driver name to use to connect to the database
`sentry.store.jdbc.password`	The JDBC password to use
`sentry.store.jdbc.url`	The JDBC URL for the backend database the Sentry server should use
`sentry.store.jdbc.user`	The JDBC username to connect as
`sentry.store.group.mapping`	The class that provides the mapping of users to groups; typically `org.apache.sentry.provider.common.HadoopGroupMappingService`

Hive Authorization

The canonical implementation of Sentry is to add role-based access controls to Hive. Without strong authorization controls, users of Hive can make changes to the Hive metastore without much restriction. Additionally, access to Hive tables is completely controlled by the underlying HDFS file permissions, which is extremely limited. With Sentry, security administrators can control which users and groups can use Hive in a very granular way to include such operations as creating tables and views, inserting new data into existing tables, or selecting data with queries.

To understand how Sentry provides authorization for Hive, it is first necessary to understand the basics of how the components of Hive work together. There are three major components in the Hive architecture: the metastore database, Hive Metastore Server, and HiveServer2. The metastore database is a relational database that contains all of the Hive metadata, such as information about databases, tables and views, locations of table data in HDFS, datatypes for columns, file formats and compression, and so on. When a client interacts with Hive, this information is necessary to make sense of the operations that are to be performed.

With older versions of Hive, this was pretty much all you had; the Hive client API would talk directly to the metastore database and perform operations. From a security standpoint, this is bad. This model meant that every Hive client had the full credentials to the Hive metastore database! The Hive Metastore Server became a component of the Hive architecture to address this problem, among others. This role's purpose is to become a middle layer between Hive clients and the metastore database. With this model, clients need only to know how to contact the Hive Metastore Server, whereas only the Hive Metastore Server holds the keys to the underlying metastore database.

The last component of the Hive architecture is HiveServer2. This component's purpose is to provide a query service to external applications using interfaces such as JDBC and ODBC. HiveServer2 fields requests from clients, communicates with the Hive Metastore Server to retrieve metadata information, and performs Hive actions as appropriate, such as spawning off MapReduce jobs. As the name implies, Hive-Server2 is the second version of such a service, with the initial version lacking concurrency and security features. The important part to understand here is that HiveServer2 was initially meant to serve external applications. The Hive command-line interface (CLI) was still interacting directly with the Hive Metastore Server and using Hive APIs to perform actions. Users could use the CLI for HiveServer2, *beeline*, to perform actions, but it was not required. This fact poses a challenge for enforcing secure authorization for *all* clients. As you might have guessed, the way to achieve this is to enforce secure authorization for HiveServer2, and ensure that all SQL clients must use HiveServer2 to perform any and all Hive SQL operations.

Another component of the Hive architecture is HCatalog. This is a set of libraries that allows non-SQL clients to access Hive Metastore structures. This is useful for users of Pig or MapReduce to determine the metadata structures of files without having to use traditional Hive clients. An extension of the HCatalog libraries is the WebHCatServer component. This component is a daemon process that provides a REST interface to perform HCatalog functions. Neither the HCatalog libraries, nor the WebHCatServer utilize HiveServer2. All communication is directly to the Hive Metastore Server. Because of this fact, the Hive Metastore Server must also be protected by Sentry to ensure HCatalog users cannot make arbitrary modifications to the Hive Metastore database.

While the 1.4 release of Sentry has the ability to provide write protection of the Hive Metastore Server, it does not currently limit reads. What this means is that a user doing something equivalent to a SHOW TABLES operation in HCatalog will return a list of *all* tables, including tables they do not have access to. This is different from the same operation performed via HiveServer2 where the user only sees the objects they have access to. However, this is only metadata exposure. Permissions of the actual data are still enforced at the time of access by HDFS. If your cluster does not have any users that utilize HCatalog, a way to force all Hive traffic to Hive-Server2 is to set the property hadoop.proxyuser.hive.groups in the *core-site.xml* configuration file to hive,impala, which allows both Hive (HiveServer2) and Impala (Catalog Server) to directly access the Hive Metastore Server, but nobody else.

Figure 7-4 shows how the Hive architecture is laid out and where the Sentry enforcements occur. As you can see, regardless of the method of access, the key enforcement is protecting the Hive metastore from unauthorized changes.

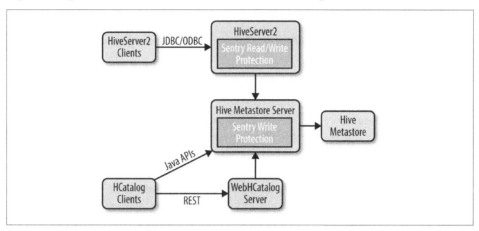

Figure 7-4. Hive sentry architecture

Hive Sentry Configuration

In this section, we take a look at what is necessary to configure Hive to leverage Sentry for authorization. Example 7-2 shows the *sentry-site.xml* configuration file that is used by both the Hive Metastore Server and HiveServer2 to leverage a Sentry service.

Example 7-2. Hive sentry-site.xml service deployment

```
<configuration>
  <property>
    <name>hive.sentry.server</name>
    <value>server1</value>
  </property>
  <property>
    <name>sentry.service.server.principal</name>
    <value>sentry/_HOST@EXAMPLE.COM</value>
  </property>
  <property>
    <name>sentry.service.security.mode</name>
    <value>kerberos</value>
  </property>
  <property>
    <name>sentry.hive.provider.backend</name>
    <value>org.apache.sentry.provider.db.SimpleDBProviderBackend</value>
  </property>
  <property>
    <name>sentry.service.client.server.rpc-address</name>
    <value>server1.example.com</value>
```

```
    </property>
    <property>
      <name>sentry.service.client.server.rpc-port</name>
      <value>8038</value>
    </property>
    <property>
      <name>hive.sentry.provider</name>
      <value>
        org.apache.sentry.provider.file.HadoopGroupResourceAuthorizationProvider
      </value>
    </property>
    <property>
      <name>sentry.metastore.service.users</name>
      <value>hive,impala,hue,hdfs</value>
    </property>
</configuration>
```

Example 7-3 shows a typical configuration for Sentry when used with HiveServer2 (and Hive Metastore Server) and a policy file–based deployment. The policy file–based configuration for Sentry is rather minimal when compared to the service-based configuration, but there are commonalities. The location of *sentry-site.xml* on the local filesystem is specified in the HiveServer2 daemon's *hive-site.xml* configuration file, as we will see later.

Example 7-3. Hive sentry-site.xml policy file deployment

```
<?xml version="1.0" encoding="UTF-8"?>

<configuration>
  <property>
    <name>hive.sentry.provider</name>
    <value>
      org.apache.sentry.provider.file.HadoopGroupResourceAuthorizationProvider
    </value>
  </property>
  <property>
    <name>sentry.hive.provider.backend</name>
    <value>org.apache.sentry.provider.file.SimpleFileProviderBackend</value>
  </property>
  <property>
    <name>hive.sentry.provider.resource</name>
    <value>/user/hive/sentry/sentry-provider.ini</value>
  </property>
  <property>
    <name>hive.sentry.server</name>
    <value>server1</value>
  </property>
</configuration>
```

First, we will look at the configuration properties that are used in both examples. The parameter `hive.sentry.server` specifies a name (label) for this particular Sentry server, which can be referenced in policies. This name has nothing to do with a machine hostname. The `sentry.hive.provider.backend` configuration tells Hive which provider backend to use. For the Sentry service, this is `org.apache.sentry.provider.db.SimpleDBProviderBackend` and for the Sentry policy file this is `org.apache.sentry.provider.file.SimpleFileProviderBackend`. `hive.sentry.provider` configures the method that Sentry will use to determine group information. `HadoopGroupResourceAuthorizationProvider`, shown here, will leverage whatever method Hadoop is configured with, such as reading groups from the local operating system or directly pulling group information from LDAP. However, this is a mere formality in Example 7-2 because the Sentry service cannot use a policy file to define local user-to-group mappings.

Next we will look at the configurations that are specific to the Sentry service example. The details of how Hive should connect to the Sentry service are provided by the following:

- `sentry.service.client.server.rpc-address`
- `sentry.service.client.server.rpc-port`

Both `sentry.service.server.principal` and `sentry.service.security.mode` set up the Kerberos configuration details. Finally, the `sentry.metastore.service.users` configuration lists the users that are allowed to bypass Sentry authorization and connect directly to the Hive Metastore Server. This likely will always be service/system users like Hive and Impala, as the example shows.

The remaining configuration that is specific to the policy file deployment example is `hive.sentry.provider.resource`. This specifies the location where the policy file is. The location specified for the Sentry policy file will assume the location is the same as is specified in *hdfs-site.xml*. For example, it will assume the path */user/hive/sentry/sentry-provider.ini* is in HDFS if *hdfs-site.xml* points to HDFS. It is also possible to be explicit in the location by providing `hdfs://` for an HDFS path or `file://` for a local filesystem path.

While the *sentry-site.xml* configuration is important for Hive, on its own it does not enable Sentry authorization for it. Additional configuration is necessary in Hive's configuration file, *hive-site.xml*. Example 7-4 shows the relevant configurations needed for the Hive Metastore Server, and Example 7-5 similarly shows what is needed for HiveServer2. The two configurations are similar, but slightly different. The last *hive-site.xml* example shown in Example 7-6 shows what is needed for Hive-Server2 in a policy file–based deployment. Note that in a policy file–based deployment, no additional configuration is needed for the Hive Metastore Server (more on that later).

Example 7-4. Hive Metastore Server hive-site.xml Sentry service configurations

```xml
<?xml version="1.0" encoding="UTF-8"?>

<configuration>
  <!-- Unrelated properties omitted -->
  <property>
    <name>hive.sentry.conf.url</name>
    <value>file:///etc/hive/conf/sentry-site.xml</value>
  </property>
  <property>
    <name>hive.metastore.pre.event.listeners</name>
    <value>org.apache.sentry.binding.metastore.MetastoreAuthzBinding</value>
  </property>
  <property>
    <name>hive.metastore.event.listeners</name>
    <value>
      org.apache.sentry.binding.metastore.SentryMetastorePostEventListener
    </value>
  </property>
</configuration>
```

Example 7-5. HiveServer2 hive-site.xml Sentry service configurations

```xml
<?xml version="1.0" encoding="UTF-8"?>

<configuration>
  <!-- Unrelated properties omitted -->
  <property>
    <name>hive.server2.enable.doAs</name>
    <value>false</value>
  </property>
  <property>
    <name>hive.server2.session.hook</name>
    <value>org.apache.sentry.binding.hive.HiveAuthzBindingSessionHook</value>
  </property>
  <property>
    <name>hive.sentry.conf.url</name>
    <value>file:///etc/hive/conf/sentry-site.xml</value>
  </property>
  <property>
    <name>hive.security.authorization.task.factory</name>
    <value>
      org.apache.sentry.binding.hive.SentryHiveAuthorizationTaskFactoryImpl
    </value>
  </property>
</configuration>
```

Example 7-6. HiveServer2 hive-site.xml Sentry policy file configurations

```
<?xml version="1.0" encoding="UTF-8"?>

<configuration>
  <!-- Unrelated properties omitted -->
  <property>
    <name>hive.server2.enable.doAs</name>
    <value>false</value>
  </property>
  <property>
    <name>hive.server2.session.hook</name>
    <value>org.apache.sentry.binding.hive.HiveAuthzBindingSessionHook</value>
  </property>
  <property>
    <name>hive.sentry.conf.url</name>
    <value>file:///etc/hive/conf/sentry-site.xml</value>
  </property>
</configuration>
```

In all three *hive-site.xml* examples, the configuration property `hive.sen try.conf.url` tells Hive where to locate the Sentry configuration file. In both Hive-Server2 examples, the property `hive.server2.session.hook` is used to specify a binding that will actually hand off authorization decisions to Sentry.

Also in both HiveServer2 examples, notice that impersonation is disabled. Disabling Hive impersonation is a critical piece of Sentry configuration. In order to truly have authorization that is enforced all the way from query to data access, Sentry and Hive need to have control of both the query interface as well as file access. To do this, HDFS permissions of the Hive warehouse need to be locked down, as shown in Example 7-7.

Example 7-7. Locking down the Hive warehouse

```
[alice@server1 ~]$ kinit hdfs
Enter password for hdfs@EXAMPLE.COM:
[alice@server1 ~]$ hdfs dfs -chown -R hive:hive /user/hive/warehouse
[alice@server1 ~]$ hdfs dfs -chmod -R 0771 /user/hive/warehouse
[alice@server1 ~]$
```

After locking down the Hive warehouse and disabling impersonation, Sentry controls authorization at the query interface. HDFS permissions are locked down because only the Hive system user is able to access the files. Not only is this better from a security perspective, but it also allows Sentry the ability to control authorization down to the view level. Views can be used for column-level security (selecting only certain columns) and as row-level security, such as providing a filtering `WHERE` clause. If impersonation is enabled and queries are thus run as the end user, view-level permissions are not realistically enforced because the user has file-level (e.g., table-level) access in

HDFS and can bypass Sentry policies by accessing files directly, such as with MapReduce.

Impala Authorization

The initial release of Sentry included support for both Hive and Impala. While both of these components have some similarities, they have some fundamental differences in architecture that need to be addressed before we can fully understand how Sentry fits into the equation. First, Impala is an entire processing framework. This differs from Hive in that Hive does not have any processing power to do the actual work a user is requesting. That work is handled by MapReduce by default (either standalone version 1, or version 2 on YARN).

Impala architecture consists of three components: *Daemon*, *StateStore*, and *Catalog Service*. The Impala Daemon, or *impalad*, is the actual worker process, which runs on every node in the cluster that runs the HDFS DataNode daemon. The Impala StateStore, or *statestored*, is responsible for keeping track of the health of all of the impalad instances in the cluster. If an instance goes bad, statestored broadcasts this information to all the rest of the impalad instances. While this might seem like a critical component of the Impala architecture, it actually is not required. If the statestored process goes down or does not exist at all, all of the work done by the impalad instances continues to operate. The only potential impact is if an impalad instance goes into bad health, the remaining instances will be slow to discover this, which can lead to a delay in total query execution time. The Impala Catalog Service, or *catalogd*, is responsible for keeping track of metadata changes. If an Impala query executes on an impalad that somehow changes metadata, the catalogd broadcasts the updated metadata to the other impalad instances. The catalogd is responsible for communicating with the Hive Metastore server to retrieve all existing metadata information.

Now that the basics of Impala architecture have been reviewed, we can cover where Sentry actually comes into play. As described earlier in our discussion of Hive, Sentry is a plug-in for Hive components HiveServer2 and Hive Metastore Server, which most of the time are each single instances on a cluster. With Impala, Sentry is not a centralized plug-in to augment a single main component, such as for the catalogd or statestored processes. Sentry is actually enabled on every impalad. When a user connects to a given impalad with Sentry enabled and issues a query, the impalad uses the Sentry policy (either from the Sentry service or a policy file) to determine if the user is authorized to perform the requested action.

Impala Sentry Configuration

Like we did in the previous section with Hive, in this section we take a look at what is necessary to configure Impala to leverage Sentry for authorization. Example 7-8 shows the *sentry-site.xml* configuration file that is used by the Impala daemons to lev-

---

erage a Sentry service. In a policy file–based deployment, a *sentry-site.xml* file is not required.

Example 7-8. Impala sentry-site.xml service deployment

```
<?xml version="1.0" encoding="UTF-8"?>

<configuration>
  <property>
    <name>sentry.service.server.principal</name>
    <value>sentry/_HOST@EXAMPLE.COM</value>
  </property>
  <property>
    <name>sentry.service.security.mode</name>
    <value>kerberos</value>
  </property>
  <property>
    <name>sentry.service.client.server.rpc-address</name>
    <value>server1.example.com</value>
  </property>
  <property>
    <name>sentry.service.client.server.rpc-port</name>
    <value>8038</value>
  </property>
</configuration>
```

As you might have noticed, the *sentry-site.xml* configuration for Impala to use a Sentry service is a subset of the configuration for Hive. The properties were already discussed in the last section, so we can move on to configuring the Impala daemons to enable Sentry authorization.

In a Sentry service deployment, the Impala daemons need just three flags configured. The first flag is `server_name`, which is a label for the Sentry server. This matches the `hive.sentry.server` configuration property. The second flag is `sentry_config`, which points the Impala daemon to the location of the *sentry-site.xml* configuration file. The third flag, `authorized_proxy_user_config`, is used to specify users that serve as impersonators for other users, such as the `hue` user. Example 7-9 shows what this looks like.

Example 7-9. Impala flags for Sentry service deployment

```
...Other unrelated flags omitted for brevity
-server_name=server1
-sentry_config=/etc/impala/conf/sentry-site.xml
-authorized_proxy_user_config=hue=*
```

In a Sentry policy file–based deployment, the Impala daemons do not need the `sen try_config` flag. Instead, the Impala daemons are configured with the `authoriza` tion_policy_file and authorization_policy_provider_class flags. These flags indicate the location of the Sentry policy file and the authorization provider class, respectively. The latter was described already with the hive.sentry.provider configuration property, which serves the same purpose. Example 7-10 shows how this looks.

Example 7-10. Impala flags for Sentry policy file deployment

```
...Other unrelated flags omitted for brevity
-server_name=server1
-authorized_proxy_user_config=hue=*
-authorization_policy_file=/user/hive/sentry/sentry-provider.ini
-authorization_policy_provider_class=\
 org.apache.sentry.provider.file.HadoopGroupResourceAuthorizationProvider
```

Solr Authorization

Authorization for Solr starts with collections. Collections are the main entry point of access, much like how databases are for SQL. Sentry authorization initially started with defining privileges at the collection level. Sentry has since evolved to provide document-level authorization. Document-level authorization is done by tagging each document with a special field name containing the value that corresponds to an associated Sentry role name defined in the Sentry policy file (described later). The tagging of documents in this fashion would be done at ingest time, so it is important to have a good sense of role names to avoid needing to reprocess documents to change tag values.

Solr Sentry Configuration

This section explains how to set up Solr with Sentry authorization. Example 7-11 shows what is needed in the *sentry-site.xml* configuration file for the Solr servers.

Example 7-11. Solr sentry-site.xml policy file deployment

```
<?xml version="1.0" encoding="UTF-8"?>

<configuration>
  <property>
    <name>sentry.provider</name>
    <value>
      org.apache.sentry.provider.file.HadoopGroupResourceAuthorizationProvider
    </value>
  </property>
  <property>
    <name>sentry.solr.provider.resource</name>
    <value>/user/solr/sentry/sentry-provider.ini</value>
```

```
    </property>
</configuration>
```

The two configuration properties shown in Example 7-11 should look very familiar at this point, but the configuration property names are slightly different with Solr. The `sentry.provider` configuration property works just like the `hive.sentry.provider` configuration for Hive and the `authorization_policy_provider_class` flag for Impala. The `sentry.solr.provider.resource` configuration property specifies the location of the Sentry policy file. Again, this policy file can be located either on the local filesystem or on HDFS. It needs to be readable by the user that the Solr servers are running as (typically the solr user).

To set up the Solr servers with Sentry authorization, some environment variables are needed. These can either be set as environment variables or as lines in the */etc/default/solr* configuration file. The first variable is `SOLR_SENTRY_ENABLED`. This obviously enables Sentry authorization when set to true. The next is `SOLR_AUTHORIZA TION_SUPERUSER`. This variable defines the user that has superuser privileges, which typically should be the solr user. The last variable is `SOLR_AUTHORIZATION_SEN TRY_SITE`, which specifies the location of the *sentry-site.xml* configuration file described earlier. Example 7-12 shows how this looks.

Example 7-12. Solr environment variables in Sentry policy file deployment

```
...Other unrelated environment variables omitted for brevity
SOLR_SENTRY_ENABLED=true
SOLR_AUTHORIZATION_SUPERUSER=solr
SOLR_AUTHORIZATION_SENTRY_SITE=/etc/solr/conf/sentry-site.xml
```

It was mentioned earlier in this section that document-level authorization can be used. In order to make that happen, a few configurations are necessary for the collection. By default, collections are configured using the *solrconfig.xml* configuration file. This file needs to look like Example 7-13.

Example 7-13. Document-level security solrconfig.xml

```
<searchComponent name="queryDocAuthorization"
class="org.apache.solr.handler.component.QueryDocAuthorizationComponent">
    <bool name="enabled">true</bool>
    <str name="sentryAuthField">sentry_auth</str>
    <str name="allRolesToken">*</str>
</searchComponent>
```

Example 7-13 shows that the class `org.apache.solr.handler.component.QueryDo cAuthorizationComponent` is used for document-level authorization decisions. It is turned on by setting the `enabled` property to `true`. The configuration property `sentryAuthField` defines the name of the field in a document that contains the authorization *token* to determine access. The default value of `sentry_auth` is shown, but this can be anything. Documents will use this tag to insert the role name that is required to access the document. The last configuration property `allRolesToken` defines the token that allows every role to access a given document. The default is *, and it makes sense to leave that as is to remain consistent with wildcard matches in other Sentry privileges.

Sentry Privilege Models

In this section, we take a look at the privilege models for the various services that Sentry provides authorization for. The privilege models identify privileges, object types that the privileges apply to, the scope of the privilege, and other useful information that will help a security administrator understand the authorization controls available, and to what granularity. Having a good grasp on the privilege models here will ensure that appropriate policies are selected to meet the desired level of authorization controls to protect data from unauthorized access.

SQL Privilege Model

Sentry provides three types of privileges for SQL access: SELECT, INSERT, and ALL. These privileges are not available for every object. Table 7-2 provides information on which privileges apply to which object in a SQL context. The SQL privilege model itself is a hierarchy, meaning privileges to container objects imply privileges to child objects. This is important to fully understand what users do or do not have access to.

Table 7-2. SQL privilege types[a]

Privilege	Object
INSERT	TABLE,URI
SELECT	TABLE,VIEW,URI
ALL	SERVER,DB,URI

[a] All privilege model tables are reproduced from cloudera.com with permission from Cloudera, Inc.

Table 7-3 lays out which container privilege yields the granular privilege on a given object. For example, the first line in the table should be interpreted as "ALL privileges on a SERVER object implies ALL privileges on a DATABASE object."

Table 7-3. SQL privilege hierarchy

Base Object	Granular Privilege	Container Object	Container Privilege That Implies Granular Privilege
DATABASE	ALL	SERVER	ALL
TABLE	INSERT	DATABASE	ALL
TABLE	SELECT	DATABASE	ALL
VIEW	SELECT	DATABASE	ALL

The final portion of the SQL privilege model is to understand how privileges map to SQL operations. Table 7-4 shows for a given SQL operation, what object scope does the operation apply to, and what privileges are required to perform the operation. For example, the first line in the table should be interpreted as "CREATE DATABASE applies to the SERVER object and requires ALL privileges on the SERVER object." Some of the SQL operations involve more than one privilege, such as creating views. Creating a new view requires ALL privileges on the DATABASE in which the view is to be created, as well as SELECT privileges on the TABLE/VIEW object(s) referenced by the view.

Table 7-4. SQL privileges

SQL Operation	Scope	Privileges
CREATE DATABASE	SERVER	ALL
DROP DATABASE	DATABASE	ALL
CREATE TABLE	DATABASE	ALL
DROP TABLE	TABLE	ALL
CREATE VIEW	DATABASE; SELECT on TABLE	ALL
DROP VIEW	VIEW/TABLE	ALL
CREATE INDEX	TABLE	ALL
DROP INDEX	TABLE	ALL
ALTER TABLE ADD COLUMNS	TABLE	ALL
ALTER TABLE REPLACE COLUMNS	TABLE	ALL
ALTER TABLE CHANGE column	TABLE	ALL

SQL Operation	Scope	Privileges
ALTER TABLE RENAME	TABLE	ALL
ALTER TABLE SET TBLPROPERTIES	TABLE	ALL
ALTER TABLE SET FILEFORMAT	TABLE	ALL
ALTER TABLE SET LOCATION	TABLE	ALL
ALTER TABLE ADD PARTITION	TABLE	ALL
ALTER TABLE ADD PARTITION location	TABLE	ALL
ALTER TABLE DROP PARTITION	TABLE	ALL
ALTER TABLE PARTITION SET FILEFORMAT	TABLE	ALL
SHOW TBLPROPERTIES	TABLE	SELECT/INSERT
SHOW CREATE TABLE	TABLE	SELECT/INSERT
SHOW PARTITIONS	TABLE	SELECT/INSERT
DESCRIBE TABLE	TABLE	SELECT/INSERT
DESCRIBE TABLE PARTITION	TABLE	SELECT/INSERT
LOAD DATA	TABLE; URI	INSERT
SELECT	TABLE	SELECT
INSERT OVERWRITE TABLE	TABLE	INSERT
CREATE TABLE AS SELECT	DATABASE; SELECT on TABLE	ALL
USE database	ANY	ANY
ALTER TABLE SET SERDEPROPERTIES	TABLE	ALL
ALTER TABLE PARTITION SET SERDEPROPERTIES	TABLE	ALL
CREATE ROLE	SERVER	ALL
GRANT ROLE TO GROUP	SERVER	ALL
GRANT PRIVILEGE ON SERVER	SERVER	ALL

SQL Operation	Scope	Privileges
GRANT PRIVILEGE ON DATABASE	DATABASE	WITH GRANT OPTION
GRANT PRIVILEGE ON TABLE	TABLE	WITH GRANT OPTION

While most of the SQL operations are supported by both Hive and Impala, some operations are supported only by Hive or Impala, or have not been implemented yet. Table 7-5 lists the SQL privileges that only apply to Hive, and Table 7-6 lists the SQL privileges that only apply to Impala.

Table 7-5. Hive-only SQL privileges

SQL Operation	Scope	Privileges
INSERT OVERWRITE DIRECTORY	TABLE; URI	INSERT
ANALYZE TABLE	TABLE	SELECT + INSERT
IMPORT TABLE	DATABASE; URI	ALL
EXPORT TABLE	TABLE; URI	SELECT
ALTER TABLE TOUCH	TABLE	ALL
ALTER TABLE TOUCH PARTITION	TABLE	ALL
ALTER TABLE CLUSTERED BY SORTED BY	TABLE	ALL
ALTER TABLE ENABLE/DISABLE	TABLE	ALL
ALTER TABLE PARTITION ENABLE/DISABLE	TABLE	ALL
ALTER TABLE PARTITION RENAME TO PARTITION	TABLE	ALL
ALTER DATABASE	DATABASE	ALL
DESCRIBE DATABASE	DATABASE	SELECT/INSERT
SHOW COLUMNS	TABLE	SELECT/INSERT
SHOW INDEXES	TABLE	SELECT/INSERT

Table 7-6. Impala-only SQL privileges

SQL Operation	Scope	Privileges
EXPLAIN	TABLE	SELECT
INVALIDATE METADATA	SERVER	ALL
INVALIDATE METADATA table	TABLE	SELECT/INSERT
REFRESH table	TABLE	SELECT/INSERT
CREATE FUNCTION	SERVER	ALL
DROP FUNCTION	SERVER	ALL
COMPUTE STATS	TABLE	ALL

Solr Privilege Model

With Solr, Sentry provides three types of privileges: QUERY, UPDATE, and * (ALL). The privilege model for Solr is broken down between privileges that apply to request handlers and those that apply to collections. In Tables 7-8 through 7-10, the *admin* collection name is a special collection in Sentry that is used to represent administrative actions. In all of the Solr privilege model tables, *collection1* denotes an arbitrary collection name.

Table 7-7. Solr privilege table for nonadministrative request handlers

Request handler	Required privilege	Collections that require privilege
select	QUERY	collection1
query	QUERY	collection1
get	QUERY	collection1
browse	QUERY	collection1
tvrh	QUERY	collection1
clustering	QUERY	collection1
terms	QUERY	collection1

Request handler	Required privilege	Collections that require privilege
elevate	QUERY	collection1
analysis/field	QUERY	collection1
analysis/document	QUERY	collection1
update	UPDATE	collection1
update/json	UPDATE	collection1
update/csv	UPDATE	collection1

Table 7-8. Solr privilege table for collections admin actions

Collection action	Required privilege	Collections that require privilege
create	UPDATE	admin, collection1
delete	UPDATE	admin, collection1
reload	UPDATE	admin, collection1
createAlias	UPDATE	admin, collection1
deleteAlias	UPDATE	admin, collection1
syncShard	UPDATE	admin, collection1
splitShard	UPDATE	admin, collection1
deleteShard	UPDATE	admin, collection1

Table 7-9. Solr privilege table for core admin actions

Collection action	Required privilege	Collections that require privilege
create	UPDATE	admin, collection1
rename	UPDATE	admin, collection1
load	UPDATE	admin, collection1
unload	UPDATE	admin, collection1
status	UPDATE	admin, collection1

Collection action	Required privilege	Collections that require privilege
persist	UPDATE	admin
reload	UPDATE	admin, collection1
swap	UPDATE	admin, collection1
mergeIndexes	UPDATE	admin, collection1
split	UPDATE	admin, collection1
prepRecover	UPDATE	admin, collection1
requestRecover	UPDATE	admin, collection1
requestSyncShard	UPDATE	admin, collection1
requestApplyUpdates	UPDATE	admin, collection1

Table 7-10. Solr privilege table for info and AdminHandlers

Request handler	Required privilege	Collections that require privilege
LukeRequestHandler	QUERY	admin
SystemInfoHandler	QUERY	admin
SolrInfoMBeanHandler	QUERY	admin
PluginInfoHandler	QUERY	admin
ThreadDumpHandler	QUERY	admin
PropertiesRequestHandler	QUERY	admin
LogginHandler	QUERY, UPDATE (or *)	admin
ShowFileRequestHandler	QUERY	admin

Sentry Policy Administration

Now that we have seen the privilege tables and the types of accesses available, we can look at how the actual policies can be added, removed, or changed. The approach to administering policies differs depending on the type of Sentry deployment, be it the newer Sentry service or the older policy file. The first, and preferred, method of administering policy is by using SQL commands.

SQL Commands

Security administrators who are accustomed to managing roles and permissions in popular relational database systems will find the SQL syntax for administering Sentry policies to be very familiar. Table 7-11 shows all of the statements available to an administrator managing Sentry policies.

Table 7-11. Sentry policy SQL syntax

Statement	Description
CREATE ROLE *role_name*	Creates a role with the specified name
DROP ROLE *role_name*	Deletes a role with the specified name
GRANT ROLE *role_name* TO GROUP *group_name*	Grants the specified role to the specified group
REVOKE ROLE *role_name* FROM GROUP *group_name*	Revokes the specified role from the specified group
GRANT privilege ON object TO ROLE *role_name*	Grants a privilege on an object to the specified role
GRANT privilege ON object TO ROLE *role_name* WITH GRANT OPTION	Grants a privilege on an object to the specified role and allows the role to further grant privileges within the object
REVOKE privilege ON object FROM ROLE *role_name*	Revokes a privilege on an object from the specified role
SET ROLE *role_name*	Sets the specified role for the current session
SET ROLE ALL	Enables all roles (that the user has access to) for the current session
SET ROLE NONE	Disables all roles for the current session
SHOW ROLES	Lists all roles in the database
SHOW CURRENT ROLES	Shows all the roles enabled for the current session
SHOW ROLE GRANT GROUP *group_name*	Shows all roles for the specified group

Statement	Description
SHOW GRANT ROLE *role_name*	Shows all grant permissions for the specified role
SHOW GRANT ROLE *role_name* ON object *object_name*	Shows all grant permissions for the specified role on the specified object.

Table 7-11 provides a good listing of the various syntaxes, a working example is warranted to see these in action (Example 7-14).

Example 7-14. Sentry SQL usage example

```
# Authenticated as the hive user, which is a member of a group listed in
# sentry.service.admin.group and accessing HiveServer2
# via the beeline CLI

# Create the role for hive administrators
0: jdbc:hive2://server1.example.com:100> CREATE ROLE hive_admin;
No rows affected (0.852 seconds)

# Grant the hive administrator role to the sqladmin group
0: jdbc:hive2://server1.example.com:100> GRANT ROLE hive_admin TO GROUP sqladmin;
No rows affected (0.305 seconds)

# Grant server-wide permissions to the hive_admin role
0: jdbc:hive2://server1.example.com:100> GRANT ALL ON SERVER server1
TO ROLE hive_admin;
No rows affected (0.339 seconds)

# Show all of the roles in the Sentry database
0: jdbc:hive2://server1.example.com:100> SHOW ROLES;
+-------------+
|    role     |
+-------------+
| hive_admin  |
+-------------+
1 row selected (0.63 seconds)

# Show all the privileges that the hive_admin role has access to
# (some columns omitted for brevity)
0: jdbc:hive2://server1.example.com:100> SHOW GRANT ROLE hive_admin;
+-----------+----------------+----------------+-----------+--------------+
| database  | principal_name | principal_type | privilege | grant_option |
+-----------+----------------+----------------+-----------+--------------+
| *         | hive_admin     | ROLE           | *         | false        |
+-----------+----------------+----------------+-----------+--------------+
+----------+
| grantor  |
+----------+
| hive     |
```

```
+----------+
1 row selected (0.5 seconds)

# Show all the roles that the sqladmin is a part of
0: jdbc:hive2://server1.example.com:100> SHOW ROLE GRANT GROUP sqladmin;
+------------+--------------+------------+----------+
|    role    | grant_option | grant_time | grantor  |
+------------+--------------+------------+----------+
| hive_admin | false        |            | hive     |
+------------+--------------+------------+----------+
1 row selected (0.5 seconds)

# Remove all of the roles for the current user session
0: jdbc:hive2://server1.example.com:100> SET ROLE NONE;
No rows affected (0.2 seconds)

# Show list of current roles
0: jdbc:hive2://server1.example.com> SHOW CURRENT ROLES;
+-------+
| role  |
+-------+
+-------+
No rows selected (0.305 seconds)

# Verify that no roles yields no access
0: jdbc:hive2://server1.example.com:100> SHOW TABLES;
+-----------+
| tab_name  |
+-----------+
+-----------+
0: jdbc:hive2://server1.example.com:100> SELECT COUNT(*) FROM sample_07;
Error: Error while compiling statement:
FAILED: SemanticException No valid privileges (state=42000,code=40000)

# Set the current role to the hive_admin role
0: jdbc:hive2://server1.example.com:100> SET ROLE hive_admin;
No rows affected (0.176 seconds)

# Show list of current roles
0: jdbc:hive2://server1.example.com:100> SHOW CURRENT ROLES;
+-------------+
|    role     |
+-------------+
| hive_admin  |
+-------------+
1 row selected (0.404 seconds)

# Execute commands that are permitted
0: jdbc:hive2://server1.example.com:100> SHOW TABLES;
+------------+
| tab_name   |
+------------+
```

```
| sample_07 |
| sample_08 |
+-----------+
2 rows selected (0.536 seconds)
0: jdbc:hive2://server1.example.com:100> SELECT COUNT(*) FROM sample_07;
+------+
| _c0  |
+------+
| 823  |
+------+
1 row selected (20.811 seconds)
```

 Using WITH GRANT OPTION is a great way to ease the administration burden on a global SQL administrator. A common example is to create a Hive database for a given line of business and delegate administrative privileges to a database-specific admin role. This gives the line of business the flexibility to manage privileges to their own data. To determine if a role has this option, use SHOW GRANT ROLE *role_name* and look at the column grant_option.

In Example 7-14, the commands are executed using the beeline CLI for HiveServer2, but they can also be run from within the impala-shell. Both components utilize the same Sentry service and thus the same Sentry policies, so changes made from one component are immediately reflected in the other. Sentry authorization decisions are not cached by the individual components because of the security ramifications of doing that.

SQL Policy File

For Sentry deployments that utilize the Sentry service for SQL components, policy administration is familiar and straightforward. This is not the case with the legacy policy file–based implementation. Sentry-enabled components need to have read access to the policy file. When using a policy file for Hive and Impala, this can be achieved by making the file group owned by the hive group and ensuring that both hive and impala users are members of this group. The policy file itself can be located either on the local system or in HDFS. For the former, the file needs to exist wherever the component that is making the authorization decision is deployed. For example, when Sentry is enabled for Hive, the local policy file needs to be on the machine where the HiveServer2 daemon is running.

It is highly recommended to specify a location in HDFS for the policy file in order to leverage HDFS replication for redundancy and availability. Because the policy file is read for every single user operation, it makes sense to increase the replication factor of the file so components reading it can retrieve it from many different nodes. This can be done with `hdfs dfs -setrep N /user/hive/sentry/sentry-provider.ini`, where *N* is the number of replicas desired. The policy file is small, so it is perfectly reasonable to set the number of replicas to the number of DataNodes in the cluster.

The format of the policy file follows a typical INI file format with configuration sections identified with braces and individual configurations specified as KEY = VALUE pairs. Example 7-15 shows a sample policy file for Sentry when used with Hive and Impala.

Example 7-15. SQL sentry-provider.ini

```
[databases]
product = hdfs://nameservice1/user/hive/sentry/product.ini

[groups]
admins = admin_role, tmp_access
analysts = analyst_role, tmp_access
developers = developer_role, tmp_access
etl = etl_role, tmp_access

[roles]
# uri accesses
tmp_access = server=server1->uri=hdfs://nameservice1/tmp

# default database accesses
analyst_role = server=server1->db=default->table=*->action=select
developer_role = server=server1->db=default
etl_role = server=server1->db=default->table=*->action=insert, \
           server=server1->db=default->table=*->action=select

# administrative role
admin_role = server=server1
```

The policy file in Example 7-15 has a lot going on and it might not be immediately apparent what it is defining. The first section of the policy file is `databases`. This section lists all of the databases and the corresponding policy files to be used to secure access to them. Having separate configuration files for each database is certainly not required. However, separating out the configuration files provides the following benefits:

- Allows for version tracking to easily tell which database was affected by a policy change and when

- Allows for delegated administrative control at a per-database level of granularity

- A misconfiguration of a given database policy file does not affect the master *sentry-provider.ini* or other database policy files

- Easily disable access for an entire database simply by changing permissions of the policy file in HDFS, which does not require a change to the policy file itself

The second section of the policy file is `groups`. This section provides a mapping between groups and the roles to which they are assigned. The syntax for this section is `group = role`. The group, as discussed earlier, comes from one of two places: the group names according to Hadoop, or locally configured groups specifically for Sentry. In Example 7-15, no locally configured groups are defined because the earlier *sentry-site.xml* in Example 7-1 is configured with `HadoopGroupResourceAuthoriza tionProvider`. A few important facts about the groups section of the policy file:

- A given group can be assigned to many roles, separated by commas

- Entries in the groups section are read top-down, thus making duplicate entries overwrite any previous entries for the same group

- Names of groups are global in scope, regardless of whether they are defined locally or provided by Hadoop

- Names of roles are local in scope in that the name of a role assigned to a group only applies to the file in which it is configured

The last section of the policy file is `roles`. This is where the meat of the policy is defined. The role configuration syntax is `role = permission`. The permission portion of the configuration looks a little odd in that it also has `key=value` syntax, but with arrows between each set of key/value configurations to indicate a more granular permission being defined. In general, the shorter the permission string, the greater the permissions. This is evidenced by the `admin_role` permission definition. This role is granted complete access to do anything at the *server* level. The next granular level of access is the database, or *db* level. The `developer_role` permission definition grants complete access to do anything with the default database. After that, the next level of access is at the *table* level. The example shows another feature of the policy file in that it supports a wildcard option to represent "any" table.

Wildcards are only valid to represent everything. They cannot be used in a leading or trailing fashion to reference any table with a partial name match. This might seem like a limiting or inconvenient implementation of wildcards, but keep in mind that these are security policies. Partial name matching with wildcards opens the door to accidental granting of privileges to unauthorized users. Imagine a scenario where access to any table starting with "pa" was being granted to a group of developers that are located in Pennsylvania, but later, users from human resources start using the cluster and create a table called "payroll" containing information about the pay stubs for all employees in the company. Now the group of developers in Pennsylvania have unintended access to confidential information. Be very careful with wildcards and security.

Still within the context of the roles definition at the highest level of granularity for permissions is the *action* portion. In the context of table objects in Hive and Impala, the only supported actions are `select` and `insert`. These actions are completely mutually exclusive. If a role is intended to be granted both select and insert on a table, both permissions are necessary. As with the groups section, multiple permissions can be given to a role. To do so, simply separate them by a comma. A backslash character can be used to carry over a list of permission definitions for ease of readability, as shown for the `etl_role` in Example 7-15.

The last part of the roles section to discuss is the notion of URIs. Example 7-15 shows a URI permission for the `tmp_access` role. This permission allows users to do two things: create external tables to data in this location, and export data from other tables they have access to into this location.

 URI accesses by default can only be specified in *sentry-provider.ini* and *not* in per-database policy files. The reason for this restriction is the case where a separate administrator maintains a database policy file but does not administer any others. If this administrator were able to define URI access in the policy file they control, they could grant themselves or anyone else access to any location in HDFS that is readable by the *hive* user by using external tables. If this behavior needs to be overridden, the Java configuration option `sentry.allow.uri.db.policyfile=true` needs to be set for Hive-Server2. This configuration should only be used if all administrators have equal access to change all Sentry policy files.

Solr Policy File

While Hive and Impala can now leverage a Sentry service and administer policies using SQL syntax, Solr has not yet migrated away from using policy files. The policy file format is similar to the SQL counterpart, with a few changes. Solr authorization operates on *collections* instead of databases and tables like SQL components do. Also, Solr privileges do not have SELECT and INSERT, but instead use Query and Update. Solr privileges can also be All, denoted by an asterisk (*).

Example 7-16 shows a similar layout to the SQL example. In the `groups` section, groups are assigned roles; and in the `roles` section, roles are assigned privileges. The analyst_role provides access to query the customer_logs collection, the etl_role provides access to update it, and finally the developer_role has full access to it. Lastly, the admin_role has full privileges to the admin collection.

Example 7-16. Solr sentry-provider.ini

```
[groups]
admins = admin_role
analysts = analyst_role
developers = developer_role
etl = etl_role

[roles]
analyst_role = collection=customer_logs->action=Query
developer_role = collection=customer_logs->action=*
etl_role = collection=customer_logs->action=Update

# administrative role
admin_role = collection=admin->action=*
```

It is important to point out that while SQL policy files allow for separate policy files per database, Solr *does not*. This means that Solr policy administrators need to be extra careful when modifying the policies because, as with the SQL policy files, a syntax error invalidates the entire policy file, thus inadvertently denying access to everyone. A nice feature to help combat typos and mistakes is to *validate* the policy file using the config-tool, which leads us into the next section.

Policy File Verification and Validation

When Sentry was first architected to use plain-text policy files, it was immediately apparent that administrators would need some kind of validation tool to perform basic sanity checks on the file prior to putting it in place. Sentry ships with a binary file, named sentry (surprise, surprise), which provides an important feature for policy file implementations: the config-tool command. This command allows an administrator to check the policy file for errors, but it also provides a mechanism to verify privileges for a given user. Example 7-17 demonstrates validating a policy file, where the first policy file has no errors and the second policy file has a typo (the word "sever" instead of "server").

Example 7-17. Sentry config-tool validation

```
[root@server1 ~]# sentry --hive-config /etc/hive/conf --command config-tool
 -s file:///etc/sentry/sentry-site.xml -i file:///etc/sentry/sentry-provider.ini -v
Using hive-conf-dir /etc/hive/conf
Configuration:
Sentry package jar: file:/var/lib/sentry/sentry-binding-hive-1.4.0.jar
Hive config: file:/etc/hive/conf/hive-site.xml
```

```
Sentry config: file:/etc/sentry/sentry-site.xml
Sentry Policy: file:///etc/sentry/sentry-provider.ini
Sentry server: server1
No errors found in the policy file
[root@server1 ~]# sentry --hive-config /etc/hive/conf --command config-tool
 -s file:///etc/sentry/sentry-site.xml -i file:///etc/sentry/sentry-provider2.ini -v
Using hive-conf-dir /etc/hive/conf
Configuration:
Sentry package jar: file:/var/lib/sentry/sentry-binding-hive-1.4.0.jar
Hive config: file:/etc/hive/conf/hive-site.xml
Sentry config: file:/etc/sentry/sentry-site.xml
Sentry Policy: file:///etc/sentry/sentry-provider2.ini
Sentry server: server1
 *** Found configuration problems ***
ERROR: Error processing file file:/etc/sentry/sentry-provider2.ini
 No authorizable found for sever=server1
ERROR: Failed to process global policy file
 file:/etc/sentry/sentry-provider2.ini
Sentry tool reported Errors:
org.apache.sentry.core.common.SentryConfigurationException:
        at org.apache.sentry.provider.file.SimpleFileProviderBackend.
         validatePolicy(SimpleFileProviderBackend.java:198)
        at org.apache.sentry.policy.db.SimpleDBPolicyEngine.
         validatePolicy(SimpleDBPolicyEngine.java:87)
        at org.apache.sentry.provider.common.ResourceAuthorizationProvider.
         validateResource(ResourceAuthorizationProvider.java:170)
        at org.apache.sentry.binding.hive.authz.SentryConfigTool.
         validatePolicy(SentryConfigTool.java:247)
        at org.apache.sentry.binding.hive.authz.
         SentryConfigTool$CommandImpl.run(SentryConfigTool.java:638)
        at org.apache.sentry.SentryMain.main(SentryMain.java:94)
        at sun.reflect.NativeMethodAccessorImpl.invoke0(Native Method)
        at sun.reflect.NativeMethodAccessorImpl.
         invoke(NativeMethodAccessorImpl.java:57)
        at sun.reflect.DelegatingMethodAccessorImpl.
         invoke(DelegatingMethodAccessorImpl.java:43)
        at java.lang.reflect.Method.invoke(Method.java:606)
        at org.apache.hadoop.util.RunJar.main(RunJar.java:212
[root@server1 ~]#
```

Verifying a user's privileges is another powerful feature offered by the config-tool.
This can be done both by listing *all* privileges for a given user, or can be more specific
by testing whether a given user would be authorized to execute a certain query.
Example 7-18 demonstrates the usage of these features.

Example 7-18. Sentry config-tool Verification

```
[root@server1 ~]# sentry --hive-config /etc/hive/conf --command config-tool \
 -s file:///etc/sentry/sentry-site.xml \
 -i file:///etc/sentry/sentry-provider.ini -l -u bob
Using hive-conf-dir /etc/hive/conf
```

```
Configuration:
Sentry package jar: file:/var/lib/sentry/sentry-binding-hive-1.4.0.jar
Hive config: file:/etc/hive/conf/hive-site.xml
Sentry config: file:/etc/sentry/sentry-site.xml
Sentry Policy: file:///etc/sentry/sentry-provider.ini
Sentry server: server1
Available privileges for user bob:
        server=server1
        server=server1->uri=hdfs://server1.example.com:8020/tmp
[root@server1 ~]# sentry --hive-config /etc/hive/conf --command config-tool \
 -s file:///etc/sentry/sentry-site.xml \
 -i file:///etc/sentry/sentry-provider.ini -l -u alice
Using hive-conf-dir /etc/hive/conf
Configuration:
Sentry package jar: file:/var/lib/sentry/sentry-binding-hive-1.4.0.jar
Hive config: file:/etc/hive/conf/hive-site.xml
Sentry config: file:/etc/sentry/sentry-site.xml
Sentry Policy: file:///etc/sentry/sentry-provider.ini
Sentry server: server1
Available privileges for user alice:
        *** No permissions available ***
[root@server1 ~]# sentry --hive-config /etc/hive/conf --command config-tool
 -s file:///etc/sentry/sentry-site.xml -i file:///etc/sentry/sentry-provider.ini
 -u bob -e "select * from sample_08"
Using hive-conf-dir /etc/hive/conf
Configuration:
Sentry package jar: file:/var/lib/sentry/sentry-binding-hive-1.4.0.jar
Hive config: file:/etc/hive/conf/hive-site.xml
Sentry config: file:/etc/sentry/sentry-site.xml
Sentry Policy: file:///etc/sentry/sentry-provider.ini
Sentry server: server1
User bob has privileges to run the query
[root@server1 ~]# sentry --hive-config /etc/hive/conf --command config-tool
 -s file:///etc/sentry/sentry-site.xml -i file:///etc/sentry/sentry-provider.ini
 -u alice  -e "select * from sample_08"
Using hive-conf-dir /etc/hive/conf
Configuration:
Sentry package jar: file:/var/lib/sentry/sentry-binding-hive-1.4.0.jar
Hive config: file:/etc/hive/conf/hive-site.xml
Sentry config: file:/etc/sentry/sentry-site.xml
Sentry Policy: file:///etc/sentry/sentry-provider.ini
Sentry server: server1
FAILED: SemanticException No valid privileges
*** Missing privileges for user alice:
        server=server1->db=default->table=sample_08->action=select
User alice does NOT have privileges to run the query
Sentry tool reported Errors: Compilation error: FAILED:
SemanticException No valid privileges
[root@server1 ~]#
```

Migrating From Policy Files

When the Sentry service was added to the project, a useful migration tool was also included. This tool allows an administrator to import the policies from the existing file into the Sentry service backend database. This alleviated the pains of needing to derive the SQL syntax for every policy and manually adding them to the database. The migration tool is a feature enhancement to the config-tool covered in the last section. Example 7-19 demonstrates the usage.

Example 7-19. Sentry Policy Import Tool

```
[root@server1 ~]# sentry --command config-tool --import \
-i file:///etc/sentry/sentry-provider.ini
Using hive-conf-dir /etc/hive/conf/
Configuration:
Sentry package jar: file:/var/lib/sentry/sentry-binding-hive-1.4.0.jar
Hive config: file:/etc/hive/conf/hive-site.xml
Sentry config: file:///etc/sentry/sentry-site.xml
Sentry Policy: file:///etc/sentry/sentry-provider.ini
Sentry server: server1
CREATE ROLE analyst_role;
GRANT ROLE analyst_role TO GROUP analysts;
# server=server1
GRANT SELECT ON DATABASE default TO ROLE analyst_role;
CREATE ROLE admin_role;
CREATE ROLE developer_role;
CREATE ROLE etl_role;
GRANT ROLE admin_role TO GROUP admins;
GRANT ALL ON SERVER server1 TO ROLE admin_role;
GRANT ROLE developer_role TO GROUP developers;
# server=server1
GRANT ALL ON DATABASE default TO ROLE developer_role;
GRANT ROLE etl_role TO GROUP etl;
# server=server1
GRANT INSERT ON DATABASE default TO ROLE etl_role;
# server=server1
GRANT SELECT ON DATABASE default TO ROLE etl_role;
[root@server1 ~]#
```

Summary

Conceptually, Sentry is a familiar and easy-to-understand concept, but as you have seen, the devil is in the details. Although Sentry is one of the newer components of the Hadoop ecosystem, it is quickly becoming an integral part of Hadoop security. Sentry has evolved rapidly in a short time and the expectation is that other ecosystem components will integrate with Sentry to provide strong authorization in a unified way.

Now that we have wrapped up the extensive topics of authentication and authorization, it is time to look at accounting to make sense of user activity in the cluster.

## CHAPTER 8

Accounting

So far in this part of the book, we've described how to properly identify and authenticate users and services, as well as how authorization controls limit what users and services can do in the cluster. While all of these various controls do a good job defining and enforcing a security model for a Hadoop cluster, they do not complete a fundamental component of a security model: accounting. Also referred to as auditing, accounting is the mechanism to keep track of what users and services are doing in the cluster. This is a critical piece of the security puzzle because without it, breaches in security can occur without anybody noticing. Accounting rounds out a security model by providing a record of what happened, which can be used for:

Active auditing

> This type of auditing is used in conjunction with some kind of alerting mechanism. For example, if a user tries to access a resource on the cluster and is denied, active auditing could generate an email to security administrators alerting them of this event.

Passive auditing

> This refers to auditing that does not generate some kind of alert. Passive auditing is often a bare-minimum requirement in a business so that designated auditors and security administrators can query audit events to look for certain events. For example, if there is a breach in security to the cluster, a security administrator can query the audit logs to find the data that was accessed during the breach.

Security compliance

> A business might be required to audit certain events to meet internal or legal compliance. This is most often the case where the data stored in HDFS contains sensitive information like personally identifiable information (PII), financial information such as credit card numbers and bank account numbers, and sensitive information about the business, like payroll records and business financials.

Hadoop components handle accounting differently depending on the purpose of the component. Components such as HDFS and HBase are data storage systems, so auditable events focus on reading, writing, and accessing data. Conversely, components such as MapReduce, Hive, and Impala are query engines and processing frameworks, so auditable events focus on end-user queries and jobs. The following subsections dig deeper into each component, and describe typical interactions with the component from an accounting point of view.

HDFS Audit Logs

HDFS provides two different audit logs that are used for two different purposes. The first, *hdfs-audit.log*, is used to audit general user activity such as when a user creates a new file, changes permissions of a file, requests a directory listing, and so on. The second, *SecurityAuth-hdfs.audit*, is used to audit service-level authorization activity. The setup for these logfiles involves hooking into `log4j.category.SecurityLogger` and `log4j.additivity.org.apache.hadoop.hdfs.server.namenode.FSNamesystem.aud it`. Example 8-1 shows how to do it.

Example 8-1. HDFS log4j.properties

```
# other logging settings omitted
hdfs.audit.logger=${log.threshold},RFAAUDIT
hdfs.audit.log.maxfilesize=256MB
hdfs.audit.log.maxbackupindex=20
log4j.logger.org.apache.hadoop.hdfs.server.namenode.FSNamesystem.audit=
  ${hdfs.audit.logger}
log4j.additivity.org.apache.hadoop.hdfs.server.namenode.FSNamesystem.audit=false
log4j.appender.RFAAUDIT=org.apache.log4j.RollingFileAppender
log4j.appender.RFAAUDIT.File=${log.dir}/hdfs-audit.log
log4j.appender.RFAAUDIT.layout=org.apache.log4j.PatternLayout
log4j.appender.RFAAUDIT.layout.ConversionPattern=%d{ISO8601} %p %c{2}: %m%n
log4j.appender.RFAAUDIT.MaxFileSize=${hdfs.audit.log.maxfilesize}
log4j.appender.RFAAUDIT.MaxBackupIndex=${hdfs.audit.log.maxbackupindex}
hadoop.security.logger=INFO,RFAS
hadoop.security.log.maxfilesize=256MB
hadoop.security.log.maxbackupindex=20
log4j.category.SecurityLogger=${hadoop.security.logger}
log4j.additivity.SecurityLogger=false
hadoop.security.log.file=SecurityAuth-${user.name}.audit
log4j.appender.RFAS=org.apache.log4j.RollingFileAppender
log4j.appender.RFAS.File=${log.dir}/${hadoop.security.log.file}
log4j.appender.RFAS.layout=org.apache.log4j.PatternLayout
log4j.appender.RFAS.layout.ConversionPattern=%d{ISO8601} %p %c: %m%n
log4j.appender.RFAS.MaxFileSize=${hadoop.security.log.maxfilesize}
log4j.appender.RFAS.MaxBackupIndex=${hadoop.security.log.maxbackupindex}
```

So what actually shows up when an auditable event occurs? For this set of examples, let's assume the following:

- The user Alice is identified by the Kerberos principal alice@EXAMPLE.COM, and she has successfully used kinit to receive a valid TGT
- She does a directory listing on her HDFS home directory
- She creates an empty file named test in her HDFS home directory
- She changes the permissions of this file to be world-writable
- She attempts to move the file out of her home directory and into the /user directory

In Example 8-2, Alice has done several actions with HDFS that are typical operations in HDFS. These are user activity events, so let's inspect *hdfs-audit.log* to see the trail that Alice left behind from her HDFS actions (the example logfile has been formatted for readability).

Example 8-2. hdfs-audit.log

```
...
2014-03-11 23:50:18,251 INFO FSNamesystem.audit: allowed=true  ugi=alice@EXAMPLE.COM
 (auth:KERBEROS) ip=/10.1.1.1 cmd=getfileinfo src=/user/alice dst=null perm=null
2014-03-11 23:50:18,280 INFO FSNamesystem.audit: allowed=true  ugi=alice@EXAMPLE.COM
 (auth:KERBEROS) ip=/10.1.1.1 cmd=listStatus src=/user/alice dst=null perm=null
2014-03-11 23:50:32,058 INFO FSNamesystem.audit: allowed=true  ugi=alice@EXAMPLE.COM
 (auth:KERBEROS) ip=/10.1.1.1 cmd=getfileinfo src=/user/alice/test dst=null perm=null
2014-03-11 23:50:32,073 INFO FSNamesystem.audit: allowed=true  ugi=alice@EXAMPLE.COM
 (auth:KERBEROS) ip=/10.1.1.1 cmd=getfileinfo   src=/user/alice dst=null perm=null
2014-03-11 23:50:32,096 INFO FSNamesystem.audit: allowed=true  ugi=alice@EXAMPLE.COM
 (auth:KERBEROS) ip=/10.1.1.1 cmd=create src=/user/alice/test dst=null
 perm=alice:alice:rw-r-----
2014-03-11 23:50:39,558 INFO FSNamesystem.audit: allowed=true  ugi=alice@EXAMPLE.COM
 (auth:KERBEROS) ip=/10.1.1.1 cmd=getfileinfo src=/user/alice/test dst=null perm=null
2014-03-11 23:50:39,587 INFO FSNamesystem.audit: allowed=true  ugi=alice@EXAMPLE.COM
 (auth:KERBEROS) ip=/10.1.1.1 cmd=setPermission src=/user/alice/test dst=null
 perm=alice:alice:rw-rw-rw-
2014-03-11 23:50:47,157 INFO FSNamesystem.audit: allowed=true  ugi=alice@EXAMPLE.COM
 (auth:KERBEROS) ip=/10.1.1.1 cmd=getfileinfo src=/user dst=null perm=null
2014-03-11 23:50:47,185 INFO FSNamesystem.audit: allowed=true  ugi=alice@EXAMPLE.COM
 (auth:KERBEROS) ip=/10.1.1.1 cmd=getfileinfo src=/user/alice/test dst=null perm=null
2014-03-11 23:50:47,187 INFO FSNamesystem.audit: allowed=true  ugi=alice@EXAMPLE.COM
 (auth:KERBEROS) ip=/10.1.1.1 cmd=getfileinfo src=/user/test dst=null perm=null
2014-03-11 23:50:47,190 INFO FSNamesystem.audit: allowed=false ugi=alice@EXAMPLE.COM
 (auth:KERBEROS) ip=/10.1.1.1 cmd=rename src=/user/alice/test dst=/user/test perm=nul
...
```

As you can see, the audit log shows pertinent information for each action Alice performed. Every action she performed required a getfileinfo command first, followed by the various actions she performed (listStatus, create, setPermission, and rename). In this log, it is clear who the user is that the event was for, what time it occurred, the IP address that action was performed from, and various other bits of information. The other important bit that was recorded was that Alice's last attempted action to move the file out of her home directory into a location she did not have permissions for was not allowed.

MapReduce Audit Logs

MapReduce follows a very similar approach to auditing in that it contains two audit logs with very similar purposes as the HDFS audit logs. The first logfile, *mapred-audit.log*, is used to audit user activity such as job submissions. The second logfile, `SecurityAuth-mapred.audit`, is used to audit service-level authorization activity just like the HDFS log equivalent. The log4j properties need to be set for these files. The hooks used to set these up are `log4j.category.SecurityLogger` and `log4j.logger.org.apache.hadoop.mapred.AuditLogger`, and Example 8-3 shows how to do it.

Example 8-3. MapReduce log4j.properties

```
# other logging settings omitted
hadoop.security.logger=INFO,RFAS
hadoop.security.log.maxfilesize=256MB
hadoop.security.log.maxbackupindex=20
log4j.category.SecurityLogger=${hadoop.security.logger}
log4j.additivity.SecurityLogger=false
hadoop.security.log.file=SecurityAuth-${user.name}.audit
log4j.appender.RFAS=org.apache.log4j.RollingFileAppender
log4j.appender.RFAS.File=${log.dir}/${hadoop.security.log.file}
log4j.appender.RFAS.layout=org.apache.log4j.PatternLayout
log4j.appender.RFAS.layout.ConversionPattern=%d{ISO8601} %p %c: %m%n
log4j.appender.RFAS.MaxFileSize=${hadoop.security.log.maxfilesize}
log4j.appender.RFAS.MaxBackupIndex=${hadoop.security.log.maxbackupindex}
mapred.audit.logger=${log.threshold},RFAAUDIT
mapred.audit.log.maxfilesize=256MB
mapred.audit.log.maxbackupindex=20
log4j.logger.org.apache.hadoop.mapred.AuditLogger=${mapred.audit.logger}
log4j.additivity.org.apache.hadoop.mapred.AuditLogger=false
log4j.appender.RFAAUDIT=org.apache.log4j.RollingFileAppender
log4j.appender.RFAAUDIT.File=${log.dir}/mapred-audit.log
log4j.appender.RFAAUDIT.layout=org.apache.log4j.PatternLayout
log4j.appender.RFAAUDIT.layout.ConversionPattern=%d{ISO8601} %p %c{2}: %m%n
log4j.appender.RFAAUDIT.MaxFileSize=${mapred.audit.log.maxfilesize}
log4j.appender.RFAAUDIT.MaxBackupIndex=${mapred.audit.log.maxbackupindex}
```

For this example, let's assume the following:

- The user Bob is identified by the Kerberos principal bob@EXAMPLE.COM, and he has already successfully used `kinit` to receive a valid TGT
- MapReduce service-level authorizations are not being used
- Bob submits a MapReduce job
- Bob kills the MapReduce job before it finishes

The result of these actions according to the logs are shown in Examples 8-4 and 8-5.

Example 8-4. mapred-audit.log

```
...
2014-03-12 18:11:46,363 INFO mapred.AuditLogger: USER=bob IP=10.1.1.1
 OPERATION=SUBMIT_JOB TARGET=job_201403112320_0001 RESULT=SUCCESS
...
```

Example 8-5. SecurityAuth-mapred.audit

```
...
2014-03-12 18:46:25,200 INFO SecurityLogger.org.apache.hadoop.ipc.Server:
 Auth successful for bob@EXAMPLE.COM (auth:SIMPLE)

2014-03-12 18:46:25,239 INFO SecurityLogger.org.apache.hadoop.security.
 authorize.ServiceAuthorizationManager: Authorization successful for
 bob@EXAMPLE.COM (auth:KERBEROS) for protocol=interface
 org.apache.hadoop.mapred.JobSubmissionProtocol

2014-03-12 18:46:29,955 INFO SecurityLogger.org.apache.hadoop.ipc.Server:
 Auth successful for job_201403112320_0002 (auth:SIMPLE)

2014-03-12 18:46:29,976 INFO SecurityLogger.org.apache.hadoop.security.
 authorize.ServiceAuthorizationManager: Authorization successful for
 job_201403112320_0002 (auth:TOKEN) for protocol=interface
 org.apache.hadoop.mapred.TaskUmbilicalProtocol

...(more)...

2014-03-12 18:47:11,598 INFO SecurityLogger.org.apache.hadoop.ipc.Server:
 Auth successful for bob@EXAMPLE.COM (auth:SIMPLE)

2014-03-12 18:47:11,638 INFO SecurityLogger.org.apache.hadoop.security.
 authorize.ServiceAuthorizationManager: Authorization successful for
 bob@EXAMPLE.COM (auth:KERBEROS) for protocol=interface
 org.apache.hadoop.mapred.JobSubmissionProtocol
...
```

Example 8-4 is pretty straightforward: the user Bob performed the operation SUBMIT_JOB, which results in a MapReduce job ID of job_201403112320_0001. Other pertinent info, as one would expect, is the date and time of the event, and the IP address. In Example 8-5, things look a little different. The first entry shows that Bob successfully authenticates to the JobTracker, whereas the second entry shows that Bob has been authorized to submit the job. The next two events (and subsequent identical events that have been removed for brevity) show the activity of the job itself. It is interesting that when Bob kills the running job, the audit events that show up are identical to the audit events that are generated when Bob submitted the job.

YARN Audit Logs

YARN audit log events are interspersed among the daemon logfiles. However, they are easily identifiable because the class name is logged in the event. For the Resource Manager, it is `org.apache.hadoop.yarn.server.resourcemanager.RMAuditLogger`; and for the Node Manager, it is `org.apache.hadoop.yarn.server.nodeman ager.NMAuditLogger`. These class names can be used to parse out audit events among normal application log events. For YARN to log audit events, the `log4j` properties need to be set. The hook to set this up is the `log4j.category.SecurityLogger` and Example 8-6 shows how to do it.

Example 8-6. YARN log4j.properties

```
# other logging settings omitted
hadoop.security.logger=INFO,RFAS
hadoop.security.log.maxfilesize=256MB
hadoop.security.log.maxbackupindex=20
log4j.category.SecurityLogger=${hadoop.security.logger}
log4j.additivity.SecurityLogger=false
hadoop.security.log.file=SecurityAuth-${user.name}.audit
log4j.appender.RFAS=org.apache.log4j.RollingFileAppender
log4j.appender.RFAS.File=${log.dir}/${hadoop.security.log.file}
log4j.appender.RFAS.layout=org.apache.log4j.PatternLayout
log4j.appender.RFAS.layout.ConversionPattern=%d{ISO8601} %p %c: %m%n
log4j.appender.RFAS.MaxFileSize=${hadoop.security.log.maxfilesize}
log4j.appender.RFAS.MaxBackupIndex=${hadoop.security.log.maxbackupindex}
```

For this example, the user Alice submits a MapReduce job via YARN, which then runs to completion. Example 8-7 shows just the audit events for the Resource Manager and Example 8-8 shows the audit events for one of the NodeManagers. Note that the repeating auditing class names have been omitted for brevity, and the events have been formatted for readability.

Example 8-7. YARN Resource Manager Audit Events

```
2014-12-27 12:49:35,182 INFO USER=alice IP=10.6.9.73
  OPERATION=Submit Application Request
  TARGET=ClientRMService  RESULT=SUCCESS
  APPID=application_1419453547005_0001
```

```
2014-12-27 12:49:43,598 INFO USER=alice OPERATION=AM Allocated Container
  TARGET=SchedulerApp RESULT=SUCCESS APPID=application_1419453547005_0001
  CONTAINERID=container_1419453547005_0001_01_000001
2014-12-27 12:49:57,288 INFO USER=alice IP=10.6.9.75 OPERATION=Register App Master
  TARGET=ApplicationMasterService RESULT=SUCCESS APPID=application_1419453547005_0001
  APPATTEMPTID=appattempt_1419453547005_0001_000001
2014-12-27 12:50:02,375 INFO USER=alice OPERATION=AM Allocated Container
  TARGET=SchedulerApp RESULT=SUCCESS APPID=application_1419453547005_0001
  CONTAINERID=container_1419453547005_0001_01_000002
2014-12-27 12:50:02,376 INFO USER=alice OPERATION=AM Allocated Container
  TARGET=SchedulerApp RESULT=SUCCESS APPID=application_1419453547005_0001
  CONTAINERID=container_1419453547005_0001_01_000003
2014-12-27 12:50:19,361 INFO USER=alice OPERATION=AM Released Container
  TARGET=SchedulerApp RESULT=SUCCESS APPID=application_1419453547005_0001
  CONTAINERID=container_1419453547005_0001_01_000002
2014-12-27 12:50:21,436 INFO USER=alice OPERATION=AM Released Container
  TARGET=SchedulerApp RESULT=SUCCESS APPID=application_1419453547005_0001
  CONTAINERID=container_1419453547005_0001_01_000003
2014-12-27 12:50:27,954 INFO USER=alice OPERATION=AM Released Container
  TARGET=SchedulerApp RESULT=SUCCESS APPID=application_1419453547005_0001
  CONTAINERID=container_1419453547005_0001_01_000001
2014-12-27 12:50:27,963 INFO USER=alice OPERATION=Application Finished - Succeeded
  TARGET=RMAppManager RESULT=SUCCESS  APPID=application_1419453547005_0001
```

Example 8-8. YARN Node Manager Audit Events

```
2014-12-27 12:49:43,956 INFO USER=alice IP=10.6.9.75
  OPERATION=Start Container Request TARGET=ContainerManageImpl RESULT=SUCCESS
  APPID=application_1419453547005_0001
  CONTAINERID=container_1419453547005_0001_01_000001
2014-12-27 12:50:27,105 INFO USER=alice OPERATION=Container Finished - Succeeded
  TARGET=ContainerImpl RESULT=SUCCESS APPID=application_1419453547005_0001
  CONTAINERID=container_1419453547005_0001_01_000001
2014-12-27 12:50:27,984 INFO USER=alice IP=10.6.9.75 OPERATION=Stop Container Request
  TARGET=ContainerManageImpl RESULT=SUCCESS APPID=application_1419453547005_0001
  CONTAINERID=container_1419453547005_0001_01_000001
```

One of the many benefits of YARN is the ability to specify resource pools. As we saw earlier, resource pools can have authorization controls set up such that only certain users and groups can submit to a given pool. In the next example, Bob tries to submit to the prod resource pool, but he does not have authorization to do so. Example 8-9 shows what the audit events look like in this case. Again, the audit logger class name has been removed for brevity and the log has been formatted for readability.

Example 8-9. YARN Resource Manager Audit Events

```
2014-12-27 13:56:35,886 INFO USER=bob IP=10.6.9.73
  OPERATION=Submit Application Request TARGET=ClientRMService
  RESULT=SUCCESS APPID=application_1419705820412_0002
2014-12-27 13:56:35,917 WARN USER=bob OPERATION=Application Finished - Failed
```

```
TARGET=RMAppManager RESULT=FAILURE  DESCRIPTION=App failed with state: FAILED
PERMISSIONS=User bob cannot submit applications to queue root.prod
APPID=application_1419705820412_0002
```

Hive Audit Logs

Hive auditing is similar to YARN in that it does not have a dedicated audit logfile. Audit events occur inside the actual Hive Metastore service log so it can be a bit of a challenge for a security administrator to get at just the pertinent audit information among regular application log events. As with YARN, however, the audit logger class names can be used to identify audit events. Other Hive components, such as Hive-Server2, do not have explicit auditing, but audit-like information can still be gleaned from the service logs. For this example, let's assume:

- The user Bob is identified by the Kerberos principal bob@EXAMPLE.COM, and he has already successfully used kinit to receive a valid TGT

- Bob is using the beeline CLI to connect to HiveServer2

- Bob first executes show tables; to list the tables in the default database

- Bob then executes select count(*) from sample_07; to count the number of records in the sample_07 table

The result of these actions is shown in Example 8-10, which has been formatted for readability.

Example 8-10. Hive Metastore audit events

```
...
2014-03-29 17:13:18,778 INFO org.apache.hadoop.hive.metastore.HiveMetaStore.audit:
  ugi=bob        ip=/10.1.1.1    cmd=get_database: default
...
2014-03-29 17:13:18,782 INFO org.apache.hadoop.hive.metastore.HiveMetaStore.audit:
  ugi=bob        ip=/10.1.1.1    cmd=get_tables: db=default pat=.*
...
2014-03-29 17:13:37,110 INFO org.apache.hadoop.hive.metastore.HiveMetaStore.audit:
  ugi=bob        ip=/10.1.1.1    cmd=get_table : db=default tbl=sample_07
```

Reviewing the audit events in Example 8-10 shows several things. First, the audit events themselves are tagged with org.apache.hadoop.hive.metastore.HiveMetaS tore.audit. This makes it a little easier to search the log specifically for audit events. Next, you will notice a slight difference in these audit events and the audit events we have seen previously with regard to user identification. With Hive, only the username is shown instead of the full Kerberos UPN. In each audit event, the action performed by the user is identified by the cmd field. As you can see, the show tables; query generates two audit events: get_database and get_tables. The actual SQL query to count rows generates a single audit event, which is for `get_table`. As with previous audit events in other components, the IP address of the user executing the action is given.

Cloudera Impala Audit Logs

Impala audit events are logged into dedicated audit logs used by each Impala daemon (impalad). The audit log directory location is specified using the flag `audit_event_log_dir`. A typical choice is the directory */var/log/impalad/audits*. These logfiles are rolled after they reach a certain "size" dictated by a number of lines, as specified using the flag `max_audit_event_log_file_size`. A reasonable setting is 5,000 lines. For the Impala example, we will assume that the exact same assumptions are made as the Hive example. The results of these actions are shown in Example 8-11.

Example 8-11. Impala daemon audit log

```
....
{"1396114935263":{"query_id":"914b9eb1591546f0:ff4419eab4de439c",
 "session_id":"e643b5e102f653ec:94e0a3d4b3646ca3",
 "start_time":"2014-03-29 17:42:15.201945000","authorization_failure":false,
 "status":"","user":"bob","impersonator":null,"statement_type":"SHOW_TABLES",
 "network_address":"::ffff:10.1.1.1:47569","sql_statement":"show tables",
 "catalog_objects":[]}}

{"1396115148996":{"query_id":"97443eddd3c172fd:34fe3f37c84d6ea8",
 "session_id":"e643b5e102f653ec:94e0a3d4b3646ca3",
 "start_time":"2014-03-29 17:45:48.850540000","authorization_failure":false,
 "status":"","user":"bob","impersonator":null,"statement_type":"QUERY",
 "network_address":"::ffff:10.1.1.1:47569","sql_statement":
 "select count(*) from sample_07","catalog_objects":
[{"name":"default.sample_07","object_type":"TABLE","privilege":"SELECT"}]}}
....
```

Reviewing Example 8-11 immediately shows that the audit events are in a much different format than other Hadoop components. These audit events are logged in JSON format, which makes it a little more difficult for human-readability, but allows for easy consumption by an external tool. The first audit event shows the type of action taken by the user under the `statement_type` field, namely `SHOW_TABLES`. This information is also available in the `sql_statement` field, which shows the exact query that Bob made. The second audit event shows the type of action taken as `QUERY`.

HBase Audit Logs

HBase logs audit events into a separate logfile, which can be configured in the associated *log4j.properties* file. HBase architecture is such that clients contact only the specific server that is responsible for the specific action taken, so audit events are spread out throughout an HBase cluster. For example, creating, deleting, and modifying tables is an action that the HBase Master is responsible for. Operations such as scans, puts, and gets are specific to a given region in a table, thus a RegionServer captures these events.

For HBase to log audit events, the `log4j` properties need to be set. The hook to set this up is the `log4j.logger.SecurityLogger` and Example 8-12 shows how to do it.

Example 8-12. HBase log4j.properties

```
# other logging settings omitted
log4j.logger.SecurityLogger=TRACE, RFAS
log4j.additivity.SecurityLogger=false
log4j.appender.RFAS=org.apache.log4j.RollingFileAppender
log4j.appender.RFAS.File=${log.dir}/audit/SecurityAuth-hbase.audit
log4j.appender.RFAS.layout=org.apache.log4j.PatternLayout
log4j.appender.RFAS.layout.ConversionPattern=%d{ISO8601} %p %c: %m%n
log4j.appender.RFAS.MaxFileSize=${max.log.file.size}
log4j.appender.RFAS.MaxBackupIndex=${max.log.file.backup.index}
```

For our example here, the following actions are performed:

- The HBase superuser creates a table called `sample`
- The HBase superuser grants RW access to user Alice on the `sample` table
- The HBase superuser grants R access to user Bob on the `sample` table
- Alice tries to create a new table called `sample2`, but is denied access
- Alice puts a value into the `sample` table
- Alice scans the `sample` table
- Bob scans the `sample` table
- Bob tries to put a value into the `sample` table, but is denied access

HBase audits can be narrowed down to a specific class, namely `SecurityLog ger.org.apache.hadoop.hbase.security.access.AccessController`, as with the log events in other components. This class is repeated throughout the logs, but is omitted in Examples 8-13 and 8-14 for brevity. Also, these examples have been formatted for readability.

Example 8-13. HBase master audit log

```
2014-12-27 21:05:56,938 TRACE Access allowed for user hbase; reason:
  Global check allowed; remote address: /10.6.9.74; request: createTable;
  context: (user=hbase@EXAMPLE.COM, scope=sample, family=cf, action=CREATE)
2014-12-27 21:06:09,484 TRACE Access allowed for user hbase; reason:
  Table permission granted; remote address: /10.6.9.74;
  request: getTableDescriptors; context: (user=hbase@EXAMPLE.COM,
  scope=sample, family=, action=ADMIN)
2014-12-27 21:06:16,620 TRACE Access allowed for user hbase; reason:
  Table permission granted; remote address: /10.6.9.74;
  request: getTableDescriptors; context: (user=hbase@EXAMPLE.COM,
  scope=sample, family=, action=ADMIN)
2014-12-27 21:07:02,102 TRACE Access denied for user alice; reason:
  Global check failed; remote address: /10.6.9.74; request:
  createTable; context: (user=alice@EXAMPLE.COM, scope=sample2,
  family=cf, action=CREATE)
```

What we can see in Example 8-13 is that table creation events are clearly logged. The *hbase* user is allowed access, whereas Alice is denied access to create a table. Also shown in this logfile is that the actual granting of permissions is not obvious in the log. While the action is logged as an ADMIN action, and it has the same scope as for the sample table, there is no indication of which user the table permissions were granted to. This is a limitation in HBase that will likely be improved in a future release.

Example 8-14. HBase region server audit log

```
2014-12-27 21:07:15,411 TRACE Access allowed for user alice; reason:
  Table permission granted; remote address: /10.6.9.74; request: put;
  context: (user=alice@EXAMPLE.COM, scope=sample,
  family=cf:col1, action=WRITE)
2014-12-27 21:07:18,705 TRACE Access allowed for user alice; reason:
  Table permission granted; remote address: /10.6.9.74; request: scan;
  context: (user=alice@EXAMPLE.COM, scope=sample, family=cf, action=READ)
2014-12-27 21:07:47,263 TRACE Access allowed for user bob; reason:
  Table permission granted; remote address: /10.6.9.74; request: scan;
  context: (user=bob@EXAMPLE.COM, scope=sample, family=cf, action=READ)
2014-12-27 21:07:57,756 TRACE Access denied for user bob; reason:
  Failed qualifier check; remote address: /10.6.9.74; request: put;
  context: (user=bob@EXAMPLE.COM, scope=sample, family=cf:col1, action=WRITE)
```

From Example 8-14, the read and write actions attempted by Alice and Bob are clearly identified. It provides the pertinent information about the table, column family, and column, as well as the reason for why the action was allowed or denied.

Accumulo Audit Logs

Similar to HBase, Accumulo can be configured to log audit events to a separate log-file. Because Accumulo clients aren't required communicate with a single, central server for every access, audit logs are spread throughout the cluster. For example, when you create, delete, or modify a table, that action will be logged by the Accumulo Master, whereas operations such as scans and writes are logged by the TabletServer handling the request.

The default Accumulo configuration templates have audit logging turned off. You can turn on logging by setting the log level of the Audit logger to INFO in the *auditLog.xml* log4j configuration file. Example 8-15 shows a sample *auditLog.xml* configuration file with audit logging turned on.

Example 8-15. Accumulo auditLog.xml

```
<?xml version="1.0" encoding="UTF-8"?>
<!DOCTYPE log4j:configuration SYSTEM "log4j.dtd">
<log4j:configuration xmlns:log4j="http://jakarta.apache.org/log4j/">

  <!-- Write out Audit info to an Audit file -->
  <appender name="Audit" class="org.apache.log4j.DailyRollingFileAppender">
    <param name="File"
     value="/var/log/accumulo/accumulo01.example.com.audit"/>
    <param name="MaxBackupIndex" value="10"/>
    <param name="DatePattern" value="'.'yyyy-MM-dd"/>
    <layout class="org.apache.log4j.PatternLayout">
      <param name="ConversionPattern"
       value="%d{yyyy-MM-dd HH:mm:ss,SSS/Z} [%c{2}] %-5p: %m%n"/>
    </layout>
  </appender>
  <logger name="Audit"  additivity="false">
    <appender-ref ref="Audit" />
    <!-- Change level from OFF to INFO. default:<level value="OFF"/> -->
    <level value="INFO"/>
  </logger>

</log4j:configuration>
```

Accumulo audits both system administration actions and normal user access. Every audit includes operation status (success, failure, permitted, or denied) and the user performing the action. Remote requests also include the client address. Failed requests log the exception that caused the failure. Individual actions differ in the details they provide, but generally they include details such as the target or targets of an action and relevant parameters such as the range of rows and columns accessed. See Table 8-1 for a list of the actions that Accumulo logs.

Table 8-1. Accumulo's audited actions

Action	Description
authenticate	A user authenticates with Accumulo
createUser	An admin creates a new user
dropUser	An admin drops a user
changePassword	An admin changes a user's password
changeAuthorizations	An admin changes a user's authorizations
grantSystemPermission	An admin grants system permissions to a user
grantTablePermission	An admin grants permissions to a user on a table
revokeSystemPermission	An admin revokes system permissions to a user
revokeTablePermission	An admin revokes permissions to a user on a table
createTable	A user creates a table
deleteTable	A user deletes a table
renameTable	A user renames a table
cloneTable	A user clones a table
scan	A user scans a range of rows
deleteData	A user delete's a table
bulkImport	A user initiates a bulk import of data
export	A user exports a table from one cluster to another
import	A user imports an exported table

Now let's see what the audit logs will look like after some actions are performed. Our examples will include the results after running the following actions:

- The Accumulo root user creates a user called `alice`
- The Accumulo root user creates a user called bob

- The Accumulo root user creates a table called `sample`

- The Accumulo root user grants `Table.READ` and `Table.WRITE` access to user `alice` on the `sample` table

- The Accumulo root user grants `Table.READ` access to user `bob` on the `sample` table

- Alice tries to create a new table called `sample2`, but is denied access

- Alice puts a value into the `sample` table

- Alice scans the `sample` table

- Bob scans the `sample` table

- Bob tries to put a value into the `sample` table, but is denied access

The audit logs shown in Examples 8-16 and 8-17 have been formatted for readibility but are otherwise unmodified.

Example 8-16. Accumulo master audit log

```
2014-12-27 16:40:11,673/-0800 [Audit] INFO : operation: permitted;
    user: root; action: createTable; targetTable: sample;
2014-12-27 16:40:28,563/-0800 [Audit] INFO : operation: denied;
    user: alice; action: createTable; targetTable: sample2;
```

In Example 8-16, we can see that the table creation operations are clearly logged. The *root* user is permitted to perform the `createTable` action while *alice* is denied. The other administrative actions appear in the `TabletServer` log.

Example 8-17. Accumulo TabletServer audit log

```
2014-12-27 16:39:49,262/-0800 [Audit] INFO : operation: success;
    user: root: action: createUser; targetUser: alice; Authorizations: ;
2014-12-27 16:40:02,226/-0800 [Audit] INFO : operation: success;
    user: root: action: createUser; targetUser: bob; Authorizations: ;
2014-12-27 16:40:13,226/-0800 [Audit] INFO : operation: success;
    user: root: action: grantTablePermission; permission: READ;
    targetTable: sample; targetUser: alice;
2014-12-27 16:40:13,292/-0800 [Audit] INFO : operation: success;
    user: root: action: grantTablePermission; permission: WRITE;
    targetTable: sample; targetUser: alice;
2014-12-27 16:40:13,442/-0800 [Audit] INFO : operation: success;
    user: root: action: grantTablePermission; permission: READ;
    targetTable: sample; targetUser: bob;
2014-12-27 16:40:30,529/-0800 [Audit] INFO : operation: permitted;
    user: alice; action: scan; targetTable: sample; authorizations: ;
    range: (-inf,+inf); columns: []; iterators: []; iteratorOptions: {};
2014-12-27 16:40:43,180/-0800 [Audit] INFO : operation: permitted;
```

```
    user: bob; action: scan; targetTable: sample; authorizations: ;
    range: (-inf,+inf); columns: []; iterators: []; iteratorOptions: {};
```

Example 8-17 shows the output of the TabletServer audit log. We can see the crea
teUser actions, the user that was created, and the authorizations that were assigned to
that user. We can also see the grantTablePermission actions along with the permission granted, the target table, and the target user. Finally, we can see that the two scan
actions includes the details of the query: the row range, columns, and iterators used.
Notably missing are the write operations. This is a current gap in Accumulo's auditing
framework. We also don't see the authentication events because they are logged by the
shell itself.

Sentry Audit Logs

In Chapter 7, we saw that the latest version of Sentry uses a service to facilitate
authorization requests and manage interaction with the policy database. Auditing
events that come as a result of modifying authorization policies is extremely critical
in the accounting process. In order to do that, Sentry needs to be configured to capture audit events. sentry.hive.authorization.ddl.logger logger class is the one
that needs to be configured. Example 8-18 shows how this can be done.

Example 8-18. Sentry server log4j.properties

```
# other log settings omitted
log4j.logger.sentry.hive.authorization.ddl.logger=${sentry.audit.logger}
log4j.additivity.sentry.hive.authorization.ddl.logger=false
sentry.audit.logger=TRACE,RFAAUDIT
sentry.audit.log.maxfilesize=256MB
sentry.audit.log.maxbackupindex=20
log4j.appender.RFAAUDIT=org.apache.log4j.RollingFileAppender
log4j.appender.RFAAUDIT.File=${log.dir}/audit/sentry-audit.log
log4j.appender.RFAAUDIT.layout=org.apache.log4j.PatternLayout
log4j.appender.RFAAUDIT.layout.ConversionPattern=%d{ISO8601} %p %c{2}: %m%n
log4j.appender.RFAAUDIT.MaxFileSize=${sentry.audit.log.maxfilesize}
log4j.appender.RFAAUDIT.MaxBackupIndex=${sentry.audit.log.maxbackupindex}
```

Now that Sentry is set up to log audit events, let's look at an example. For this example, Alice is a Sentry administrator and Bob is not. Alice uses the beeline shell to
create a new role called analyst, assign the role to the group analystgrp, and grant
SELECT privileges on the default database to the role. Next, Bob tries to create a new
role using the impala-shell, but is denied access. Example 8-19 shows the record of
these actions.

Example 8-19. Sentry server audit log

```
2015-01-02 11:17:10,753 INFO ddl.logger:
  {"serviceName":"Sentry-Service","userName":"alice","impersonator":
  "hive/server1.example.com@EXAMPLE.COM","ipAddress":"/10.6.9.74",
  "operation":"CREATE_ROLE","eventTime":"1420215430742","operationText":
  "CREATE ROLE analyst","allowed":"true","databaseName":null,
  "tableName":null,"resourcePath":null,"objectType":"ROLE"}
2015-01-02 11:17:37,537 INFO ddl.logger:
  {"serviceName":"Sentry-Service","userName":"alice","impersonator":
  "hive/server1.example.com@EXAMPLE.COM","ipAddress":"/10.6.9.74",
  "operation":"ADD_ROLE_TO_GROUP","eventTime":"1420215457536",
  "operationText":"GRANT ROLE analyst TO GROUP analystgrp","allowed":"true",
  "databaseName":null,"tableName":null,"resourcePath":null,"objectType":"ROLE"}
2015-01-02 11:17:52,408 INFO ddl.logger:
  {"serviceName":"Sentry-Service","userName":"alice","impersonator":
  "hive/server1.example.com@EXAMPLE.COM","ipAddress":"/10.6.9.74",
  "operation":"GRANT_PRIVILEGE","eventTime":"1420215472407","operationText":
  "GRANT SELECT ON DATABASE default TO ROLE analyst","allowed":"true",
  "databaseName":"default","tableName":"","resourcePath":"","objectType":"PRINCIPAL"}
2015-01-02 11:33:20,199 INFO ddl.logger:
  {"serviceName":"Sentry-Service","userName":"bob","impersonator":
  "impala/server1.example.com@EXAMPLE.COM","ipAddress":"/10.6.9.73",
  "operation":"CREATE_ROLE","eventTime":"1420216400199","operationText":
  "CREATE ROLE temp","allowed":"false","databaseName":null,"tableName":null,
  "resourcePath":null,"objectType":"ROLE"}
```

As you can see from the logs, the actual audit record is in JSON format. This makes for easy consumption by external log aggregation and management systems, which are important in larger enterprises.

Log Aggregation

Audit logs often span across many, if not all, nodes in the cluster. The sheer number of nodes multiplied by the individual audit log files generated can be a large undertaking to make sense of what is happening. It is typical, and highly recommended, to use some kind of log aggregation system to pull audit events from all of the nodes in the cluster into a central place for storage and analysis. There certainly are Hadoop-specific options out there that overlay additional intelligence as to what is going on the cluster. Even so, general-purpose log aggregation systems already in place in the enterprise can be a great way to manage Hadoop audit logs.

Another interesting option for log aggregation is to ingest them back into the Hadoop cluster for analysis. Security use cases for Hadoop are common and analyzing audit events from Hadoop fits the bill as well. As shown in this chapter, audit events are generally in a structured form and make for easy querying using SQL tools like Hive or Impala.

Summary

In this chapter, we took a look at several of the components in the Hadoop ecosystem and described the types of audit events that are recorded when users interact with the cluster. These log events are critical for accounting to ascertain what regular users are doing, but also to discover what unauthorized users are attempting to do. Although the Hadoop ecosystem does not have native alerting capabilities, the structure of the log events are conducive to allow additional tools to consume the events in a more general way. Active alerting is a newer capability that is still being worked on in the Hadoop ecosystem. Still, many general-purpose log aggregation tools possess the capabilities to alert when certain criteria are met, with many of these tools being common in the enterprise.

All of the auditing capabilities covered in this chapter wrap up the accounting portion of AAA. In the next part of the book, we will dive into how actual data, the lifeblood of Hadoop and big data, is secured.

## PART III

Data Security

## CHAPTER 9

Data Protection

—By Eddie Garcia

So far, we have covered how Hadoop can be configured to enforce standard AAA controls. In this chapter, we will understand how these controls, along with the CIA principles discussed in Chapter 1, provide the foundation for protecting data. Data protection is a broad concept that involves topics ranging from data privacy to acceptable use. One of the topics we will specifically focus on is *encryption*.

Encryption is a common method to protect data. There are two primary flavors of data encryption: *data-at-rest encryption* and *data-in-transit encryption*, also referred to as *over-the-wire encryption*. Data at rest refers to data that is stored even after machines are powered off. This includes data on hard drives, flash drives, USB sticks, memory cards, CDs, DVDs, or even some old floppy drives or tapes in storage boxes. Data in transit, as its name implies, is data on the move, such as data traveling on the Internet, a USB cable, a coffee shop WiFi, cell phone towers, or from a remote space station to Earth.

Encryption Algorithms

Before diving into the two flavors of data encryption, we'll briefly discuss encryption algorithms. Encryption algorithms define the mathematical technique used to encrypt data. A common encryption algorithm is the *Advanced Encryption Standard*, or *AES*. It is a specification established by the U.S. National Institute of Standards and Technology (NIST) in FIPS-197 (*http://1.usa.gov/1GFoIdU*).

Describing how AES encryption works is beyond the scope of this text, and we recommend Chapter 4 of *Understanding Cryptography* by Christof Paar and Jan Palzl (Springer, 2010). Other common encryption algorithms include DES, RC4, Twofish, and Blowfish.

When encrypting data, key size is important. In general, the larger the key, the harder it is to crack. On the downside, encrypting data with larger keys is slower. When dealing with extremely small data, the encryption key should not be larger than the data itself.

When using AES, the commonly supported sizes are 128-bit, 192-bit, and 256-bit keys. The industry standard today is AES-256 (256-bit key) encryption, but history has shown that this can and will change. At one point, DES and triple DES (three rounds of DES) was the industry standard, but with today's computers both can be easily cracked with brute force.

Because of the performance overhead that encryption incurs, chip vendors created on-hardware functions to improve the performance of encryption. These enhancements can yield several orders of magnitude of improvement over software encryption. One popular hardware encryption technology is Intel's AES-NI.

With a basic understating of the encryption methods and algorithms, we can now dig a little deeper into two of the methods: full disk and filesystem encryption. These are much easier to implement because they do not require special hardware.

Encrypting Data at Rest

Let's say Alice places a message for Bob on a USB stick and hands it to him. But Bob somehow in his excitement misplaces the USB stick and Eve happens to find it. Eve, being curious, connects the USB and attempts to read the contents. Luckily, Alice encrypted the message; otherwise, it would have been an embarrassing situation for her. In this simple example, encryption has helped assure the confidentiality of the message. Nobody but Bob knows the password to decrypt the data.

At the core of the Hadoop ecosystem is HDFS, which is the filesystem for many other components. Until recently, encrypting data in HDFS was not natively supported, which means that other methods of encryption needed to be adopted.

Over the years, there have been many cases of sensitive data breaches as a result of laptops and cell phones misplaced during transport, improper hard drive disposal, and physical hardware theft. Data-at-rest encryption helps mitigate these types of breaches because encryption makes it more difficult (but not impossible) to view the data.

In addition to native HDFS encryption, we will explore three other options, but we will not go into depth for every method because some are vendor specific. These methods work transparently below HDFS and thus don't require any Hadoop-specific configuration. All of these methods protect data in the case of a drive being physically removed from a drive array:

Encrypted drives
> This method is completely independent of the operating system. The physical drives on which HDFS stores its data support encryption natively. One limitation is that encrypted drives don't offer protection for data from rogue users and processes running on the system.

Full disk encryption
> This method typically works at system boot. This method does not require special drives or hardware like encrypted drives do. Several implementations of this technology exist, and typically vary by operating system. Some full disk encryption methods support operating system root partition encryption, while other methods only support encryption of the data partitions or volumes where the HDFS blocks are stored. Full disk encryption also has the limitation of encrypted drives in that it does not offer protection for data from rogue users and processes running on the system.

Filesystem encryption
> This method works at the operating-system level. This method also does not require special drives or hardware. Several implementations of this technology exist and vary by operating system. Filesystem encryption of the root partition is not supported because it becomes a chicken and the egg situation; the encrypted OS would need to boot to decrypt the OS. One of the benefits of filesystem encryption is that it offers protection for data against rogue users and processes running on the system. If an encrypted home directory is protected by a password known to a user and that user has not logged on to the system since boot, it would be impossible for a rogue user or process to gain access to the key to unlock the user's data, even as *root*.

Encryption and Key Management

Production Hadoop clusters typically have 8–12 drives per node across hundreds to thousands of nodes. Extending data-at-rest encryption to additional components beyond HDFS increases the potential complexity. As you begin rolling out encryption, it's important to consider additional questions:

- How do you configure more than one disk partition with encryption?
- How can you avoid providing passwords at boot time or in clear text scripts?

Ultimately, the hard part of large-scale at-rest encryption is key management. Native HDFS data-at-rest encryption, as we'll discuss in the next section, uses a combination of collocating encrypted keys with the file metadata and reliance on an external key server for managing key material. The other encryption-at-rest technologies discussed also require the use of a key management service at scale.

Picking a vendor for your key management system is complicated and we can't provide a recommendation for your environment. However, here are some key criteria to consider:

- Does the solution support hardware security modules?
- How scalable is the solution (number of keys as well as key retrieval per second)?
- Does the solution support Hadoop standards (e.g., KeyProvider interface)?
- How easy is it to manage authorization controls for hundreds or thousands of keys?

If you're using a prepackaged Hadoop distribution, the easiest way to find vendors for key management systems is to look at the security vendors that are certified by your Hadoop vendor.

HDFS Data-at-Rest Encryption

Starting with Hadoop 2.6, HDFS supports native encryption at rest. This feature is not considered full disk encryption or filesystem encryption. Rather it is another variation typically called *application-level encryption*. In this method, data is encrypted at the application layer before it is sent in transit and before it reaches storage. This method of encryption runs above the operating system layer and no special operating system packages or hardware are required other than what is provided by Hadoop. For more details on the design of native HDFS encryption beyond the description given here, you can read the HDFS Data at Rest Encryption Design Document (*http://bit.ly/1KZMeph*).

Within HDFS, directory paths that require encryption are broken down into *encryption zones*. Each file in an encryption zone is encrypted with a unique *data encryption key* (DEK). This is where the encryption zone distinction matters. The plain text DEKs are *not* persisted. Instead, a zone-level encryption key called an *encryption zone key* (EZK), is used to encrypt the DEK into an *encrypted DEK* (EDEK). The EDEK is then persisted as an extended attribute in the NameNode metadata for a given file.

HDFS encryption zones provide a tool for mirroring external security domains. Take a company with multiple divisions that need to maintain some division-only datasets. By creating an encryption zone per division, you can protect data on a per-division basis without the overhead of keeping a unique key per file in an authenticated keystore.

If the EDEK is stored in the HDFS metadata, where are the EZKs stored? These keys need to be kept secure because compromising an EZK provides access to all data stored in that encryption zone. To prevent Hadoop administrators from having access to the EZKs, and thus the ability to decrypt any data, the EZKs must not be stored in HDFS. EZKs need to be accessed through a secure *key server*. The key server itself is a separate piece of software that handles the storage and retrieval of EZKs. In larger enterprises, the actual storage component is handled by a dedicated *hardware security module* (HSM). With this deployment, the key server acts as the software interface between the clients requesting keys and the backend secure storage.

In order to have a separation of duties, there needs to be an intermediary between HDFS, HDFS clients, and the key server. This is solved with the introduction of the Hadoop *Key Management Server* (KMS). The KMS handles generating encryption keys (both EZKs and DEKs), communicating with the key server, and decrypting EDEKs. The KMS communicates with the key server through a Java API called the *KeyProvider*. The KeyProvider implementation and configuration is covered a bit later.

To better understand what is happening, let's take a look at the sequence of events that happens when an HDFS client is writing to a new file that's stored in an encryption zone in HDFS:

1. The HDFS client calls `create()` to write to the new file.
2. The NameNode requests the KMS to create a new EDEK using the EZK-id/ version.
3. The KMS generates a new DEK.
4. The KMS retrieves the EZK from the key server.
5. The KMS encrypts the DEK, resulting in the EDEK.
6. The KMS provides the EDEK to the NameNode.
7. The NameNode persists the EDEK as an extended attribute for the file metadata.
8. The NameNode provides the EDEK to the HDFS client.
9. The HDFS client provides the EDEK to the KMS, requesting the DEK.
10. The KMS requests the EZK from the key server.
11. The KMS decrypts the EDEK using the EZK.
12. The KMS provides the DEK to the HDFS client.
13. The HDFS client encrypts data using the DEK.
14. The HDFS client writes the encrypted data blocks to HDFS.

The sequence of events for reading an encrypted file is:

1. The HDFS client calls open() to read a file.
2. The NameNode provides the EDEK to the client.
3. The HDFS client passes the EDEK and EZK-id/version to the KMS.
4. The KMS requests the EZK from the key server.

5. The KMS decrypts the EDEK using the EZK.

6. The KMS provides the DEK to the HDFS client.

7. The HDFS client reads the encrypted data blocks, decrypting them with the DEK.

In both the read and write sequences, HDFS authorization was not mentioned. Authorization checks still happen before the file can be created or opened. The encryption/decryption steps only happen after the HDFS authorization checks.

 Because the KMS plays such an important role in HDFS encryption, this component should *not* be collocated on servers running other Hadoop ecosystem components, or servers used as edge nodes for clients. There needs to be a proper security separation of duties, and isolation between encryption key operations and other operations.

Because the communication between the KMS and both the key server and HDFS clients involves passing encryption keys, it is absolutely paramount that this communication also be encrypted using TLS. We will see how to do this in the next section.

Configuration

We have covered a lot in this section about HDFS encryption, but so far we have not discussed how any of this actually gets configured. In the *core-site.xml* on each HDFS node and client node, set the following parameter:

hadoop.security.key.provider.path
> The URI for the KeyProvider to use when interacting with encryption keys as a client. Example: kms://https@kms.example.com:16000/kms.

On the HDFS server (NameNode and DataNode) side, the following properties are available:

dfs.encryption.key.provider.uri
> The URI for the KeyProvider to use when interacting with encryption keys used when reading and writing to an encryption zone. Example: kms:// https@kms.example.com:16000/kms.

hadoop.security.crypto.cipher.suite
> Cipher suite for the crypto codec. Default: AES/CTR/NoPadding

hadoop.security.crypto.codec.classes.aes.ctr.nopadding
> Comma-separated list of crypto codec implementations for AES/CTR/NoPadding. The first implementation will be used if available; others are fallbacks.

Default: `org.apache.hadoop.crypto.OpensslAesCtrCryptoCodec`, `org.apache.hadoop.crypto.JceAesCtrCryptoCodec`

`hadoop.security.crypto.jce.provider`
The JCE provider. Default: None

`hadoop.security.crypto.buffer.size`
The buffer size used by `CryptoInputStream` and `CryptoOutputStream`. Default: 8192

As you can see, the HDFS configuration is minimal. HDFS uses sensible defaults for the cryptography aspect of it, so the only requirement to enable HDFS encryption is to set the first two configurations, namely `hadoop.security.key.provider.path` and `dfs.encryption.key.provider.uri`.

In order to configure the Hadoop KMS, the configuration file *kms-site.xml* is used. Configure the following properties on the Hadoop KMS node:

`hadoop.kms.key.provider.uri`
The URI for the EZK provider. Example: `jceks://file@/var/lib/kms/kms.keystore`.

`hadoop.kms.authentication.type`
The authentication mechanism to use. Example: simple or kerberos

`hadoop.kms.authentication.kerberos.keytab`
The location of the Kerberos keytab file to use for service authentication

`hadoop.kms.authentication.kerberos.principal`
The SPN that the service should use for authentication. Example: `HTTP/kms.example.com@EXAMPLE.COM`.

`hadoop.kms.authentication.kerberos.name.rules`
Kerberos `auth_to_local` rules to use. Example: `DEFAULT`

`hadoop.kms.proxyuser.<user>.groups`
The list of groups that *<user>* (e.g., hdfs, hive, oozie) is allowed to impersonate

hadoop.kms.proxyuser.<user>__.hosts++
The list of hosts from which *<user>* (e.g., hdfs, hive, oozie) is allowed to impersonate

An example is listed in the KMS configuration properties that shows the ability to use a file-based KeyProvider. This is just a Java keystore file that stores EZKs. While this is a quick and easy way to get up and running with HDFS encryption, it is only recommended in POC or development environments for testing. Using a file-based KeyProvider collocates the KMS and key server functions on the same machine, which does not offer the desired security separation of duties or the ability to enforce additional isolation controls. Also, the key storage is just a basic file on disk. As mentioned before, most enterprises will want to utilize a separate service as the KeyProvider, which uses a more secure storage for EZKs, such as what is provided by HSMs.

As you can see from the KMS configuration, strong authentication with Kerberos is possible. This is absolutely the recommended configuration. Non-Kerberos deployment should not be used due to the sensitivity of what the KMS is providing. The actual KMS operates over the HTTP protocol, so Kerberos authentication with KMS clients happens over SPNEGO. For this reason, the Kerberos principal that the KMS uses should be of the `HTTP/kms.example.com@EXAMPLE.COM` variety, which uses the HTTP service name.

We mentioned briefly in the last section that setting up the KMS with TLS wire encryption is important. To do this, set two environment variables for the KeyStore and password in `kms-env.sh`. The KeyStore file is just a Java KeyStore and the location of it is specified with the `KMS_SSL_KEYSTORE_FILE` environment variable. If this KeyStore is protected with a password (and it should be!), specify the password in the `KMS_SSL_KEYSTORE_PASS` environment variable.

KMS authorization

The KMS, like other Hadoop components, has the ability to restrict access to certain functions through the use of access control lists (ACLs). The file *kms-acls.xml* stores information about which users and groups can perform which functions with the KMS. Example 9-1 shows an example of one.

Example 9-1. KMS kms-acls.xml

```
<?xml version="1.0" encoding="UTF-8"?>
<configuration>
  <property>
    <name>hadoop.kms.blacklist.CREATE</name>
    <value>hdfs supergroup</value>
  </property>
  <property>
    <name>hadoop.kms.blacklist.DELETE</name>
    <value>hdfs supergroup</value>
```

```
  </property>
  <property>
    <name>hadoop.kms.blacklist.ROLLOVER</name>
    <value>hdfs supergroup</value>
  </property>
  <property>
    <name>hadoop.kms.blacklist.GET</name>
    <value>hdfs supergroup</value>
  </property>
  <property>
    <name>hadoop.kms.blacklist.GET_KEYS</name>
    <value>hdfs supergroup</value>
  </property>
  <property>
    <name>hadoop.kms.blacklist.SET_KEY_MATERIAL</name>
    <value>hdfs supergroup</value>
  </property>
  <property>
    <name>hadoop.kms.blacklist.DECRYPT_EEK</name>
    <value>hdfs supergroup</value>
  </property>
  <property>
    <name>default.key.acl.MANAGEMENT</name>
    <value> infosec</value>
  </property>
  <property>
    <name>default.key.acl.GENERATE_EEK</name>
    <value>hdfs supergroup</value>
  </property>
  <property>
    <name>default.key.acl.DECRYPT_EEK</name>
    <value> hadoopusers</value>
  </property>
  <property>
    <name>default.key.acl.READ</name>
    <value> infosec</value>
  </property>
</configuration>
```

Each of the entries in Example 9-1 have a value format of user1,user2 group1,group2, just like as described in "Service-Level Authorization" on page 101. You'll notice the usage of *blacklists*. In order to enforce the separation of Hadoop administrators from the actual data, Hadoop administrators should not have the ability to interact and perform operations on the KMS. Hadoop administrators that are part of the supergroup have the ability to traverse the entire HDFS directory tree. Encrypted data should not be able to be decrypted by administrators of the cluster, so blacklisting these users is important.

Keep in mind that the Hadoop KMS is a general-purpose key management server. The keys it works with have no meaning or difference in how they are handled. This means that EZKs and DEKs are equivalent from the KMS point of view. This is why using KMS ACLs is important. For example, by default the CREATE operation returns the actual key material. This is bad if regular users are able to retain the actual EZK, as it can be used to decrypt EDEKs for the entire encryption zone.

 Allowing any user to create keys opens up several potential security risks. For example, a rogue user could easily write a script to continually create new keys until the KMS and/or key server fails, such as running out of storage. This effectively creates a denial-of-service scenario that prevents *all* encrypted data from being accessible! Use restrictive KMS ACLs to authorize only a small set of security administrators the ability to create and manage keys.

It is recommended to come up with (at least) three different roles to apply ACLs to: Hadoop administrators, security administrators, and regular users. With this model, Hadoop administrators only need the ability to request the KMS to generate new EDEKs. The security administrators are responsible for creating and maintaining EZKs. Lastly, regular users of the cluster are only able to request the KMS decrypt a provided EDEK.

Following this model, Example 9-1 shows that Hadoop administrators, namely the *hdfs* user and the *supergroup* group, are blacklisted from all the operations that are unnecessary. Furthermore, the *infosec* group is the only group allowed to perform the MANAGEMENT and READ functions. Lastly, the *hadoopusers* group is allowed to perform the DECRYPT_EEK function, but nothing else.

While Example 9-1 shows default ACLs, denoted by the prefix default.key.acl, it is also possible to define ACLs to specific keys by name, such as key.acl.foo.READ where foo is the name of the key. We'll discuss how the keynames come into the picture in the next section, which covers HDFS encryption client operations.

Client operations

So far we've covered HDFS encryption both from a workflow perspective and a configuration perspective. Now we need to look at the actual client operations to set this all up. First, let's start with the creation of a new EZK. To do this, use the hadoop key command, which outputs details of the key created and the KMS that performed the request:

```
[bob@server1 ~]$ hadoop key -create myzonekey
myzonekey has been successfully created with options
 Options{cipher='AES/CTR/NoPadding', bitLength=128, description='null', attr
ibutes=null}.
KMSClientProvider[https://kms.example.com:16000/kms/v1/] has been updated.
[bob@server1 ~]$
```

Now we can create a new encryption zone in HDFS. To do this, use the `hdfs crypto` command:

```
[bob@server1 ~]$ hdfs dfs -mkdir /myzone
[bob@server1 ~]$ hdfs crypto -createZone -keyName myzonekey -path /myzone
[bob@server1 ~]$ hdfs crypto -listZones
/myzone    myzonekey
[bob@server1 ~]$
```

From here, HDFS clients can read and write files in the */myzone* directory and have them be transparently encrypted or decrypted.

 HDFS encryption zone creation requires an empty directory. It is not possible to create an encryption zone on a directory that already has data in it. To encrypt data that already resides in HDFS, rename the desired directory to a temporary name, create the desired directory again, set up the encryption zone, and copy the data back into the zone. Keep in mind that the original data was persisted to disk unencrypted. Rewriting the data as encrypted does not remove the original exposure of the unencrypted sensitive data on disk.

MapReduce2 Intermediate Data Encryption

When HDFS encryption is enabled, it is important that temporary, intermediate versions of the data also be protected. It is possible to encrypt the intermediate output from MapReduce jobs, but there are some caveats:

- Intermediate data encryption is on a per-job basis (client configuration)
- Users might not know that the source data came from an encryption zone
  - Users might not enable intermediate data encryption properly
  - Users might *disable* intermediate data encryption because of performance impacts
- Intermediate data encryption is only available for MR2 not MR1

The job configuration properties shown in Table 9-1 are used to enable intermediate data encryption.

Table 9-1. Intermediate data encryption properties

Property	Description
`mapreduce.job.encrypted-intermediate-data`	Set to `true` to enable (default: `false`)
`mapreduce.job.encrypted-intermediate-data-key-size-bits`	The key length size for encryption (default: 128)
`mapreduce.job.encrypted-intermediate-data.buffer.kb`	The buffer size to use in KB (default: 128)

It is certainly desirable to have intermediate data encryption that is both enforced and enabled when actually necessary. We hope that in a later Hadoop release this implementation will improve such that MapReduce tasks will encrypt intermediate files automatically if it detects that it is reading data sourced from an encryption zone, and that this feature is not able to be overridden by a client.

Impala Disk Spill Encryption

Impala has the ability to encrypt data that is spilled to disk when all of the data being processed cannot fit in memory. Without disk spill encryption, sensitive data could be written back to disk unencrypted. This poses a risk to the sensitive data and defeats the advantages of encrypting the data in the first place.

To configure Impala daemons to protect data it spills to disk, the following startup flags are needed:

`disk_spill_encryption`
Set this to `true` to turn on the encryption of all data spilled to disk during a query. Default: `false`. When data is about to be spilled to disk, it is encrypted with a randomly generated AES 256-bit key. When read back from disk, it's decrypted.

`disk_spill_integrity`
Set this to `true` to turn on an integrity check of all data spilled to disk during a query. Default: `false`. When data is about to be spilled to disk, a SHA256 hash of the data is taken. When read back in from disk, a SHA256 is again taken and compared to the original. This prevents tampering of data spilled to disk.

Full Disk Encryption

If you're using a version of HDFS that doesn't support native encryption or if you need to encrypt the data used by other Hadoop ecosystem components, then you might want to consider full disk encryption or filesystem encryption. Let's take a look at full disk encryption using the *Linux Unified Key Setup* (LUKS). In addition to LUKS, there are several products for full disk encryption. We will focus on LUKS, as it is a common open source tool for enabling full disk encryption on Linux.

 Data encryption is not something you want to experiment with in production or on real data. A mistake could cause your data to be permanently unrecoverable.

Most LUKS implementations use `cryptsetup` and `dm-crypt` found in Linux distributions:

- `cryptsetup` provides the user space tools to create, configure, and administer the encrypted volumes
- `dm-crypt` provides the Linux kernel space logic to encrypt the block device

In Example 9-2, we show how to configure LUKS on a device using the command line. Some Linux distributions have tools that allow for simple configuration during OS installation. This can be as easy as checking a box or selecting an option to enable full-disk encryption when setting up storage drives, adding additional drives, or re-partitioning existing drives. This hides all the complexity of using `cryptsetup` and `dm-crypt`. We encourage you to use the distribution-provided tools when possible.

 When you set up LUKS on a device, data on the device is overwritten. If you're setting up LUKS on a device that already has data, first make a backup of the entire device and then restore the data after LUKS is configured. Exercise caution when performing the LUKS configuration.

Example 9-2. LUKS encryption

1. Install `crypsetup`.

   On CentOS/RHEL:

   ```
   [root@hadoop01 ~]# yum install cryptsetup-luks
   ```

   On Debian/Ubuntu:

   ```
   [root@hadoop01 ~]# apt-get install cryptsetup
   ```

2. Set up the LUKS storage device.

   ```
   [root@hadoop01 ~]# cryptsetup -y -v luksFormat /dev/xvdc
   WARNING!
   ========
   ```

```
This will overwrite data on /dev/xvdc irrevocably.

Are you sure? (Type uppercase yes): YES
Enter LUKS passphrase:
Verify passphrase:
Command successful.
```

3. Open the device and map it to a new device:

```
[root@hadoop01 ~]# cryptsetup luksOpen /dev/xvdc data1
```

This creates a new mapping device on */dev/mapper/data1.*

4. Clear all the data on the device (this is mainly to clear the header, but it's a good security practice to clear it all):

```
[root@hadoop01 ~]# dd if=/dev/zero of=/dev/mapper/data1
```

The preceding operation is writing zeros over the entire storage device so it can take minutes to hours to complete, depending on the size of the device and the speed of your system.

5. When the dd command completes, you can create your filesystem; in this case, we will use ext4, but you can also use XFS or your desired filesystem format:

```
[root@hadoop01 ~]# mkfs.ext4 /dev/mapper/data1
```

6. Now that you have an encrypted device with a filesystem, you can mount it like a regular filesystem:

```
[root@hadoop01 ~]# mkdir /data/dfs/data1
[root@hadoop01 ~]# mount /dev/mapper/data1 /data/dfs/data1
[root@hadoop01 ~]# df -H
[root@hadoop01 ~]# ls -l /data/dfs/data1
```

7. Repeat the previous steps for your other drives mounted on */data/dfs/data[2-N]* and then install Hadoop using */data/dfs/data[1-N]* for HDFS storage.

This example is meant to be just that, an example. It does not cover many other aspects such as how you might provide the password on boot or how to perform backups. What happens if you need to add a drive? What if you want to resize the partition? These are all questions that you should consider for any production deployment.

Filesystem Encryption

There are many products that provide filesystem encryption, but we will focus on eCryptfs because it is a common open source filesystem encryption solution for Linux.

eCryptfs has two main components, `ecryptfs-utils` and `ecryptfs`:

- `ecryptfs-utils` provides the user space tools to create, configure, and administer the encrypted directories
- `ecryptfs` provides the Linux kernel space logic to layer the encrypted filesystem over the directories on the existing filesystem

In Example 9-3, we show you how to configure eCryptfs using the command line. Some Linux distributions have tools that allow for simple configuration during OS install. This can be as easy as checking a box or selecting an option to set up storage drives, add additional drives, or repartition existing drives. This hides all the complexity of using `ecryptfs-utils` and `ecryptfs` for you. We encourage you to use the distribution-provided tools when possible.

Example 9-3. eCryptfs encryption

1. Install ecryptfs-utils.

   On CentOS/RHEL:

   ```
   [root@hadoop01 ~]# yum install ecryptfs-utils
   ```

   On Debian/Ubuntu:

   ```
   [root@hadoop01 ~]# apt-get install ecryptfs-utils
   ```

2. Mount a new encrypted filesystem over your empty HDFS data directory.

   ```
   [root@hadoop01 ~]# mount -t ecryptfs /data/dfs/data1 /data/dfs/data1
   Select key type to use for newly created files:
   1) passphrase
   2) tspi
   3) openssl
   Selection: 1
   Passphrase:

   Select cipher:
   1) aes: blocksize = 16; min keysize = 16; max keysize = 32 (not loaded)
   2) blowfish: blocksize = 16; min keysize = 16; max keysize = 56 (not loaded)
   3) des3_ede: blocksize = 8; min keysize = 24; max keysize = 24 (not loaded)
   4) twofish: blocksize = 16; min keysize = 16; max keysize = 32 (not loaded)
   5) cast6: blocksize = 16; min keysize = 16; max keysize = 32 (not loaded)
   6) cast5: blocksize = 8; min keysize = 5; max keysize = 16 (not loaded)
   ```

```
Selection [aes]: aes

Select key bytes:
1) 16
2) 32
3) 24
Selection [16]: 32
Enable plaintext passthrough (y/n) [n]: n
Enable filename encryption (y/n) [n]: n
Attempting to mount with the following options:
ecryptfs_unlink_sigs
ecryptfs_key_bytes=32
ecryptfs_cipher=aes
ecryptfs_sig= 9808e34a098f3814
WARNING: Based on the contents of [/root/.ecryptfs/sig-cache.txt],
it looks like you have never mounted with this key
before. This could mean that you have typed your
passphrase wrong.
Would you like to proceed with the mount (yes/no)? : yes
Would you like to append sig [9808e34a098f3814] to
[/root/.ecryptfs/sig-cache.txt]
in order to avoid this warning in the future (yes/no)? : yes
Successfully appended new sig to user sig cache file
Mounted eCryptfs
```

 During the mount command, you'll be prompted for the size of the key in bytes. Previously, we described the desired key size as 256 bits. Because there are 8 bits in a byte, we will select a 32-byte key.

3. Repeat the preceding steps for your other drives mounted on */data/dfs/data[2-N]* and then install Hadoop using */data/dfs/data[1-N]* for HDFS storage.

This example does not cover other aspects like how to provide the password on boot, how to perform backups, or what happens if the password is forgotten. These are additional considerations to make when rolling out an encryption solution at such a large scale.

Important Data Security Consideration for Hadoop

If you are configuring encryption for data at rest for Hadoop, you should take notice that sensitive data may not only land in HDFS, but in other areas such as shuffles, spill fills, temporary files, logfiles, swap files, indexes, and metadata stores that run on MySQL, PostgreSQL, SQLite, Oracle, or Derby. In Chapter 10, we will cover some of the areas where Hadoop offers encryption for those other data sets outside of HDFS.

Encrypting Data in Transit

In the previous section, we described how you can proect data at rest with encryption, but what about data while it's being transmitted over the network? Let's start with an abstract example. When Alice and Bob were children, they liked to exchange notes in class. Because they didn't always sit next to each other, they often had to trust other children to pass the notes along. How would they deal with nosy kids that might want to read the note before passing it, or worse, what happens if the teacher catches them and reads the note aloud to the whole class?

Being a clever kid, Alice came up with her own alphabet with symbols that map one-to-one to letters in the English alphabet. Instead of writing their messages using English letters, they use this custom alphabet. Alice and Bob can exchange a copy of the mapping in advance or even memorize the alphabet (there are only 26 symbols after all). Now when they send their notes, only those with a copy of the alphabet map can read them.

This method is simple and effective, but it's not absolutely secure. More sophisticated methods might include having multiple alphabets or the same alphabet with randomized mappings along with a key that tells the recipient which mapping to use. This is probalby overkill for passing notes, but it becomes very important when designing encryption systems for data in transit.

Transport Layer Security

Transport Layer Security (TLS) is a cryptographic protocol for encrypting data in transit. TLS replaced the *Secure Socket Layer* (SSL), an early standard for encrypting data in transit. TLS was first defined in RFC 2246 based on the SSL 3.0 protocol designed by Paul Kocher. Given the shared history of TLS and SSL, the two are often used interchangeably even though they are not the same. It is also common to use the same library for implementing either SSL or TLS. For example, the OpenSSL library includes implementations of SSL 2.0 and 3.0, as well as TLS 1.0, 1.1, and 1.2.

Whereas Chapter 4 is a protocol for enabling strong authentication, SSL/TLS are protocols for securing data as it moves through the network. While most commonly associated with web traffic in the form of the HTTPS protocol, SSL/TLS are generic protocols that can be used to secure any socket connection. This lets you create an encrypted pipe that other protocols can then be layered on top of. In the same way that Kerberos clients rely on trusting the KDC, clients using SSL/TLS trust a central *certificate authority* (CA).

The following are basic concepts that underpin SSL/TLS:

Private key
> An asymmetric encryption key that is known only to the owner of a signed certificate.

Public key
> An asymmetric encryption key that is shared publicly and can be used to encrypt data that is only decryptable by the corresponding private key.

Certificate signing request (CSR)
> A cryptographic message sent to a certificate authority to apply for a specific identity.

Signed certificate
> The result of sending the CSR to the CA. The signed certificate includes a copy of the public key that was generated alongside the private key. It is possible to use certificates that are self-signed rather than signed by a CA, but this is only recommended for test and development systems.

PKCS #12
> A file format that bundles the private key and the signed certificate.

While there are many technical details of SSL/TLS that we will not cover here, there are a few things you should understand which are covered in the following basic workflow example.

Generating a new certificate

1. An administrator for the service seeking to accept SSL/TLS connections generates a public and private key pair.

2. The administrator then generates a CSR and sends it to the CA.

3. The CA validates the identity of the server/service (and sometimes business entity), and then generates a signed certificate.

4. The administrator of the service can then install the signed certificate.

SSL/TLS handshake

1. Alice connects to the Bob service, which presents an SSL/TLS certificate to Alice.

2. Alice looks up the CA certificate that signed Bob's certificate in her chain of trusted third parties.

3. Alice and the Bob service exchange public keys, and then agree to a newly created symmetric encryption key for the current session.

4. Alice sends messages to the Bob service that are encrypted in transit by the securely exchanged symmetric key.

5. If Eve captures the packet of messages going from Alice to Bob, she is unable to decrypt them because she does not possess the symmetric key.

One well-known implementation of this scheme is the RSA key exchange algorithm. In this method, private and public key pairs are generated, followed by a secure exchange of public keys, which allows the two parties to send encrypted messages that only the intended recipients can decrypt.

 RSA comes from the surname initials of Ron Rivest, Adi Shamir, and Leonard Adlemanwho, who wrote a paper on this algorithm while at MIT in 1977. As you can see in this book, along with Kerberos, many security technologies we use today originate from MIT.

For a more in-depth understanding on SSL/TLS, we recommend reading Network Security with OpenSSL by John Viega, Matt Messier, Pravir Chandra (O'Reilly), and Chapter 14, "SSL and HTTPS," in Java Security, Second Edition by Scott Oaks (O'Reilly).

Hadoop Data-in-Transit Encryption

Hadoop has several methods of communication over the network, including RPC, TCP/IP, and HTTP. API clients of MapReduce, JobTracker, TaskTracker, NameNode and DataNodes use RPC calls. HDFS clients use TCP/IP sockets for data transfers. The HTTP protocol is used for MapReduce shuffles and also by many daemons for their web UIs.

Each of these three network communications have a different in-transit encryption method. We will explore the basics of these next, and in Chapter 10 we will cover a detailed example of Flume SSL/TLS configuration. In Chapters 11 and 12, we also cover the use of SSL/TLS with Oozie, HBase, Impala, and Hue.

Hadoop RPC Encryption

Hadoop's RPC implementation supports SASL, which in addition to supporting authentication, provides optional message integrity and encryption. Hadoop uses the Java SASL implementation, which supports the following modes:

- `auth`, for authentication between client and server
- `auth-int`, for authentication and integrity
- `auth-conf`, for authentication, integrity, and confidentiality

RPC protection in Hadoop is configured with the `hadoop.rpc.protection` property in the *core-site.xml* file. This property can be set to the values:

- `authentication`, the default, puts SASL into `auth` mode and provides only authentication

- `integrity` puts SASL into `auth-int` mode and adds integrity checking in addition to authenticaiton

- `privacy` puts SASL into `auth-conf` mode and adds encryption to ensure full confidentiality

To configure Hadoop RPC protection, set the value in your *core-site.xml* as shown here (keeping in mind that all daemons need to be restarted for it to take effect):

```
<property>
  <name>hadoop.rpc.protection</name>
  <value>privacy</value>
</property>
```

HDFS data transfer protocol encryption

When HDFS data is transferred from one DataNode to another or between DataNodes and their clients, a direct TCP/IP socket is used in a protocol known as the *HDFS data transfer protocol*. The Hadoop RPC protocol is used to exchange an encryption key for use in the data transfer protocol when data transfer encryption is enabled.

To configure data transfer encryption, set `dfs.encrypt.data.transfer` to true in the *hdfs-site.xml* file. This change is required only on the DataNodes. RPC will be used to exchange the encryption keys, so ensure that RPC encryption is enabled by setting the `hadoop.rpc.protection` configuration to `privacy`, as described earlier. The encryption algorithm should also be configured to use AES. In the following code, we configure AES encryption:

```
<property>
  <name>dfs.encrypt.data.transfer</name>
  <value>true</value>
</property>
<property>
  <name>dfs.encrypt.data.transfer.cipher.suites</name>
  <value>AES/CTR/NoPadding</value>
</property>
<property>
  <name> dfs.encrypt.data.transfer.cipher.key.bitlength</name>
  <value>256</value> <!-- can also be set to 128 or 192 -->
</property>
```

> Setting AES encryption using the `dfs.encrypt.data.trans fer.cipher.suites` setting is a more recent Hadoop feature, added in version 2.6. For earlier releases, you can set `dfs.encrypt.data.transfer.algorithm` to `3des` (default) or `rc4` to choose between triple-DES or RC4 respectively.

You will need to restart your DataNode and NameNode daemons after this is set to take effect. The entire process can be done manually, and Hadoop distributions might also offer automated methods to enable HDFS data transfer encryption.

Hadoop HTTP encryption

When it comes to HTTP encryption, there is a well-known and proven method to encrypt the data in transit using *HTTPS*, which is an enhancement of HTTP with SSL/TLS. While HTTPS is very standardized, configuring it in Hadoop is not. Several Hadoop components support HTTPS, but they are not all configured with the same steps.

As you may recall from the description of the basic SSL/TLS concepts, a few additional files are required, like private keys, certificates, and PKCS #12 bundles. When using Java, these files are stored in a Java *keystore*. Many of the HTTPS configuration steps for Hadoop generate these objects, store them in the Java keystore, and finally, configure Hadoop to use them.

Some Hadoop components are both HTTPS servers and clients to other services. A few examples are:

- HDFS, MapReduce, and YARN daemons act as both SSL servers and clients
- HBase daemons act as SSL servers only
- Oozie daemons act as SSL servers only
- Hue acts as an SSL client to all of the above

We will not cover HTTPS configuration in depth. Instead we will focus on the Map-Reduce encrypted shuffle and encrypted web UI configuration as a starting point to configure other components.

Encrypted shuffle and encrypted web UI

Encrypted shuffle is supported for both MR1 and MR2. In MR1, setting the `hadoop.ssl.enabled` property in the *core-site.xml* file enables both the encrypted shuffle and the encrypted web UI. In MR2, setting the `hadoop.ssl.enabled` property enables the encrypted web UI feature only; setting the `mapreduce.shuf fle.ssl.enabled` property in the *mapred-site.xml* file enables the encrypted shuffle feature.

 When configuring HTTPS, just as with Kerberos, it is important to set up all your servers with their full hostnames and to configure DNS to resolve correctly to these names across the cluster.

For both MR1 or MR2, set the `ssl` property in *core-site.xml*; this will enable the encrypted web UI. For MR1, this also enables the encrypted shuffle:

```
<property>
  <name>hadoop.ssl.enabled</name>
  <value>true</value>
  <final>true</final>
</property>
```

For MR2 only, set the encrypted shuffle SSL property in *mapred-site.xml*:

```
<property>
  <name>mapreduce.shuffle.ssl.enabled</name>
  <value>true</value>
  <final>true</final>
</property>
```

You can also optionally set the `hadoop.ssl.hostname.verifier` property to control how hostname verification happens. Valid values are:

DEFAULT

> The hostname must match either the first CN or any of the subject-alt names. If a wildcard exists on either the CN or one of the subject-alt names, then it matches all subdomains.

DEFAULT_AND_LOCALHOST

> This behaves the same as DEFAULT with the addition that a host of `localhost`, `localhost.localdomain`, `127.0.0.1`, and `::1` will always pass.

STRICT

> This behaves like DEFAULT, but only matches wildcards on the same level. For example, `*.example.com` matches `one.example.com` but not `two.one.example.com`.

ALLOW_ALL

> Accepts any hostname. This mode should only be used in testing because it is not secure.

For example, to support default plus localhost mode, set the following:

```
<property>
  <name>hadoop.ssl.hostname.verifier</name>
  <value>DEFAULT_AND_LOCALHOST</value>
  <final>true</final>
</property>
```

You will also need to update your *ssl-server.xml* and *ssl-client.xml* files. These files are typically located in the */etc/hadoop/conf* directory. The settings that go into the *ssl-server.xml* file are shown in Table 9-2.

Table 9-2. Keystore and Truststore settings for ssl-server.xml

Property	Default value	Description
`ssl.server.key store.type`	`jks`	The keystore file type
`ssl.server.key store.location`	`NONE`	The path to the keystore file; this file should be owned by the mapred user and the mapred user must have exclusive read access to it (i.e., permission 400)
`ssl.server.key store.password`	`NONE`	The password to the keystore file
`ssl.server.trust store.type`	`jks`	The truststore file type
`ssl.server.trust store.location`	`NONE`	The path to the truststore file; this file should be owned by the mapred user and the mapred user have exclusive read access to it (i.e., permission 400)
`ssl.server.trust store.password`	`NONE`	The password to the truststore file
`ssl.server.trust store.reload.interval`	`10000`	Number of milliseconds between reloading the truststore file

An example, fully configured *ssl-server.xml* file looks like this:

```
<configuration>
  <!-- Server keystore -->
  <property>
    <name>ssl.server.keystore.type</name>
    <value>jks</value>
  </property>
  <property>
    <name>ssl.server.keystore.location</name>
    <value>/etc/hadoop/ssl/server/hadoop01.example.com.jks</value>
  </property>
  <property>
    <name>ssl.server.keystore.password</name>
    <value>super-secret-squirrel</value>
  </property>

  <!-- Server truststore -->
  <property>
    <name>ssl.server.truststore.type</name>
    <value>jks</value>
  </property>
```

```
      <property>
        <name>ssl.server.truststore.location</name>
        <value>/etc/hadoop/ssl/server/truststore.jks</value>
      </property>
      <property>
        <name>ssl.server.truststore.password</name>
        <value>changeit</value>
      </property>
      <property>
        <name>ssl.server.truststore.reload.interval</name>
        <value>10000</value>
      </property>
    </configuration>
```

The settings that go into the *ssl-client.xml* file are shown in Table 9-3.

Table 9-3. Keystore and truststore settings for ssl-client.xml

Property	Default value	Description
ssl.client.keystore.type	jks	The keystore file type.
ssl.client.keystore.loca tion	NONE	The path to the keystore file; this file should be owned by the mapred user and all users that can run a MapReduce job should have read access (i.e., permission 444).
ssl.client.keystore.pass word	NONE	The password to the keystore file.
ssl.client.trust store.type	jks	The truststore file type.
ssl.client.trust store.location	NONE	The path to the keystore file; this file should be owned by the mapred user and all users that can run a MapReduce job should have read access (i.e., permission 444).
ssl.client.trust store.password	NONE	The password to the truststore file.
ssl.client.trust store.reload.interval	10000	Number of milliseconds between reloading the truststore file.

An example, fully configured *ssl-client.xml* file looks like this:

```
    <configuration>
      <!-- Client keystore -->
      <property>
        <name>ssl.client.keystore.type</name>
        <value>jks</value>
```

```
    </property>
    <property>
      <name>ssl.client.keystore.location</name>
      <value>/etc/hadoop/ssl/client/hadoop01.example.com.jks</value>
    </property>
    <property>
      <name>ssl.client.keystore.password</name>
      <value>super-secret-squirrel</value>
    </property>

    <!-- Client truststore -->
    <property>
      <name>ssl.client.truststore.type</name>
      <value>jks</value>
    </property>
    <property>
      <name>ssl.client.truststore.location</name>
      <value>/etc/hadoop/ssl/client/truststore.jks</value>
    </property>
    <property>
      <name>ssl.client.truststore.password</name>
      <value>changeit</value>
    </property>
    <property>
      <name>ssl.client.truststore.reload.interval</name>
      <value>10000</value>
    </property>
</configuration>
```

 When configuring SSL/TLS, be sure to disable the clear text services. For example, if a service runs on HTTP port 80 and HTTPS is configured and running on port 443, be sure to disable the HTTP service running on port 80. For a stronger level of protection, you can configure a firewall, such as the `iptables` software firewall, to disable access to port 80.

After you set up your *ssl-server.xml* and *ssl-client.xml* files, you need to restart all the TaskTrackers in MR1 and NodeManagers in MR2 for the changes to take effect.

Data Destruction and Deletion

When dealing with data security, *how* you delete the data is important. If you happen to reuse servers in your cluster that may have previously been used with sensitive data, you will want to destroy the data first—for instance, in Example 9-2, we used `dd` to zero out the LUKS partition.

You can do a more thorough destruction of data using the GNU `shred` utility. The `shred` utility will overwrite a file or device with random patterns to better obfuscate the previous data that was written. You can pass `shred` a number of iterations to run, with three passes being the default. The old DoD 5220.22-M standard mandated that a 7-pass overwrite was required to securely erase sensitive data. The most secure mode implements the Gutmann method, which requires 35 passes using a combination of random data and specially selected data patterns.

Performing 35 overwrite passes on a large disk is a time-consuming operation. Assuming your disk can write at a sustained 100 MB/s, it will take over 200 hours, or roughly 8.5 days, to fully overwrite a 2 TB drive 35 times. When dealing with a cluster of hundreds of machines and thousands of disks, this is a huge undertaking even if you perform the sanitization in parallel.

DoD standards have advanced in recent years to the point where no amount of overwrite is sufficient for particularly sensitive data. In these cases, only degaussing or physical destruction is acceptable. It's also important to remember that a damaged drive cannot be overwritten, so degaussing or physical destruction are the only options. For large clusters where you expect disk failures to be common and data to be sufficiently sensitive, a physical destruction plan should be in place. There are many facilities where drives can be physically destroyed, and some companies offer on-site services where they will bring shredding equipment to you.

Summary

In this chapter, we discussed how encryption is used to protect data from unauthorized access by users and administrators of a Hadoop cluster. We compared and contrasted protecting data at rest and data in transit. We described how HDFS has recently added native data-at-rest encryption along with alternative approaches applicable to earlier versions, as well as to data that lives outside of HDFS. We also showed how intermediate data that is generated during a data processing job or query can also be encrypted to provide end-to-end protection.

Next, we discussed methods of protecting data in transit starting with Hadoop RPC encryption. We followed this with protection of data from HDFS clients to DataNodes and between DataNodes in the form of HDFS data transfer protocol encryption. We also discussed how to encrypt the HTTP endpoints and the MapReduce shuffle with SSL/TLS. Lastly, we described extending the protection of data to the operational end of life for hardware by describing methods of permanent data destruction.

The next two chapters will explore holistically securing your Hadoop environment by extending data security to your data ingest pipeline and client access, respectively.

CHAPTER 10

Securing Data Ingest

The preceding chapters have focused on securing Hadoop from a storage and data processing perspective. We've assumed that you have data in Hadoop and you want to secure access to it or to control how users share analytic resources, but we've neglected to explain how data gets into Hadoop in the first place.

There are many ways for data to be ingested into Hadoop. The simplest method is to copy files from a local filesystem (e.g., a local hard disk or an NFS mount) to HDFS using Hadoop's put command, as shown in Example 10-1.

Example 10-1. Ingesting files from the command line

```
[alice@hadoop01 ~]$ hdfs dfs -put /mnt/data/sea*.json /data/raw/sea_fire_911/
```

While this method might work for some datasets, it's much more common to ingest data from existing relational systems or set up flows of event- or log-oriented data. For these use cases, users use Sqoop and Flume, respectively.

Sqoop is designed to either pull data from a relational database into Hadoop or to push data from Hadoop into a remote database. In both cases, Sqoop launches a Map-Reduce job that does that actual data transfer. By default, Sqoop uses JDBC drivers to transport data between the map tasks and the database. This is called *generic mode* and it makes it easy to use Sqoop with new data stores, as the only requirement is the availability of JDBC drivers. For performance reasons, Sqoop also supports connectors that can use vendor-specific tools and interfaces to optimize the data transfer. To enable these optimizations, users specify the --direct option to enable *direct mode*. For example, when enabling direct mode for MySQL, Sqoop will use the mysqldump and mysqlimport utilities to extract from or import to MySQL much more efficiently.

Flume is a distributed service for efficiently collecting, aggregating, and moving large volumes of event data. Users of Flume deploy agents, which are Java processes that transfer events. An event is the smallest unit of data that flows through Flume. Events have a binary (byte array) payload and an optional set of attributes defined by string key/value pairs. Each agent is configured with sources, sinks, and a channel. A source is a component that consumes events from an external data source; a source can either pull events from the external source or it can have events pushed to it by the external source. The Flume source connects to a channel, which makes the event available for consumption by a sink. The channel is completely passive in that it accepts events from sources and keeps them until they are consumed by a sink. A Flume sink transfers the event to an external data store or process.

Flume includes an AvroSource and an AvroSink that uses Avro RPC to transfer events. You can configure the AvroSink of one Flume agent to send events to the AvroSource of another Flume agent in order to build complex, distributed data flows. While Flume also supports a wide variety of sources and sinks, the primary ones used to implement inter-agent data flow are the AvroSource and AvroSink, so we'll restrict the rest of our discusion to this pair. The reliability of Flume is determined by the configuration of the channel. There are in-memory channels for data flows that prioritize speed over reliability, as well as disk-backed channels that support full recoverability. Figure 10-1 shows a two-tier Flume data flow showing the components internal to the agents as well as their interconnection.

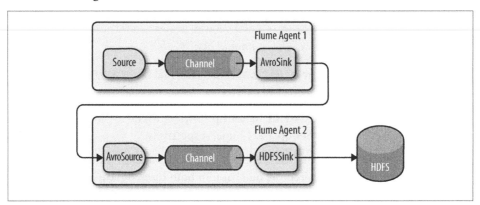

Figure 10-1. Flume architecture

Because Sqoop and Flume can be used to transfer sensitive data, it is important to consider the security implications of your ingest pipeline in the context of the overall deployment. In particular, you need to worry about the confidentiality, integrity, and availability (CIA) of your ingest pipeline. Confidentiality refers to limiting access to the data to a set of authorized users. Systems typically guarantee confidentiality by a combination of authentication, authorization, and encryption. Integrity refers to how much you can trust that data hasn't been tampered with. Most systems employ checksums or signatures to verify the integrity of data. Availability refers to keeping information resources available. In the context of data ingest, it means that your ingestion system is robust against the loss of some capacity and that it has the ability to preserve in-transit data while it's dealing with the outage of some downstream system or service.

Integrity of Ingested Data

The value of an analytic process is directly tied to the value of the data and data is only of value if it can be trusted. Thus, the integrity of data is essential. Hadoop is a complex, distributed system, so it's not surprising that data ingest flows are often equally complex and distributed. That means there are multiple places where data can be worked with, corrupted, and tampered with. Your specific threat model will determine the level of integrity your ingest pipeline requires. Most use cases are concerned with accidentally corrupted data, and for those a simple checksum of records or files is sufficient. To prevent tampering by malicious users, you can add cryptographic signatures and/or encryption of records.

One of the primary ways that Flume guarantees integrity is through its built-in, reliable channel implementations. Flume channels present a very simple interface that resembles an unbounded queue. Channels have a put(Event event) method for putting an event into a channel and a take() method for taking the next event from the channel. The default channel implementation is an in-memory channel. This implementation is reliable but only so long as the Flume agent stays up. This means that in the event of a process or server crash, data will be lost. Furthermore, because the events never leave memory, Flume assumes that events can't be tampered with and does not calculate or verify event checksums.

For users that care about reliable delivery of events and integrity, Flume offers a file-based channel. The file channel essentially implements a write-ahead log that is persisted to stable storage as each event is put into the channel. In addition to persisting the events to disk, the file channel calculates a checksum of each event and writes the checksum to the write-ahead log along with the event. When events are taken from the channel, the checksum is verified to ensure that the event has not been corrupted. This provides some integrity guarantees but is limited to the integrity of the event as it passes through the channel. Currently, Flume does not calculate checksums when passing events from one agent to another from the AvroSink to the AvroSource. TCP will still protect against accidental corruption of packets, but a man-in-the-middle who is able to manipulate packets could still corrupt data in a manner that is not detected. In the next section, we'll see that Flume does have the ability to encrypt the RPC protocol, which would prevent undetected corruption by a man-in-the-middle attack.

Before moving on to the integrity offered by Sqoop, let's quickly cover how Flume approaches availability. Flume lets users build a distributed data flow that guarantees at-least-once delivery semantics. Strictly speaking, Flume is available from the point-of-view of a particular data source as long as the first agent that communicates with the external source is available. As events proceed from agent to agent, any downtime of a downstream agent can be handled by using a failover sink processor that targets two or more downstream Flume agents as the target. You can also have both failure handling and load balancing by using the load balancing sink processor. This processor will send events to a set of downstream sinks in either a round robin or random fashion. If the downstream sink fails, it will retry with the next sink.

Both of these mechanisms improve availability of the overall data flow, but they don't guarantee availability of any particular event. There is a proposal to add a replicating channel that would replicate events to multiple agents before acknowledging the source, but until that is in place, events will be unavailable while nodes in the Flume cluster are down. No events will be lost unless the stable storage where the file channel logs data is unrecoverable. When building an ingest flow, it's important to keep these considerations in mind. We'll go into more detail on these kinds of trade-offs in "Enterprise Architecture" on page 235.

Unlike Flume, Sqoop does not have built-in support to verify the integrity of imports. Sqoop does have the advantage of having the same process pull data from the database as writes the data to HDFS. This means the probability of data corruption is relatively lower than it is with a complex Flume flow. As we'll see in the next section, it is possible to guarantee confidentiality with Sqoop by enabling SSL encryption. This will also improve integrity by making it much more difficult to tamper with records as they transit the network, but does nothing to prove that what made it to HDFS matches what was stored in the database. The current state of the art for verifying a Sqoop import is to round-trip the table—from the database, to Hadoop, and back to the database. You can then checksum the original table and the round-tripped table to verify that no data was lost. Unfortunately, this is a very expensive process and may require multiple full table scans depending on your database's checksum capabilities.

Data Ingest Confidentiality

Determining the level of confidentiality that your ingest flow requires depends on the type of data you're ingesting, the threat models that you're concerned with, and any regulatory requirements you may need to adhere to. While data is being ingested, it's vulnerable to be viewed by unauthorized persons while it is transiting the network and while it is staged on intermediate servers. Even when running on a trusted, corporate network, there may be certain classes of data that must always be encrypted to prevent unauthorized users that might have the access to sniff network traffic from seeing sensitive data. Likewise, the administrators of the servers that data transits through might not be authorized to access some of the data that is being ingested. In those cases, it is useful to encrypt the data prior to it hitting stable storage in order to prevent that unauthorized access.

Flume Encryption

)To solve the problem of unauthorized access to data as it transits the network, Flume supports enabling SSL encryption on your AvroSource and AvroSink. In addition to providing encryption, you can configure the AvroSource and AvroSink with trust policies to ensure that a sink is only sending data to a trusted source. Let's suppose we want to send events from a Flume agent running on flume01.example.com to a second agent running on flume02.example.com. The first thing we have to do is create an RSA private key for flume02 using the openssl command-line tool, as shown in Example 10-2.

Example 10-2. Creating a private key

```
[alice@flume02 ~]$ mkdir certs
[alice@flume02 ~]$ cd certs
[alice@flume02 certs]$ openssl genrsa -des3 -out flume02.key 1024
Generating RSA private key, 1024 bit long modulus
...............................................................
........++++++
....................++++++
e is 65537 (0x10001)
Enter pass phrase for flume02.key:
Verifying - Enter pass phrase for flume02.key:
[alice@flume02 certs]$
```

In Example 10-3, we generate a certificate signing request so that a certificate can be issued to the private key we just created.

Example 10-3. Creating a certificate signing request

```
[alice@flume02 certs]$ openssl req -new -key flume02.key -out flume02.csr
Enter pass phrase for flume02.key:
You are about to be asked to enter information that will be incorporated
into your certificate request.
What you are about to enter is what is called a Distinguished Name or a DN.
There are quite a few fields but you can leave some blank
For some fields there will be a default value,
If you enter '.', the field will be left blank.
---
Country Name (2 letter code) [XX]:US
State or Province Name (full name) []:California
Locality Name (eg, city) [Default City]:San Francisco
Organization Name (eg, company) [Default Company Ltd]:Cluster, Inc.
Organizational Unit Name (eg, section) []:
```

```
Common Name (eg, your name or your server's hostname) []:flume02.example.com
Email Address []:admin@example.com

Please enter the following 'extra' attributes
to be sent with your certificate request
A challenge password []:
An optional company name []:
[alice@flume02 certs]$
```

Once we have the certificate signing request, we can generate a certificate signed by a trusted key. In our example, we don't have a root signing authority, so we'll just create a self-signed certificate (a certificate signed by the same key that requested the certificate). In a real deployment, you'd send the certificate signing request to your corporate signing authority and they would provide the signed certificate. A self-signed certificate will work just fine for Example 10-4.

Example 10-4. Creating a self-signed certificate

```
[alice@flume02 certs]$ openssl x509 -req -days 365 -in flume02.csr \
  -signkey flume02.key -out flume02.crt
Signature ok
subject=/C=US/ST=California/L=San Francisco/O=Cluster, Inc./CN=flume02.cluster.
com/emailAddress=admin@example.com
Getting Private key
Enter pass phrase for flume02.key:
[alice@flume02 certs]$
```

We will be configuring the AvroSink on flume02 to use the key and certificate we've just made, but first we need to create a truststore that flume01 will be able to use to verify the authenticity of our key. In a real deployment, this truststore could be loaded with the certificate authority (CA) certificate of your corporate signing authority or a sub CA that is only trusted by your Flume cluster. This time we'll use Java's keytool to import the certificate into a Java truststore.

Example 10-5. Creating a Java truststore

```
[alice@flume02 certs]$ keytool -import -alias flume02.example.com \
  -file flume02.crt -keystore flume.truststore
Enter keystore password:
Re-enter new password:
Owner: EMAILADDRESS=admin@example.com, CN=flume02.example.com, O="Cluster, Inc.
", L=San Francisco, ST=California, C=US
Issuer: EMAILADDRESS=admin@example.com, CN=flume02.example.com, O="Cluster, Inc
.", L=San Francisco, ST=California, C=US
Serial number: 86a6cb314f86328b
Valid from: Tue Jun 24 11:31:50 PDT 2014 until: Wed Jun 24 11:31:50 PDT 2015
Certificate fingerprints:
        MD5:  B6:4A:A7:98:9B:60:3F:A2:5E:0B:BA:BA:12:B4:8D:68
        SHA1: AB:F4:AB:B3:2D:E1:AF:71:28:8B:60:54:2D:C1:C9:A8:73:18:92:31
```

```
        SHA256: B1:DD:C9:1D:AD:57:FF:47:28:D9:7F:A8:A3:DF:9C:BE:30:C1:49:CD:85
:D3:95:AD:95:36:DC:40:4C:72:15:AB
        Signature algorithm name: SHA1withRSA
        Version: 1
Trust this certificate? [no]:  yes
Certificate was added to keystore
[alice@flume02 certs]$
```

Before we can use our certificate and key with Flume, we need to load them into a file format that Java can read. Generally, this will be either a Java keystore *.jks* file or a PKCS12 *.p12*. Because Java's keytool doesn't have support for importing a separate key and certificate, we'll use `openssl` to generate a PKCS12 file and configure Flume to use that directly, as shown in Example 10-6.

Example 10-6. Creating a PKCS12 file with our key and certificate

```
[alice@flume02 certs]$ openssl pkcs12 -export -in flume02.crt \
  -inkey flume02.key -out flume02.p12 -name flume02.example.com
Enter pass phrase for flume02.key:
Enter Export Password:
Verifying - Enter Export Password:
[alice@flume02 certs]$
```

Prior to configuring Flume to use our certificate, we need to move the PKCS12 file into Flume's configuration directory, as shown in Example 10-7.

Example 10-7. Moving PKCS12 file to /etc/flume-ng/ssl

```
[root@flume02 ~]# mkdir /etc/flume-ng/ssl
[root@flume02 ~]# cp ~alice/certs/flume02.p12 /etc/flume-ng/ssl
[root@flume02 ~]# chown -R root:flume /etc/flume-ng/ssl
[root@flume02 ~]# chmod 750 /etc/flume-ng/ssl
[root@flume02 ~]# chmod 640 /etc/flume-ng/ssl/flume02.p12
```

In Example 10-8, you'll see that we also need to copy the truststore to `flume01.exam` `ple.com` so that the sink will know it can trust the source on `flume02.example.com`.

Example 10-8. SCP truststore to flume01.example.com

```
[root@flume02 ~]# scp ~alice/certs/flume.truststore flume01.example.com:/tmp/
```

Next, in Example 10-9, we move the truststore into Flume's configuration directory.

Example 10-9. Moving truststore to /etc/flume-ng/ssl

```
[root@flume01 ~]# mkdir /etc/flume-ng/ssl
[root@flume01 ~]# mv /tmp/flume.truststore /etc/flume-ng/ssl
[root@flume01 ~]# chown -R root:flume /etc/flume-ng/ssl
```

```
[root@flume01 ~]# chmod 750 /etc/flume-ng/ssl
[root@flume01 ~]# chmod 640 /etc/flume-ng/ssl/flume.truststore
```

Now that the PKCS12 and truststore files are in place, we can configure Flume's source and sink. We'll start with the sink on `flume01.example.com`. The key configuration parameters are as follows:

ssl

> Set to `true` to enable SSL for this sink. When SSL is enabled, you also need to configure the `trust-all-certs`, `truststore`, `truststore-password`, and `truststore-type` parameters.

trust-all-certs

> Set to `true` to disable certificate verification. It's highly recommended that you set this parameter to `false`, as that will ensure that the sink checks that the source it connects to is using a trusted certificate.

truststore

> Set this to the full path of the Java truststore file. If left blank, Flume will use the default Java certificate authority files. The Oracle JRE ships with a file called *$JAVA_HOME/jre/lib/security/cacerts*, which will be used unless a site-specific truststore is created in *$JAVA_HOME/jre/lib/security/jssecacerts*.

truststore-password

> Set this to the password that protects the truststore.

truststore-type

> Set this to JKS or another supported truststore type.

Example 10-10 shows an example configuration.

Example 10-10. Avro SSL sink configuration

```
a1.sinks = s1
a1.channels = c1
a1.sinks.s1.type = avro
a1.sinks.s1.channels = c1
a1.sinks.s1.hostname = flume02.example.com
a1.sinks.s1.port = 4141
a1.sinks.s1.ssl = true
a1.sinks.s1.trust-all-certs = false
a1.sinks.s1.truststore = /etc/flume-ng/ssl/flume.truststore
a1.sinks.s1.truststore-password = password
a1.sinks.s1.truststore-type = JKS
```

On `flume02.example.com`, we can configure the AvroSource to use our certificate and private key to listen for connections. The key configuration parameters are as follows:

ssl
> Set to `true` to enable SSL for this sink. When SSL is enabled, you also need to configure the `keystore`, `keystore-password`, and `keystore-type` parameters.

keystore
> Set this to the full path of the Java keystore.

keystore-password
> Set this to the password that protects the keystore.

keystore-type
> Set this to `JKS` or `PKCS12`.

Example 10-11. Avro SSL source configuration

```
a2.sources = r1
a2.channels = c1
a2.sources.r1.type = avro
a2.sources.r1.channels = c1
a2.sources.r1.bind = 0.0.0.0
a2.sources.r1.port = 4141
a2.sources.r1.ssl = true
a2.sources.r1.keystore = /etc/flume-ng/ssl/flume02.p12
a2.sources.r1.keystore-password = password
a2.sources.r1.keystore-type = PKCS12
```

In addition to protecting your data over the wire, you might need to ensure that data is encrypted on the drives where Flume writes events as they transit a channel. One option is to use a third-party encryption tool that supports full disk encryption on the drives your Flume channel writes to. This could also be done with dm-crypt/LUKS.[1] However, full disk encryption might be overkill, especially if Flume is not the only service using the log drives or if not all events need to be encrypted.

For those use cases, Flume offers the ability to encrypt the logfiles used by the file channel. The current implementation only supports AES encryption in Counter mode with no padding (AES/CTR/NOPADDING), but it is possible to add additional algorithms and modes in the future. Flume currently only supports the *JCE keystore implementation* (JCEKS) as the key provider. Again, nothing precludes adding support for additional key providers but it would require a modification to Flume itself, as there is not currently a pluggable interface for adding key providers. Despite these limitations, Flume does support key rotation to help improve security. Because the file channel logfiles are relatively short lived, you can rotate keys as frequently as nec-

---

[1] To make setup of dm-crypt/LUKS easier, you can use the cryptsetup tool. Instructions for setting up dm-crypt/LUKS using cryptsetup are available on the cryptsetup FAQ page (*http://bit.ly/1Hc9zCz*).

essary to meet your requirements. In order to ensure that logfiles written with the previous key are still readable, you must maintain old keys for reading while only the newest key is used for writing.

To set up Flume's on-disk encryption for the file channel, start by generating a key, as shown in Example 10-12.

Example 10-12. Generating the key for on-disk encrypted file channel

```
[root@flume01 ~]# mkdir keys
[root@flume01 ~]# cd keys/
[root@flume01 keys]# keytool -genseckey -alias key-0 -keyalg AES -keysize 256 \
  -validity 9000 -keystore flume.keystore -storetype jceks
Enter keystore password:
Re-enter new password:
Enter key password for <key-0>
        (RETURN if same as keystore password):
Re-enter new password:
[root@flume01 keys]#
```

In our example, we set the keystore password to keyStorePassword and the key password to keyPassword. In a real deployment, stronger passwords should be used. Keytool won't show what you are typing nor will it show the familiar asterisk characters, so type carefully. You can also provide the keystore password and key password on the command line with -storepass *keyStorePassword* and -keypass *keyPassword*, respectively. It's generally not recommended to include passwords on the command line, as they will typically get written to your shell's history file, which should not be considered secure. Next, let's copy the keystore to Flume's configuration directory in Example 10-13.

Example 10-13. Copying the keystore to Flume's configuration directory

```
[root@flume01 ~]# mkdir /etc/flume-ng/encryption
[root@flume01 ~]# cp ~/keys/flume.keystore /etc/flume-ng/encryption/
[root@flume01 ~]# cat > /etc/flume-ng/encryption/keystore.password
keyStorePassword
^D
[root@flume01 ~]# cat > /etc/flume-ng/encryption/key-0.password
keyPassword
^D
[root@flume01 ~]# chown -R root:flume /etc/flume-ng/encryption
[root@flume01 ~]# chmod 750 /etc/flume-ng/encryption
[root@flume01 ~]# chmod 640 /etc/flume-ng/encryption/*
[root@flume01 ~]#
```

Notice that we also created files that contain the keystore password and key passwords. Where the listing shows ^D, you should hold down the Control key and type the letter D on the keyboard. Generating these files helps to keep the passwords protected, as they won't be accessible to the same users that can read Flume's configuration file. Now we can configure Flume to enable encryption on the file channel, as shown in Example 10-14.

Example 10-14. Encrypted file channel configuration

```
a1.channels = c1
a1.channels.c1.type = file
a1.channels.c1.checkpointDir = /data/01/flume/checkpoint
a1.channels.c1.dataDirs = /data/02/flume/data,/data/03/flume/data
a1.channels.c1.encryption.cipherProvider = AESCTRNOPADDING
a1.channels.c1.encryption.activeKey = key-0
a1.channels.c1.encryption.keyProvider = JCEKSFILE
a1.channels.c1.encryption.keyProvider.keyStoreFile =
  /etc/flume-ng/encryption/flume.keystore
a1.channels.c1.encryption.keyProvider.keyStorePasswordFile =
  /etc/flume-ng/encryption/keystore.password
a1.channels.c1.encryption.keys = key-0
a1.channels.c1.encryption.keys.key-0.passwordFile =
  /etc/flume-ng/encryption/key-0.password
```

 Examples 10-14 through 10-16 show some configuration settings (`a1.channels.c1.encryption.keyProvider.keyStorePassword File`, `a1.channels.c1.encryption.keys.key-0.passwordFile`) split across two lines. These are meant to improve readability of the examples, but are not valid for a Flume configuration file. All setting names and values must be on the same line.

Over time, it might become necessary to rotate in a new encryption key to mitigate the risk of an older key becoming compromised. Flume supports configuring multiple keys for decryption while only using the latest key for encryption. The old keys must be maintained to ensure that old logfiles that were written before the rotation can still be read. We can extend our example in Example 10-15 by generating a new key and updating Flume to make it the active key.

Example 10-15. Generating a new key for on-disk encrypted file channel

```
[root@flume01 ~]# keytool -genseckey -alias key-1 -keyalg AES -keysize 256 \
  -validity 9000 -keystore /etc/flume-ng/encryption/flume.keystore \
  -storetype jceks
Enter keystore password:
Enter key password for <key-1>
       (RETURN if same as keystore password):
Re-enter new password:
[root@flume01 ~]# cat > /etc/flume-ng/encryption/key-1.password
key1Password
^D
```

```
[root@flume01 ~]# chmod 640 /etc/flume-ng/encryption/*
[root@flume01 ~]#
```

Now that we've added our new key to the keystore and created the associate key password file, we can update Flume's configuration to make the new key the active key, as shown in Example 10-16.

Example 10-16. Encrypted file channel new key configuration

```
a1.channels = c1
a1.channels.c1.type = file
a1.channels.c1.checkpointDir = /data/01/flume/checkpoint
a1.channels.c1.dataDirs = /data/02/flume/data,/data/03/flume/data
a1.channels.c1.encryption.cipherProvider = AESCTRNOPADDING
a1.channels.c1.encryption.activeKey = key-1
a1.channels.c1.encryption.keyProvider = JCEKSFILE
a1.channels.c1.encryption.keyProvider.keyStoreFile =
  /etc/flume-ng/encryption/flume.keystore
a1.channels.c1.encryption.keyProvider.keyStorePasswordFile =
  /etc/flume-ng/encryption/keystore.password
a1.channels.c1.encryption.keys = key-0 key-1
a1.channels.c1.encryption.keys.key-0.passwordFile =
  /etc/flume-ng/encryption/key-0.password
a1.channels.c1.encryption.keys.key-1.passwordFile =
  /etc/flume-ng/encryption/key-1.password
```

Here is a summary of the parameters for configuring file channel encryption:

encryption.activeKey
: The alias for the key used to encrypt new data.

encryption.cipherProvider
: The type of the cipher provider. Supported providers: *AESCTRNOPADDING*

encryption.keyProvider
: The type of the key provider. Supported providers: *JCEKSFILE*

encryption.keyProvider.keyStoreFile
: The path to the keystore file.

encryption.keyProvider.keyStorePasswordFile
: The path to a file that contains the password for the keystore.

encryption.keyProvider.keys
: A space-delimited list of key aliases that are or have been the active key.

encryption.keyProvider.keys.*<key>*.passwordFile
: An optional path to a file that contains the password for the key *key*. If omitted, the password from the keystore password file is used for all keys.

Sqoop Encryption

Unlike Flume, Sqoop does not have its own native support for encryption over the wire. This isn't surprising because Sqoop relies on standard JDBC drivers and/or optimized connectors that are database specific. However, Sqoop can be configured to connect to a database that supports SSL with SSL enabled. This will enable encryption for data that flows through the JDBC channel.

This support is not necessarily limited to the generic JDBC implementation. If the tool that is used to implement `--direct` mode supports SSL, you can still encrypt data even when using the direct connector.

Let's take a look at how we can use SSL to encrypt traffic between Sqoop and MySQL.[1] Examples 10-17 and 10-18 assume that SSL is already configured for MySQL.[2] If you have not already done so, download the MySQL JDBC drivers from MySQL's connector download page (*http://dev.mysql.com/downloads/connector/j/5.1.html*). After you download the connector, install it in a location to make it available to Sqoop, as shown in Example 10-17.

Example 10-17. Installing the MySQL JDBC driver for Sqoop

```
[root@sqoop01 ~]# SQOOP_HOME=/usr/lib/sqoop
[root@sqoop01 ~]# tar -zxf mysql-connector-java-*.tar.gz
[root@sqoop01 ~]# cp mysql-connector-java-*/mysql-connector-java-*-bin.jar \
  ${SQOOP_HOME}/lib
[root@sqoop01 ~]#
```

When the driver is in place, you can test the connection by using Sqoop's `list-tables` command, as shown in Example 10-18.

Example 10-18. Testing SSL connection by listing tables

```
[alice@sqoop01 ~]$ URI="jdbc:mysql://mysql01.example.com/sqoop"
[alice@sqoop01 ~]$ URI="${URI}?verifyServerCertificate=false"
[alice@sqoop01 ~]$ URI="${URI}&useSSL=true"
[alice@sqoop01 ~]$ URI="${URI}&requireSSL=true"
[alice@sqoop01 ~]$ sqoop list-tables --connect ${URI} \
  --username sqoop -P
Enter password:
cities
```

---

1 The Sqoop examples are based on the Apache Sqoop Cookbook by Kathleen Ting and Jarek Jarcec Cecho (O'Reilly). The example files and scripts used are available from the *Apache Sqoop Cookbook* project page (*https://github.com/jarcec/Apache-Sqoop-Cookbook*).

2 If SSL has not yet been configured for MySQL, you can follow the instructions in the MySQL manual (*http://dev.mysql.com/doc/refman/5.7/en/ssl-connections.html*).

```
countries
normcities
staging_cities
visits
[alice@sqoop01 ~]$
```

The parameters that tell the MySQL JDBC driver to use SSL encryption are provided as options to the JDBC URI passed to Sqoop:

verifyServerCertificate
> Controls whether the client should validate the MySQL server's certificate. If set to true, you also need to set trustCertificateKeyStoreUrl, trustCertificate KeyStoreType, and trustCertificateKeyStorePassword.

useSSL
> When set to true, the client will attempt to use SSL when talking to the server.

requireSSL
> When set to true, the client will reject connections if the server doesn't support SSL.

Now let's try importing a table over SSL in Example 10-19.

Example 10-19. Importing a MySQL table over SSL

```
[alice@sqoop01 ~]$ URI="jdbc:mysql://mysql01.example.com/sqoop"
[alice@sqoop01 ~]$ URI="${URI}?verifyServerCertificate=false"
[alice@sqoop01 ~]$ URI="${URI}&useSSL=true"
[alice@sqoop01 ~]$ URI="${URI}&requireSSL=true"
[alice@sqoop01 ~]$ sqoop import --connect ${URI} \
  --username sqoop -P --table cities
Enter password:
...
14/06/27 16:09:07 INFO mapreduce.ImportJobBase: Retrieved 3 records.
[alice@sqoop01 ~]$ hdfs dfs -cat cities/part-m-*
1,USA,Palo Alto
2,Czech Republic,Brno
3,USA,Sunnyvale
[alice@sqoop01 ~]$
```

You can see that it is as simple as once again including the SSL parameters in the JDBC URI. We can confirm that the SSL parameters are used while the job executes by looking at the configuration of the job in the Job History Server's page, as shown in Figure 10-2.

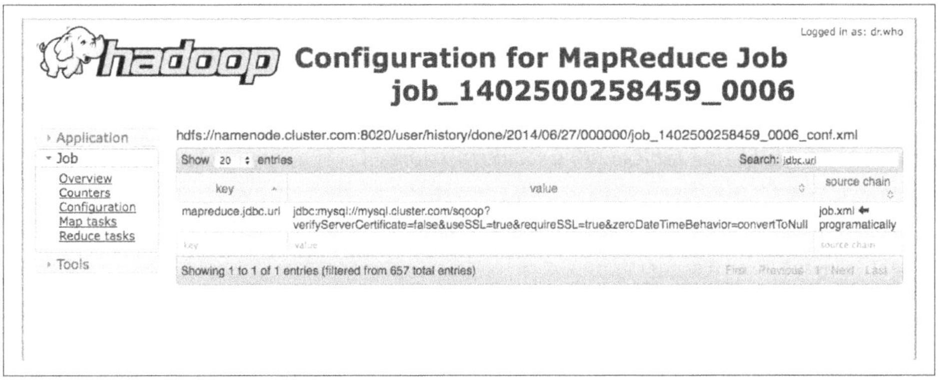

Figure 10-2. Job History Server page showing use of SSL JDBC settings

In the previous example, we set `verifyServerCertificate` to `false`. While this is useful for testing, in a production setting we'd much rather verify that the server we're connecting to is in fact the server we expect it to be. Let's see what happens if we attempt to set that parameter to true in Example 10-20.

Example 10-20. Certificate verification fails without a truststore

```
[alice@sqoop01 ~]$ URI="jdbc:mysql://mysql01.example.com/sqoop"
[alice@sqoop01 ~]$ URI="${URI}?verifyServerCertificate=true"
[alice@sqoop01 ~]$ URI="${URI}&useSSL=true"
[alice@sqoop01 ~]$ URI="${URI}&requireSSL=true"
[alice@sqoop01 ~]$ sqoop list-tables --connect ${URI} \
  --username sqoop -P
Enter password:
14/06/30 10:52:29 ERROR manager.CatalogQueryManager: Failed to list tables
com.mysql.jdbc.exceptions.jdbc4.CommunicationsException: Communications link failure

The last packet successfully received from the server was 1,469 milliseconds ago.  Th
e last packet sent successfully to the server was 1,464 milliseconds ago.
        at sun.reflect.NativeConstructorAccessorImpl.newInstance0(Native Method)
...
        at org.apache.sqoop.Sqoop.main(Sqoop.java:240)
Caused by: javax.net.ssl.SSLHandshakeException: sun.security.validator.ValidatorExcep
tion: PKIX path building failed: sun.security.provider.certpath.SunCertPathBuilderExc
eption: unable to find valid certification path to requested target
...
[alice@sqoop01 ~]$
```

Unsurprisingly, this didn't work, as Java's standard certificate truststores don't include our MySQL server's certificate as a trusted certificate. The key error message to look for when diagnosing these kinds of trust issues is `unable to find valid certifica tion path to requested target`. That basically means that there is no signing path from any of our trusted certificates to the server's certificate. The easiest way to remedy this is to import the MySQL server's certificate into a truststore and instruct the MySQL JDBC driver to use that truststore when connecting, as shown in Example 10-21.

Example 10-21. Listing tables with a local truststore

```
[alice@sqoop01 ~]$ keytool \
  -import \
  -alias mysql.example.com \
  -file mysql.example.com.crt \
  -keystore sqoop-jdbc.ts
Enter keystore password:
Re-enter new password:
Owner: EMAILADDRESS=admin@example.com, CN=mysql.example.com, O="Cluster, Inc.",
L=San Francisco, ST=California, C=US
Issuer: EMAILADDRESS=admin@example.com, CN=mysql.example.com, O="Cluster, Inc."
, L=San Francisco, ST=California, C=US
Serial number: d7f528349bee94f3
Valid from: Fri Jun 27 13:59:05 PDT 2014 until: Sat Jun 27 13:59:05 PDT 2015
Certificate fingerprints:
         MD5:  38:9E:F4:D0:4C:14:A8:DF:06:EC:A5:59:76:D1:0C:21
         SHA1: AD:D0:CB:E2:70:C1:89:83:22:32:DE:EF:E5:2B:E5:4F:7E:49:9E:0A
         Signature algorithm name: SHA1withRSA
         Version: 1
Trust this certificate? [no]:  yes
Certificate was added to keystore
[alice@sqoop01 ~]$ URI="jdbc:mysql://mysql01.example.com/sqoop"
[alice@sqoop01 ~]$ URI="${URI}?verifyServerCertificate=true"
[alice@sqoop01 ~]$ URI="${URI}&useSSL=true"
[alice@sqoop01 ~]$ URI="${URI}&requireSSL=true"
[alice@sqoop01 ~]$ URI="${URI}&trustCertificateKeyStoreUrl=file:sqoop-jdbc.ts
[alice@sqoop01 ~]$ URI="${URI}&trustCertificateKeyStoreType=JKS"
[alice@sqoop01 ~]$ URI="${URI}&trustCertificateKeyStorePassword=password"
[alice@sqoop01 ~]$ sqoop list-tables --connect ${URI} \
  --username sqoop -P
Enter password:
cities
countries
normcities
staging_cities
visits
[alice@sqoop01 ~]$
```

Here, we first create a truststore with the MySQL server's certificate and then we point the MySQL JDBC driver to the truststore. This requires us to set some additional parameters in the JDBC URI, namely:

trustCertificateKeyStoreUrl

A URL pointing to the location of the keystore used to verify the MySQL server's certificate.

trustCertificateKeyStoreType

The type of the keystore used to verify the MySQL server's certificate.

trustCertificateKeyStorePassword

The password of the keystore used to verify the MySQL server's certificate.

Notice that we specify the location of the truststore with a relative file:*<URI>*. This will become important in the next example. Now that we can list tables, lets try doing an import in Example 10-22.

Example 10-22. Importing tables with a truststore

```
[alice@sqoop01 ~]$ URI="jdbc:mysql://mysql01.example.com/sqoop"
[alice@sqoop01 ~]$ URI="${URI}?verifyServerCertificate=true"
[alice@sqoop01 ~]$ URI="${URI}&useSSL=true"
[alice@sqoop01 ~]$ URI="${URI}&requireSSL=true"
[alice@sqoop01 ~]$ URI="${URI}&trustCertificateKeyStoreUrl=file:sqoop-jdbc.ts"
[alice@sqoop01 ~]$ URI="${URI}&trustCertificateKeyStoreType=JKS"
[alice@sqoop01 ~]$ URI="${URI}&trustCertificateKeyStorePassword=password"
[alice@sqoop01 ~]$ sqoop import \
  -files sqoop-jdbc.ts \
  --connect ${URI} \
  --username sqoop \
  -P \
  --table cities
Enter password:
...
14/06/30 10:57:13 INFO mapreduce.ImportJobBase: Retrieved 3 records.
[alice@sqoop01 ~]$
```

Not much has changed, except we're using the same URI as the last list-tables example and we've added a -files command-line argument. The -files switch will place the list of files into Hadoop's distributed cache. The distributed cache copies the files to each node in the cluster and places them in the working directory of the running task. This is useful, as it means our specification for the trustCertificateKeyS toreUrl works for both the local machine and all of the nodes where tasks are executed. That is why we wanted the truststore to be in the working directory where we launched the Sqoop job.

Encryption support is not limited to generic mode. In particular, MySQL's direct mode uses the mysqldump and mysqlimport tools, which support SSL. Let's see how we'd enable SSL in direct mode in Example 10-23.

Example 10-23. Importing tables with a truststore using direct mode

```
[alice@sqoop01 ~]$ URI="jdbc:mysql://mysql01.example.com/sqoop"
[alice@sqoop01 ~]$ URI="${URI}?verifyServerCertificate=true"
[alice@sqoop01 ~]$ URI="${URI}&useSSL=true"
```

```
[alice@sqoop01 ~]$ URI="${URI}&requireSSL=true"
[alice@sqoop01 ~]$ URI="${URI}&trustCertificateKeyStoreUrl=file:sqoop-jdbc.ts"
[alice@sqoop01 ~]$ URI="${URI}&trustCertificateKeyStoreType=JKS"
[alice@sqoop01 ~]$ URI="${URI}&trustCertificateKeyStorePassword=password"
[alice@sqoop01 ~]$ sqoop import \
  -files sqoop-jdbc.ts,mysql.example.com.crt \
  --connect ${URI} \
  --username sqoop \
  -P \
  --table cities \
  --direct \
  -- \
    --ssl \
    --ssl-ca=mysql.example.com \
    --ssl-verify-server-cert
Enter password:
...
14/06/30 15:32:43 INFO mapreduce.ImportJobBase: Retrieved 3 records.
[alice@sqoop01 ~]$
```

Again, this is very similar to our last example. The main differences are that we added
mysql.example.com.crt to the -files switch so that the nodes will have the PEM-
formatted certificate file that will be required by the mysqldump tool. We also added
the --direct switch to enable direct mode. Finally, we added a -- switch followed by
--ssl, --ssl-ca=mysql.example.com, and --ssl-verify-server-cert. The --
switch indicates that all following arguments should be passed to the tool that implements direct mode. The rest of the arguments will be processed by mysqldump to
enable SSL, set the location of the CA certificate, and to tell mysqldump to verify the
MySQL server's certificate.

Ingest Workflows

So far, we've looked at how data is commonly ingested into a Hadoop environment
and the different options for confidentiality, integrity, and availability for those ingest
pipelines. However, ingesting data is typically part of an overall ETL process and
additional considerations must be made in the context of the overall ETL flow.

One detail that we glossed over is *where* tools like Sqoop are launched from. Typically,
you want to limit the interfaces that users have access to. As described in "Remote
Access Controls" on page 43, there are numerous ways that access to remote protocols can be secured, and the exact architecture will depend on your needs. The most
common way of limiting access to edge services, including ingest, is to deploy services like Flume and Sqoop to *edge nodes*. Edge nodes are simply servers that have
access to both the internal Hadoop cluster network and the outside world. Typical
cluster deployments will lock down access to specific ports on specific hosts through
the use of either host or network firewalls. In the context of data ingest, we can

restrict the ability to *push* data to a Hadoop cluster through the edge nodes while still deploying *pull*-based mechanisms, such as Sqoop, to perform parallel ingest without opening up access to sensitive Hadoop services to the world.

Limiting remote login capabilities to only edge nodes goes a long way toward mitigating the risk of having users be physically logged into a Hadoop cluster. It allows you to concentrate your monitoring and security auditing while at the same time reducing the population of potential bad actors. When building production data flows, it's common to set up dedicated ETL accounts or groups that will execute the overall workflow. For organizations that require detailed auditing, it's recommended that actions be initiated by individual user accounts to better track activity back to a person.

In addition to Flume and Sqoop, edge nodes may run proxy services or other remote user protocols. For example, HDFS supports a proxy server called HttpFS, which exposes a read/write REST interface for HDFS. Just as with HDFS itself, HttpFS fully supports Kerberos-based authentication, and the same authorization controls built into HDFS apply when it's accessed through HttpFS. Running HttpFS on an edge node can be useful for allowing limited access to the data stored in HDFS and can even be used for certain data ingest use cases.

Another common edge node service is Oozie. Ooze is a workflow execution and scheduling tool. Complex workflows that combine Sqoop jobs, Hive queries, Pig scripts, and MapReduce jobs can be composed into single units and can be reliably executed and scheduled using Oozie. Oozie also provides a REST interface that supports Kerberos-based authentication and can be safely exposed to an edge node.

For some use cases, it is necessary to stage files on an edge node before they are pushed into HDFS, HBase, or Accumulo. When creating these local disk (or sometimes NFS-mounted) staging directories, it is important to use your standard operating system controls to limit access to only those users authorized to access the data. Again, it's useful to define one or more ETL groups and limit the access to raw data to these relatively trusted groups.

Enterprise Architecture

This discussion of data ingest helps to illustrate a useful point: Hadoop is never deployed in a vacuum. Hadoop necessarily integrates with your existing and evolving enterprise architecture. This means that you can't consider Hadoop security on its own. When deciding how to secure your cluster, you must look at the requirements that already apply to your data and systems. These requirements will be driven by enterprise security standards, threat models, and specific dataset sensitivity. In particular, it doesn't make sense to lock down a Hadoop cluster or the data ingest pipeline that feeds the cluster if the source of the data has no security wrapped around it.

This is no different than when data warehousing systems were introduced to the enterprise. In a typical deployment, applications are tightly coupled with the transactional systems that back them. This makes security integration straightforward because access to the backend database is typically limited to the application that is generating and serving the data. Some attention to security detail gets introduced as soon as that transactional data is important enough to back up. However, this is still a relatively easy integration to make, because the backups can be restricted to trusted administrators that already have access to the source systems.

Where things get interesting is when you want to move data from these transactional systems into analytic data warehouses so that analysis can be performed independently of the application. Using a traditional data warehouse system, you would compare the security configuration of the transactional database with the features of the new data warehouse. This works fine for securing that data once it's in the warehouse and you can apply the same analysis to the database-based authorization features available in Sentry. However, care must be taken in how the data is handled between the transactional system and the analysis platform.

With these traditional systems, this comes down to securing the ETL grid that is used to load data into the data warehouse. It's clear that the same considerations that you make to your ETL grid would apply to the ingest pipeline of a Hadoop cluster. In particular, you have to consider when and where encryption was necessary to protect the confidentiality of data. You need to pay close attention to how to maintain the integrity of your data. This is especially true of traditional ETL grids that might not have enough storage capacity to maintain raw data after it has been transformed. And lastly, you care about the availability of the ETL grid to make sure that it does not impact the ability of the source systems or data warehouse to meet the requirements of their users. This is exactly the same process we went through in our discussion of data ingest into Hadoop in general, and with Flume and Sqoop in particular.

Again, this works in both directions. It doesn't make sense to apply security controls to Hadoop at ingest or query time that are not maintained in source systems, just as it doesn't make sense to leave Hadoop wide open after careful work has gone into designing the security protections of your existing transactional or analytic tools. The perfect time to consider all of these factors is when you're designing your ingest pipeline. Because that is where Hadoop will integrate with the rest of your enterprise architecture, it's the perfect time to compare security and threat models and to carefully consider the security architecture of your overall Hadoop deployment.

Summary

In this chapter, we focused on the movement of data from external sources to Hadoop. After briefly talking about batch file ingest, we moved on to focus on the ingestion of event-based data with Flume, and the ingestion of data sourced from relational databases using Sqoop. What we found is that these common mechanisms for ingest have the ability to protect the integrity of data in transit. A key takeaway from this chapter is that the protection of data inside the cluster needs to be extended all the way to the source of ingest. This mode of protection should match the level in place at the source systems.

Now that we have covered protection of both data ingestion and data inside the cluster, we can move on to the final topic of data protection, which is to secure data extraction and client access.

## CHAPTER 11

Data Extraction and Client Access Security

One of the core philosophies of Hadoop is to bring processing to the data rather than the other way around, so our focus has been on how security works inside the cluster. In this chapter, we'll cover the last mile of securing a Hadoop cluster, namely securing client access and data extraction. While most of the processing of Hadoop data is done on the cluster itself, users will access that data via external tools, and some use cases, such as an enterprise data warehouse, require extracting potentially large volumes of data for use in specialized tools.

The most basic form of client access comes in the form of command-line tools. As we described in "Edge Nodes" on page 42, it's common for clusters to limit external access to a small set of *edge nodes*. Users use ssh to remotely log into an edge node and then use various command-line tools to interact with the cluster. A brief description of the most common commands is shown in Table 11-1.

Table 11-1. Common command-line tools for client access

Command	Description
hdfs dfs -put <src> <dst>	Copy a local file into HDFS
hdfs dfs -get <src> <dst>	Download a file from HDFS to the local filesystem
hdfs dfs -cat <path>	Print the contents of a file to standard out
hdfs dfs -ls <path>	List the files and directories in a path
hdfs dfs -mkdir <path>	Make a directory in HDFS
hdfs dfs -cp <src> <dst>	Copy an HDFS file to a new location

Command	Description
`hdfs dfs -mv <src> <dst>`	Move an HDFS file to a new location
`hdfs dfs -rm <path>`	Remove a file from HDFS
`hdfs dfs -rmdir <path>`	Remove a directory from HDFS
`hdfs dfs -chgrp <group> <path>`	Change the group of a file or directory
`hdfs dfs -chmod <mode> <path>`	Change the permissions on a file or directory
`hdfs dfs -chown <owner>[:<group>] <path>`	Change the owner of a file or directory
`yarn jar <jar> [<main-class>] <args>`	Run a JAR file, typically used to launch a MapReduce or other YARN job
`yarn application -list`	List running YARN applications
`yarn application -kill <app-id>`	Kill a YARN application
`mapred job -list`	List running MapReduce jobs
`mapred job -status <job-id>`	Get the status of a MapReduce job
`mapred job -kill <job-id>`	Kill a MapReduce job
`hive`	Start a Hive SQL shell (deprecated; use beeline instead)
`beeline`	Start a SQL shell for Hive or Impala
`impala-shell`	Start an Impala SQL shell
`hbase shell`	Start an HBase shell
`accumulo shell`	Start an Accumulo shell
`oozie job`	Run, inspect, and kill Oozie jobs
`sqoop export`	Export a table from HDFS to a database
`sqoop import`	Import a table from a database to HDFS

Hadoop Command-Line Interface

The core Hadoop command-line tools (hdfs, yarn, and mapred) only support Kerberos or delegation tokens for authentication. The easiest way to authenticate these commands is to obtain your Kerberos ticket-granting ticket[1] using kinit before executing a command. If you don't obtain your TGT before executing a Hadoop command, you'll see an error similar to Example 11-1. In particular, you're looking for the message failed to find any Kerberos tgt.

Example 11-1. Executing a Hadoop command with no Kerberos ticket-granting ticket

```
[alice@hadoop01 ~]$ hdfs dfs -cat movies.psv
cat: Failed on local exception: java.io.IOException: javax.security.sasl.SaslExc
eption: GSS initiate failed [Caused by GSSException: No valid credentials provid
ed (Mechanism level: Failed to find any Kerberos tgt)]; Host Details : local hos
t is: "hadoop01.example.com/172.25.2.196"; destination host is: "hadoop02.exampl
e.com":8020;
```

Now let's see what happens after Alice first obtains her TGT using kinit (Example 11-2).

Example 11-2. Executing a Hadoop command after kinit

```
[alice@hadoop01 ~]$ kinit
Password for alice@EXAMPLE.COM:
[alice@hadoop01 ~]$ hdfs dfs -cat movies.psv
1|Toy Story (1995)|01-Jan-1995|||http://us.imdb.com/M/title-exact?Toy%20Story%20(
...
```

This time the command completes successfully and prints the contents of the file *movies.psv*. One of the advantages to using Kerberos for authentication is that the user doesn't need to authenticate individually for each command. If you kinit at the beginning of your session or have your Linux system configured to obtain your Kerberos TGT during login, then you can run any number of Hadoop commands and all of the authentication will happen behind the scenes.

While not typically done, it is possible for command-line tools to authenticate with HDFS using delegation tokens. In order to fetch a delegation token, you need to be authenticated with Kerberos. HDFS provides a command-line tool for fetching a delegation token to a file. That token can then be used for subsequent HDFS commands by setting the HADOOP_TOKEN_FILE_LOCATION environment variable. See Example 11-3 for an example using delegation tokens.

---

1 Refer back to Table 4-1 for a refresher on TGTs.

Example 11-3. Executing a Hadoop command using delegation tokens

```
[alice@hadoop01 ~]$ kinit
Password for alice@EXAMPLE.COM:
[alice@hadoop01 ~]$ hdfs fetchdt --renewer alice nn.dt
14/10/21 19:19:32 INFO hdfs.DFSClient: Created HDFS_DELEGATION_TOKEN token 2 for
 alice on 172.25.3.210:8020
Fetched token for 172.25.3.210:8020 into file:/home/alice/nn.dt
[alice@hadoop01 ~]$ kdestroy
[alice@hadoop01 ~]$ export HADOOP_TOKEN_FILE_LOCATION=nn.dt
[alice@hadoop01 ~]$ hdfs dfs -cat movies.psv
1|Toy Story (1995)|01-Jan-1995||http://us.imdb.com/M/title-exact?Toy%20Story%20(
...
```

Delegation tokens are completely separate from Kerberos-based authentication. Once issued, a delegation token is valid for 24 hours by default and can be renewed for up to 7 days. You can change how long the token is initially valid for by setting `dfs.namenode.delegation.token.renewal-interval`, which is expressed as the amount of time in milliseconds the token is valid before needing to be renewed. You can set `dfs.namenode.delegation.token.max-lifetime` to change the max renewal lifetime of a token. This setting is also in milliseconds. These tokens are separate from the Kerberos system, so if your Kerberos credentials are revoked in the KDC, your delegation tokens will continue to remain valid for their designated lifetime. There is no administrative way to forcibly revoke delegation tokens.

The Hadoop command-line tools don't have their own authorization model. Rather, they rely on the cluster configuration to control what users can access. For a refresher on Hadoop authorization, refer back to "HDFS Authorization" on page 97, "Service-Level Authorization" on page 101, and "MapReduce and YARN Authorization" on page 114.

Securing Applications

When developing an application there are a lot of design choices that must be made, such as what framework to use for the user interface or what system to use for back-end storage. One of the most critical factors in application design is how to secure an application. This is often made more complicated by the large number of interfaces that the application will integrate with.

There are generally two schools of thought when it comes to where data authorization should take place. On the one hand, security in general (and authorization in particular) is viewed as an application-level concern. This view makes sense as applications typically have a lot more context with respect to how data should be controlled. The downside to punting authorization to applications is that it means each application has to re-implement common services. Over time, databases evolved so that the database can store and enforce authorization controls while letting the application push authorization labels down to the database. This was one of the major motivations for adding cell-level visibility tags to Accumulo and cell-level ACLs and visibility tags to HBase.

Closely related to where authorization decisions are made is how deep do user accounts go? Historically, databases have maintained their own private identity directories. This often made it complicated to try and replicate each user in a corporate directory in the database. Accumulo still uses its own identity directory so it shares this drawback. In response to this, many application developers adopted a pattern where the database would store application-level accounts and it was the application's responsibility to downgrade its access to take advantage of database-level authorizations.

The ability to downgrade access is why Accumulo requires users to pass in a list of authorizations when accessing Accumulo via the Java API. This allows an application to perform authentication with the end user and to look up the user's authorizations using a central service. The application will then pass these end user authorizations when reading data. Accumulo will automatically intersect the application's authorizations with the end user's authorizations. This means that you can control the maximum level of data that an application can access while still providing end users with finer-grained access based on their individual level.

Ultimately, it's an application developer's prerogative how deep they want end-user authentication to go. Over time, as applications and the Hadoop-based data stores integrate into the same identity directories, it will be easier for application developers to make an informed design decision. This is not an area of security where one size fits all, and it's constantly evolving.

HBase

In Chapter 5, we saw how to configure HBase to use Kerberos for authentication. HBase clients can access HBase via the shell, the Java API, or through one of the HBase gateway servers. All of the client access APIs support Kerberos for authentication and require that the user first obtain a Kerberos TGT before connecting.

The method of client access depends on your use case. For database administrative access such as creating, modifying, or deleting tables, the HBase shell is commonly used. When using MapReduce or another data processing framework, access is through the Java API. Other types of HBase applications may use the Java API directly or access HBase through a gateway. It's especially common to use one of the gateway APIs when accessing HBase from a language other than Java. The gateways also provide a choke point for administrators to restrict direct access to HBase. Next, we'll see how to securely interact with HBase via the shell before discussing how to configure the HBase gateways with security.

HBase Shell

When using the shell, the user typically obtains their TGT by executing `kinit`. If you try to run the shell without running `kinit`, you'll see something similar to Example 11-4. What you're looking for is again the `Failed to find any Kerberos tgt` at the end of the stack trace.

Example 11-4. Using the HBase shell with no Kerberos ticket-granting ticket

```
[alice@hadoop01 ~]$ hbase shell
14/11/13 14:45:53 INFO Configuration.deprecation: hadoop.native.lib is depre
cated. Instead, use io.native.lib.available
HBase Shell; enter 'help<RETURN>' for list of supported commands.
Type "exit<RETURN>" to leave the HBase Shell
Version 0.98.6, rUnknown, Sat Oct 11 15:15:15 PDT 2014

hbase(main):001:0> list
TABLE
14/11/13 14:46:00 WARN ipc.RpcClient: Exception encountered while connecting
 to the server : javax.security.sasl.SaslException: GSS initiate failed [Cau
sed by GSSException: No valid credentials provided (Mechanism level: Failed
to find
any Kerberos tgt)]
14/11/13 14:46:00 FATAL ipc.RpcClient: SASL authentication failed. The most
likely cause is missing or invalid credentials. Consider 'kinit'.
javax.security.sasl.SaslException: GSS initiate failed [Caused by GSSExcepti
on: No valid credentials provided (Mechanism level: Failed to find any Kerberos tgt)]
...

ERROR: No valid credentials provided (Mechanism level: Failed to find any Ke
rberos tgt)

Here is some help for this command:
List all tables in hbase. Optional regular expression parameter could
be used to filter the output. Examples:

  hbase> list
  hbase> list 'abc.*'
  hbase> list 'ns:abc.*'
  hbase> list 'ns:.*'


hbase(main):002:0>
```

Now let's try that again in Example 11-5, but this time we'll obtain our TGT using `kinit` before executing the shell.

Example 11-5. Using the HBase shell after kinit

```
[alice@hadoop01 ~]$ kinit
Password for alice@EXAMPLE.COM:
[alice@hadoop01 ~]$ hbase shell
14/11/13 14:53:56 INFO Configuration.deprecation: hadoop.native.lib
 is deprecated. Instead, use io.native.lib.available
HBase Shell; enter 'help<RETURN>' for list of supported commands.
Type "exit<RETURN>" to leave the HBase Shell
Version 0.98.6, rUnknown, Sat Oct 11 15:15:15 PDT 2014

hbase(main):001:0> list
TABLE
analytics_demo
document_demo
2 row(s) in 3.1900 seconds

=> ["analytics_demo", "document_demo"]
hbase(main):002:0> whoami
alice@EXAMPLE.COM (auth:KERBEROS)
    groups: alice, hadoop-users

hbase(main):003:0>
```

The HBase shell doesn't have unique authorization configuration and all access will be authorized per the configuration of HBase authorization. See "HBase and Accumulo Authorization" on page 126 for a refresher on HBase authorization.

HBase REST Gateway

HBase ships with two implementations of gateway servers, a REST server and a Thrift server. Both implementations allow access to HBase from languages other than Java and they both support authentication, impersonation, and confidentiality in the form of encryption. The decision of which gateway to deploy depends on the needs of application developers. Direct access to a gateway from a web application via JavaScript will typically use the REST interface, whereas access from other languages will typically use the Thrift API. Now let's see how to configure the REST gateway with authentication.

The first step is to create a Kerberos principal for the REST gateway to talk to the rest of HBase. This is a service principal and should include the hostname of the server running the REST gateway—for example, `rest/rest.example.com@EXAMPLE.COM` where `rest.example.com` is replaced with the fully qualified domain name of the server the REST gateway is run on. After creating the principal and exporting a keytab file with the principal's key, you need to configure the REST server to use Kerberos to talk to a secure HBase cluster. Let's set the following in the *hbase-site.xml* file:

```
<property>
  <name>hbase.rest.keytab.file</name>
```

```
    <value>/etc/hbase/conf/hbase-rest.keytab</value>
  </property>
  <property>
    <name>hbase.rest.kerberos.principal</name>
    <value>rest/_HOST@EXAMPLE.COM</value>
  </property>
```

If HBase authorization is turned on, you also need to create a top-level ACL for the principal the REST server is using. Assuming you want to grant everything (including administrative access) through the REST gateway, then you would use the HBase shell to execute the following (see "HBase and Accumulo Authorization" on page 126 for a refresher on HBase authorization):

```
hbase(main):001:0> list grant 'rest', 'RWCA'
```

If you used a different principal name, then replace rest with the short name for your principal. The next step is to enable authentication with REST clients through SPNEGO/Kerberos. Per the SPNEGO specification, you need to create a principal with the format HTTP/rest.example.com@EXAMPLE.COM where rest.example.com is replaced with the fully qualified domain name of the server the REST gateway is run on. Let's set the following in *hbase-site.xml* to turn on authentication:

```
  <property>
    <name>hbase.rest.authentication.type</name>
    <value>kerberos</value>
  </property>
  <property>
    <name>hbase.rest.authentication.kerberos.principal</name>
    <value>HTTP/_HOST@EXAMPLE.COM</value>
  </property>
  <property>
    <name>hbase.rest.authentication.kerberos.keytab</name>
    <value>/etc/hbase/conf/hbase-rest.keytab</value>
  </property>
```

In this example, we configured the REST authentication keytab to the same location as the HBase authentication keytab. This means that you either need to export both keys at the same time or use ktutil to combine the keys for both principals into a single keytab file. Alternatively, you can use different keytab files for the REST client authentication and the HBase authentication.

The REST server always authenticates with HBase using the hbase.rest.ker beros.principal, but it will perform actions on behalf of the user that authenticated with the REST server. In order to do this, the REST server must have privileges to *impersonate* other users. We can use the same hadoop.proxyuser.<*proxy*>.groups and hadoop.proxyuser.<*proxy*>.hosts settings we described in "Impersonation" on page 82. As a refresher, these settings control which users the *proxy* user can impersonate and which hosts they can impersonate *from*. The values of those settings are comma-separated lists of the groups and hosts, respectively, or * to mean all groups/

hosts. For example, if you want the *rest* user to impersonate any users in the *hbase-users* group from any host, you'd add the following on the *hbase-site.xml* file on the HBase Master:

```
<property>
  <name>hadoop.security.authorization</name>
  <value>true</value>
</property>
<property>
  <name>hadoop.proxyuser.rest.groups</name>
  <value>hbase-users</value>
</property>
<property>
  <name>hadoop.proxyuser.rest.hosts</name>
  <value>*</value>
</property>
```

The REST server also supports remote REST clients impersonating end users. This is called two-level user impersonation because the REST client impersonates a user who is then impersonated by the REST server. This lets you run an application that accesses HBase through the REST server where the application can pass user credentials all the way to HBase. This level of impersonation is enabled by setting `hbase.rest.support.proxyuser` to true. You can control which end users an application accessing the REST server can impersonate by setting the `hadoop.proxyuser.<app user>.groups` configuration setting. Let's say we have an application called *whizbang* that can impersonate any of the users in the *whizbang-users* group. We would set the following in the *hbase-site.xml* file on the REST server:

```
<property>
  <name>hbase.rest.support.proxyuser</name>
  <value>true</value>
</property>
<property>
  <name>hadoop.security.authorization</name>
  <value>true</value>
</property>
<property>
  <name>hadoop.proxyuser.whizbang.groups</name>
  <value>whizbang-users</value>
</property>
<property>
  <name>hadoop.proxyuser.whizbang.hosts</name>
  <value>*</value>
</property>
```

Figure 11-1 shows how two-level impersonation works through the HBase REST server. The end user, Alice, authenticates with an LDAP username and password to prove her identity to Hue (1). Hue then authenticates with Kerberos using the `hue/hue.example.com@EXAMPLE.COM` principal and passing a `doAs` user of `alice` (2).

Finally, the HBase REST server authenticates with Kerberos using the `rest/ rest.example.com@EXAMPLE.COM` principal and passing a `doAs` user of `alice` (3). This effectively propagates Alice's credentials all the way from the user to HBase.

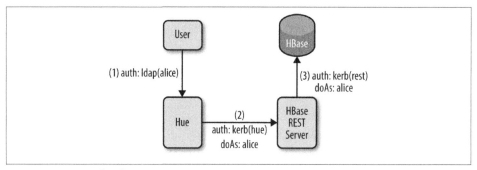

Figure 11-1. Two-level user impersonation

The REST server supports encrypting the connection between clients and the REST server by enabling TLS/SSL. We can enable SSL by setting `hbase.rest.ssl.enabled` to `true` and configuring the REST server to use a Java keystore file with the private key and certificate. If our keystore is in */etc/hbase/conf/rest.example.com.jks* and the key and keystore use the password `secret`, then we'd set the following in the *hbase-site.xml* file on the REST server:

```
<property>
  <name>hbase.rest.ssl.enabled</name>
  <value>true</value>
</property>
<property>
  <name>hbase.rest.ssl.keystore.store</name>
  <value>/etc/hbase/conf/rest.example.com.jks</value>
</property>
<property>
  <name>hbase.rest.ssl.keystore.password</name>
  <value>secret</value>
</property>
<property>
  <name>hbase.rest.ssl.keystore.keypassword</name>
  <value>secret</value>
</property>
```

If the REST server certificate isn't signed by a trusted certificate, then you need to import the certificate into the Java central truststore using the `keytool` command-line tool:

```
[hbase@rest ~]$ keytool -import -trustcacerts -file rest.example.com.crt \
  -keystore $JAVA_HOME/jre/lib/security/cacerts
```

The preceding keytool command imports a certificate into Java's central trusted certificates store. That means that any certificate you import will be trusted by any Java application—not just HBase —that is using the given JRE.

HBase Thrift Gateway

Like the REST gateway, the HBase Thrift gateway supports user authentication with Kerberos. The first step is to create a Kerberos principal for the Thrift gateway to talk to the rest of HBase. This is a service principal and should include the hostname of the server running the Thrift gateway (e.g., `thrift/thrift.example.com@EXAM PLE.COM`). After creating the principal and exporting a keytab file with the principal's key, you need to configure the Thrift server to use Kerberos to talk to a secure HBase cluster. Let's set the following in the *hbase-site.xml* file:

```
<property>
  <name>hbase.thrift.keytab.file</name>
  <value>/etc/hbase/conf/hbase.keytab</value>
</property>
<property>
  <name>hbase.thrift.kerberos.principal</name>
  <value>thrift/_HOST@EXAMPLE.COM</value>
</property>
```

If HBase authorization is turned on, you also need to create a top-level ACL for the principal the Thrift server is using. Assuming you want to grant everything, including administrative access, through the Thrift gateway, then you would use the HBase shell to execute the following:

```
hbase(main):001:0> list grant 'thrift', 'RWCA'
```

At this point, the Thrift gateway will be able to access a secure HBase cluster but won't do user authentication. You need to set `hbase.thrift.security.qop` to one of the following three values to enable authentication:

auth
   Enable authentication

auth-int
   Enable authentication and integrity checking

auth-conf
   Enable authentication, confidentiality (encryption), and integrity checking

As with the REST gateway, we need to enable the Thrift user to impersonate the users that authenticate with the Thrift gateway. Again, we'll use the `hadoop.proxyuser` settings in the HBase Master's *hbase-site.xml* file:

```
<property>
  <name>hadoop.security.authorization</name>
  <value>true</value>
</property>
<property>
  <name>hadoop.proxyuser.thrift.groups</name>
  <value>hbase-users</value>
</property>
<property>
  <name>hadoop.proxyuser.thrift.hosts</name>
  <value>*</value>
</property>
```

Unlike the REST gateway, the Thrift gateway does not support application users impersonating end users. This means that if an application is accessing HBase through the Thrift gateway, then all access will proceed as the *app* user. In the upcoming HBase 1.0, the ability for the Thrift gateway to do impersonation is being added when the Thrift gateway is configured to use HTTPS as the transport. The work for this is being tracked in HBASE-12640 (*https://issues.apache.org/jira/browse/ HBASE-12640*).

Figure 11-2 shows how impersonation works with the Thrift gateway. Suppose you have a web application that uses the Thrift gateway to access HBase. The user, Alice, authenticates with the web application using PKI (1). The application then authenticates with the Thrift gateway using Kerberos (2). Because one level of impersonation is supported, the Thrift gateway authenticates with HBase using the `thrift/ thrift.example.com@EXAMPLE.COM` principal and a `doAs` of `app` (3). HBase won't know that the original end user was Alice and it will be up to the web application to apply additional authorization controls before showing results to Alice. Take a look back at Figure 11-1 and compare and contrast one-level and two-level user impersonation.

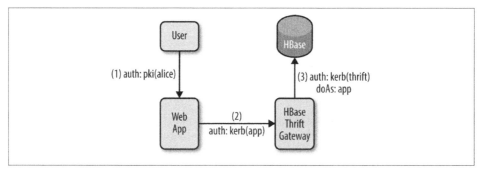

Figure 11-2. Thrift gateway application-level impersonation

Accumulo

Accumulo client access can be achieved with two mechanisms: the shell and the proxy server. The Accumulo shell is similar to the HBase shell, whereas the proxy server is similar to the HBase thrift server gateway.

Accumulo Shell

Unlike HBase, Accumulo uses usernames and passwords for authentication. Support for Kerberos authentication of clients is coming in Accumulo 1.7.0 and is tracked in ACCUMULO-1815 (*https://issues.apache.org/jira/browse/ACCUMULO-2815*). That means that clients must provide both when connecting to Accumulo. When using the Accumulo shell, you can pass a username with the -u or --user command-line parameters or you can let it default to the Linux username where you're running the shell. If you don't pass any parameters, Accumulo will prompt you for the password on stdin. Alternatively, you can have the password provided on the command line, in a file, or in an environment variable. These methods are enabled by passing the -p or --password parameters with an option of pass:*<literal password>*, file:*<path to file with password>*, or env:*<environment variable with password>*, respectively. You can also change the user after launching the Accumulo shell using the user command. The user will be prompted for their password. See Example 11-6 to see the various methods of passing a password to the Accumulo shell. Notice that when the wrong password is provided, the shell will print the message Username or Password is Invalid.

Example 11-6. Authenticating with the Accumulo shell

```
[alice@hadoop01 ~]$ accumulo shell
Password: ***
2014-11-13 15:19:54,225 [shell.Shell] ERROR: org.apache.accumulo.core.client
.AccumuloSecurityException: Error BAD_CREDENTIALS for user alice - Username
or Password is Invalid
[alice@hadoop01 ~]$ accumulo shell
Password: ******

Shell - Apache Accumulo Interactive Shell
-
- version: 1.6.0
- instance name: accumulo
- instance id: 382edcfb-5078-48b4-8570-f61d92915015
-
- type 'help' for a list of available commands
-
alice@accumulo> quit
[alice@hadoop01 ~]$ accumulo shell -p pass:secret
```

```
Shell - Apache Accumulo Interactive Shell
-
- version: 1.6.0
- instance name: accumulo
- instance id: 382edcfb-5078-48b4-8570-f61d92915015
-
- type 'help' for a list of available commands
-
alice@accumulo> quit
[alice@hadoop01 ~]$ accumulo shell -p file:accumulo_pass.txt

Shell - Apache Accumulo Interactive Shell
-
- version: 1.6.0
- instance name: accumulo
- instance id: 382edcfb-5078-48b4-8570-f61d92915015
-
- type 'help' for a list of available commands
-
alice@accumulo> quit
[alice@hadoop01 ~]$ accumulo shell -p env:ACCUMULO_PASS

Shell - Apache Accumulo Interactive Shell
-
- version: 1.6.0
- instance name: accumulo
- instance id: 382edcfb-5078-48b4-8570-f61d92915015
-
- type 'help' for a list of available commands
-
alice@accumulo> user bob
Enter password for user bob: ***
bob@accumulo>
```

The Accumulo shell doesn't have unique authorization configuration and all access
will be authorized per the configuration of Accumulo authorization. See "HBase and
Accumulo Authorization" on page 126 for a refresher on Accumulo authorization.

Accumulo Proxy Server

Accumulo has a service called the proxy server, which is similar to HBase's Thrift
gateway. The proxy server can be deployed to any server where the Java client API
would work. Specifically, that means the server must be able to communicate with the
Accumulo Master, ZooKeeper quorum, NameNodes, and DataNodes. The configuration for the Accumulo proxy server is set in the $ACCUMULO_HOME/proxy/proxy.prop
erties file. The protocolFactory determines the underlying Thrift protocol that will
be used by the server and the clients. Changing this setting must be coordinated with
the protocol implementation that clients are using. If you need to support multiple
Thrift protocols, you should deploy multiple proxy servers.

The other setting that must be synced between clients and the proxy server is the tokenClass. The proxy server doesn't authenticate clients directly and instead passes the authentication token provided by the user to Accumulo for authentication. If you need to support multiple types of authentication tokens simultaneously, you need to deploy multiple proxy servers.

An example *proxy.properties* file is shown here:

```
protocolFactory=org.apache.thrift.protocol.TCompactProtocol$Factory
tokenClass=org.apache.accumulo.core.client.security.tokens.PasswordToken
port=42424
instance=accumulo-instance
zookeepers=zoo-1.example.com,zoo-2.example.com,zoo-3.example.com
```

Because Accumulo passes the authentication token from the application accessing the proxy server to Accumulo, you get the equivalent of one level of impersonation, as shown in Figure 11-2. Accumulo supports *downgrading* the access of the application user, so it's possible for the web application to look up Alice's authorizations and have Accumulo's authorization filter limit access to data that Alice is authorized for.

Oozie

Oozie is a very important tool from a client access perspective. In addition to being the workflow executor and scheduler for your cluster, Oozie can be used as a gateway service for clients to submit any type of job. This allows you to shield direct access to your YARN or MR1 servers from clients while still allowing remote job submission. If you choose to use this style of architecture, it's very important to secure your Oozie server by enabling authentication and authorization. We previously described how to configure Kerberos authentication in "Oozie" on page 92 while authorization was detailed in "Oozie Authorization" on page 125.

Once those features are enabled on the server side, they can be used by clients with little additional configuration. To authenticate with Oozie, you simply need to have a Kerberos TGT cached on your workstation. This can easily be handled by running kinit before issuing an Oozie command from the command line. If you run an Oozie command and see an error that says Failed to find any Kerberos tgt, then you probably didn't run kinit:

```
[alice@edge01 ~]$ oozie jobs -oozie http://oozie01.example.com:11000/oozie
Error: AUTHENTICATION : Could not authenticate, GSSException: No valid crede
ntials provided (Mechanism level: Failed to find any Kerberos tgt)
[alice@edge01 ~]$ klist
klist: No credentials cache found (ticket cache FILE:/tmp/krb5cc_1236000001)
[alice@edge01 ~]$ kinit
Password for alice@EXAMPLE.COM:
[alice@edge01 ~]$ oozie jobs -oozie http://oozie01.example.com:11000/oozie
No Jobs match your criteria!
```

While we've configured Oozie with authentication and authorization, we haven't done anything to guarantee confidentiality of the communication between the Oozie client and the Oozie server. Fortunately, Oozie supports using HTTPS to encrypt the connection and provide integrity checks. In order to enable HTTPS, you must get a certificate issued to the Oozie server by your certificate authority. See "Flume Encryption" on page 221 for an example of creating a self-signed certificate.

Once your certificate authority has issued a certificate and you have the certificate and private key in a PKCS12 file, you can import the certificate and private key into a Java keystore file. In the following example, we use the same pass phrase, secret, for both the keystore and the certificate's private key:

```
[root@oozie01 ~]# mkdir /etc/oozie/ssl
[root@oozie01 ~]# keytool -v -importkeystore \
  -srckeystore /etc/pki/tls/private/oozie01.example.com.p12 \
  -srcstoretype PKCS12 \
  -destkeystore /etc/oozie/ssl/oozie01.example.com.keystore -deststoretype JKS \
  -deststorepass secret -srcalias oozie01.example.com -destkeypass secret
Enter source keystore password:
[Storing /etc/oozie/ssl/oozie01.example.com.keystore]
[root@oozie01 ~]# chown -R oozie:oozie /etc/oozie/ssl
[root@oozie01 ~]# chmod 400 /etc/oozie/ssl/*
[root@oozie01 ~]# chmod 700 /etc/oozie/ssl
```

Next, set the environment variables that control the keystore location and password in the *oozie-env.sh* file:

```
export OOZIE_HTTPS_KEYSTORE_FILE=/etc/oozie/ssl/oozie01.example.com.keystore
export OOZIE_HTTPS_KEYSTORE_PASS=secret
```

> The keystore password used here will be visible to anyone that can perform a process listing on the server running Oozie. You must protect the keystore file itself with strong permissions to prevent users from reading or modifying the keystore.

Before you configure Oozie to use HTTPS, you need to make sure the Oozie server isn't running. To configure Oozie to use HTTPS, run the following command:

```
[oozie@oozie01 ~]$ oozie-setup.sh prepare-war -secure
```

Now if you start the server it will use HTTPS over port 11443. The port can be changed by setting the OOZIE_HTTPS_PORT environment variable in the *oozie-env.sh* file.

On client machines that will be accessing Oozie, you can simply change the Oozie URL to *https://oozie01.example.com:11443/oozie* on the command line. For example:

```
[alice@edge01 ~]$ oozie jobs -oozie https://oozie01.example.com:11443/oozie
No Jobs match your criteria!
```

If you get a `SSLHandshakeException` error instead of the expected output as shown here:

```
[alice@edge01 ~]$ oozie jobs -oozie https://oozie01.example.com:11443/oozie
Error: IO_ERROR : javax.net.ssl.SSLHandshakeException: sun.security.validato
r.ValidatorException: PKIX path building failed: sun.security.provider.certp
ath.SunCertPathBuilderException: unable to find valid certification path to
requested target
```

Then it means your Oozie server is using a certificate that isn't signed by a trusted certificate authority. This can happen if you're using a self-signed certificate or an internal CA that isn't signed by one of the root CAs. Let's say we have a certificate authority for the `EXAMPLE.COM` realm in a file called *example-ca.crt*. Because we'll be importing this into Java's central truststore, this certificate will be trusted by all Java applications running on this server, not just Oozie. We can import the certificate into Java's central truststore using the following command:

```
[root@edge01 ~]# keytool -import -alias EXAMPLE.COM -file example-ca.crt \
  -keystore ${JAVA_HOME}/jre/lib/security/cacerts
Enter keystore password:
Owner: CN=Certificate Authority, O=EXAMPLE.COM
Issuer: CN=Certificate Authority, O=EXAMPLE.COM
Serial number: 1
...
Trust this certificate? [no]:  yes
Certificate was added to keystore
```

The default password for the Java `cacerts` file is `changeit`. If Oozie is configured with HA, then you need to configure your load balancer to do TLS pass-through. This will allow clients to see the certificate presented by the Oozie servers and won't require the load balancer to have its own certificate. When you're doing TLS pass-through, you should either use a wildcard certificate or certificates with subject alternate names that include the load balancer's fully qualified domain name as a valid name.

Sqoop

In Chapter 10, we discussed how to protect the confidentiality, integrity, and availability of your data ingest pipeline. The same principles hold for securing data extraction pipelines. In the case of Sqoop, confidentiality isn't provided by Sqoop itself but it may be provided by the drivers that Sqoop uses to talk to an RDBMS server. In "Sqoop Encryption" on page 229, we showed how you can configure the MySQL driver to use SSL to encrypt traffic between the MySQL server and the tasks executed by Sqoop. You can use the same parameters to encrypt the data during an export as shown in Example 11-7.

Example 11-7. Exporting a MySQL table over SSL

```
[alice@sqoop01 ~]$ hdfs dfs -cat cities/*
1,USA,Palo Alto
2,Czech Republic,Brno
3,USA,Sunnyvale
[alice@sqoop01 ~]$ URI="jdbc:mysql://mysql01.example.com/sqoop"
[alice@sqoop01 ~]$ URI="${URI}?verifyServerCertificate=false"
[alice@sqoop01 ~]$ URI="${URI}&useSSL=true"
[alice@sqoop01 ~]$ URI="${URI}&requireSSL=true"
[alice@sqoop01 ~]$ sqoop export --connect ${URI} \
  --username sqoop -P --table cities \
  --export-dir cities
Enter password:
...
14/06/28 17:27:22 INFO mapreduce.ExportJobBase: Exported 3 records.
[alice@sqoop01 ~]$
```

SQL Access

As described in Chapter 1, there are two popular ways for accessing Hadoop data using SQL: Hive and Impala. Both Hive and Impala support both Kerberos and LDAP-based username/password authentication. Users don't typically interact with Hive or Impala directly and instead rely on SQL shells or JDBC drivers.

The rest of this section covers configuring Impala and Hive with their supported authentication protocols and how to pass authentication details as a client. Authorization for Impala and Hive is provided by Sentry, which is covered in Chapter 7.

Impala

Impala can be configured to use Kerberos-only, LDAP-only, or both LDAP and Kerberos for authentication. When Impala is run on a Hadoop cluster that has Kerberos enabled, it must be configured with Kerberos so that Impala can securely communicate with HDFS and YARN.

Using Impala with Kerberos authentication

When Kerberos is enabled for communication with Hadoop, then Kerberos-based client authentication is automatically enabled. Impala uses command-line parameters for configuration. You should set the `--principal` and `--keytab_file` parameters on the `impalad`, `statestored`, and `catalogd` daemons. The `--principal` should be set to the Kerberos principal that Impala uses for authentication. This will typically be of the format `impala/<fully qualified domain name>@<realm>` where *<fully quali fied domain name>* is the host name of the server running `impalad` and *<realm>* is the Kerberos realm. The first component of the principal, `impala`, must match the name of the user starting the Impala process. The `--keytab_file` parameter must point to a keytab file that contains the previously mentioned principal and the HTTP principal for the server running `impalad`. You can create a keytab file with both principals from two independent keytabs using the `ktutil` command, as shown in Example 11-8.

Example 11-8. Merging the Impala and HTTP keytabs

```
[impala@impala01 ~]$ ktutil
ktutil: rkt impala.keytab
ktutil: rkt http.keytab
ktutil: wkt impala-http.keytab
ktutil: quit
```

To make it easier to configure, you can set the command-line parameters that the `impalad` process uses by setting the `IMPALA_SERVER_ARGS`, `IMPALA_STATE_STORE_ARGS`, and `IMPALA_CATALOG_ARGS` variables in the */etc/default/ impala* file. Example 11-9 shows how to enable Kerberos for Impala.

Example 11-9. Configuring Impala with Kerberos authentication

```
IMPALA_SERVER_ARGS="${IMPALA_SERVER_ARGS} \
  --principal=impala/impala01.example.com@EXAMPLE.COM \
  --keytab_file=/etc/impala/conf/impala-http.keytab"

IMPALA_STATE_STORE_ARGS="${IMPALA_STATE_STORE_ARGS} \
  --principal=impala/impala01.example.com@EXAMPLE.COM \
  --keytab_file=/etc/impala/conf/impala-http.keytab"

IMPALA_CATALOG_ARGS="${IMPALA_CATALOG_ARGS} \
  --principal=impala/impala01.example.com@EXAMPLE.COM \
  --keytab_file=/etc/impala/conf/impala-http.keytab"
```

If users access Impala behind a load balancer, then the configuration changes slightly. When building the combined keytab, you also need to include the keytab for the proxy server principal and you need to add the `--be_principal` parameter. The `--be_principal` is the principal that Impala uses for talking to backend services like HDFS. This should be set to the same value that `--principal` was set to before, and `--principal` should be changed to the principal for the load balancer. If your load balancer is on the `impala-proxy.example.com` server then you would set the `IMPALA_SERVER_ARGS` as shown in Example 11-10.

Example 11-10. Configuring Impala behind a load balancer with Kerberos authentication

```
IMPALA_SERVER_ARGS="${IMPALA_SERVER_ARGS} \
  --principal=impala/impala-proxy.example.com@EXAMPLE.COM \
```

```
--be_principal=impala/impala01.example.com@EXAMPLE.COM \
--keytab_file=/etc/impala/conf/impala-http.keytab"
```

Impala supports using YARN for resource management via a project called Llama.
Llama mediates resource management between YARN and low-latency execution
engines such as Impala. Llama has two components, a long-running application master and a node manager plug-in. The application master handles reserving resources
for Impala while the node manager plug-in coordinates with the local Impala daemon
regarding changes to available resources on the local node.

When enabling Kerberos for Impala, you must also configure Kerberos for Llama by
configuring the following properties in the *llama-site.xml* file.

lama.am.server.thrift.security
> Set to `true` to enable Thrift SASL/Kerberos-based security for the application
> master.

llama.am.server.thrift.security.QOP
> Set the quality of protection when security is enabled. Valid values are `auth` for
> authentication only, `auth-int` for authentication and integrity, and `auth-conf` for
> authentication, integrity, and confidentiality (encryption).

llama.am.server.thrift.kerberos.keytab.file
> Set the location of the application master keytab file. If this is a relative path, then
> it it is looked up under the Llama configuration directory.

llama.am.server.thrift.kerberos.server.principal.name
> The fully qualified principal name for the Llama application server. This setting
> must include both the short name and the fully qualified hostname of the server
> running the Llama application master.

llama.am.server.thrift.kerberos.notification.principal.name
> The short name used for client notifications. This short name is combined with
> the client hostname provided by the impalad process during registration. You can
> override the hostname that the impalad process registers with by configuring the
> `--hostname` parameter in the `IMPALA_SERVER_ARGS` variable.

Example 11-11 shows a snippet of the *llama-site.xml* file configured to enable Kerberos security.

Example 11-11. Configuring Llama application master with Kerberos authentication

```
<property>
  <name>llama.am.server.thrift.security</name>
  <value>true</value>
</property>
<property>
```

```
    <name>llama.am.server.thrift.kerberos.keytab.file</name>
    <value>/etc/llama/conf/llama.keytab</value>
  </property>
  <property>
    <name>llama.am.server.thrift.kerberos.server.principal.name</name>
    <value>llama/llama.example.com@EXAMPLE.COM</value>
  </property>
  <property>
    <name>llama.am.server.thrift.kerberos.notification.principal.name</name>
    <value>impala</value>
  </property>
```

Once Impala is configured to use Kerberos authentication, then clients can authenticate by having a cached Kerberos TGT (i.e., running `kinit` before executing the shell). Example 11-12 shows Alice obtaining her Kerberos TGT and then authenticating with Kerberos using the Impala shell.

Example 11-12. Impala shell with Kerberos authentication

```
[alice@hadoop01 ~]$ kinit
Password for alice@EXAMPLE.COM:
[alice@hadoop01 ~]$ impala-shell -i impala-proxy
Starting Impala Shell without Kerberos authentication
Error connecting: TTransportException, TSocket read 0 bytes
Kerberos ticket found in the credentials cache, retrying the connection with a s
ecure transport.
Connected to impala-proxy:21000
Server version: impalad version 2.0.0 RELEASE (build ecf30af0b4d6e56ea80297df218
9367ada6b7da7)
Welcome to the Impala shell. Press TAB twice to see a list of available commands.

Copyright (c) 2012 Cloudera, Inc. All rights reserved.

(Shell build version: Impala Shell v2.0.0 (ecf30af) built on Sat Oct 11 13:56:06
 PDT 2014)
[impala-proxy:21000] > show tables;
Query: show tables
+-----------+
| name      |
+-----------+
| sample_07 |
| sample_08 |
+-----------+
Fetched 2 row(s) in 0.18s
[impala-proxy:21000] >
```

When using Kerberos authentication with JDBC drivers, you need to first obtain a Kerberos TGT and then include the name of the Impala principal in the connection string. Example 11-13 shows how to set up the JDBC connection string for Kerberos authentication with Impala.

Example 11-13. JDBC connection string for Kerberos authentication

```
// Start with the basic JDBC URL string
String url = "jdbc:hive2://impala-proxy.example.com:21050/default";

// Add the Impala Kerberos principal name, including the FQDN and realm
url = url + ";principal=impala/impala-proxy.example.com@EXAMPLE.COM";

// Create the connection from the URL
Connection con = DriverManager.getConnection(url);
```

Using Impala with LDAP/Active Directory authentication

Impala can also be configured to use an LDAP directory, such as Active Directory, for authentication. The advantage of LDAP authentication is that it doesn't require that clients be able to obtain their Kerberos credentials before connecting to Impala. This is especially useful for business intelligence tools which may not have native support for Kerberos-based authentication. LDAP authentication is configured independently of Kerberos although the two are typically configured together as it doesn't make that much sense to enable authentication for Impala when Hadoop doesn't have authentication enabled.

You can enable LDAP authentication by setting the --enable_ldap_auth and --ldap_uri parameters on the impalad daemons. When configuring LDAP authentication you can optionally set bind parameters depending on the type of LDAP provider you're using. If you're using Active Directory, you often don't need additional configuration, but you can explicitly set the domain name so that the username used to bind to AD will be passed as user@*<domain name>*. The domain name is set by specifying the --ldap_domain parameter. For OpenLDAP or freeIPA, you can configure a base distinguished name and the username used to bind to LDAP will be passed as uid=user,*<base dn>*. This setting is enabled by specifying the --ldap_baseDN parameter. If your LDAP provider doesn't use uid=user to specify the username in distinguished names, then you can provide a pattern that will become the distinguished name. The pattern works by replacing all instances of #UID with the username prior to binding. This setting is enabled by specifying the --ldap_bind_pattern parameter.

Regardless of the LDAP provider, it's strongly recommend that you use TLS to encrypt the connection between Impala and the LDAP server. This can be done by either using an ldaps:// URL or by enabling StartTLS. You can enable StartTLS by setting the --ldap_tls parameter to true. For either mode, you have to configure the certificate authority (CA) certificate so that Impala trusts the certificate used by the LDAP server. You can set the --ldap_ca_certificate parameter to configure the location of the CA certificate.

Refer to Examples 11-14 through pass:[11-16 for sample configuration when using Active Directory, OpenLDAP, and custom LDAP providers, respectively.

Example 11-14. Configuring Impala with Active Directory

```
IMPALA_SERVER_ARGS="${IMPALA_SERVER_ARGS} \
  --enable_ldap_auth=true \
  --ldap_uri=ldaps://ad.example.com \
  --ldap_ca_certificate=/etc/impala/pki/ca.crt \
  --ldap_domain=example.com"
```

Example 11-15. Configuring Impala with OpenLDAP

```
IMPALA_SERVER_ARGS="${IMPALA_SERVER_ARGS} \
  --enable_ldap_auth=true \
  --ldap_uri=ldaps://ldap.example.com \
  --ldap_ca_certificate=/etc/impala/pki/ca.crt \
  --ldap_baseDN=ou=People,dc=example,dc=com"
```

Example 11-16. Configuring Impala with other LDAP provider

```
IMPALA_SERVER_ARGS="${IMPALA_SERVER_ARGS} \
  --enable_ldap_auth=true \
  --ldap_uri=ldaps://ldap.example.com \
  --ldap_ca_certificate=/etc/impala/pki/ca.crt \
  --ldap_bind_pattern=user=#UID,ou=users,dc=example,dc=com"
```

Specify the -l command-line option to the impala-shell to connect to Impala using LDAP authentication. You'll be prompted for the user password before the connection is complete. If you want to connect as a user other than current Linux user, you can specify the -u option to change the username. Example 11-17 shows how to authenticate using LDAP with the Impala shell.

Example 11-17. Impala shell with LDAP/Active Directory authentication

```
[alice@hadoop01 ~]$ impala-shell -i impala-proxy -l
Starting Impala Shell using LDAP-based authentication
LDAP password for alice:
Connected to impala-proxy:21000
Server version: impalad version 2.0.0 RELEASE (build ecf30af0b4d6e56ea80297d
f2189367ada6b7da7)
Welcome to the Impala shell. Press TAB twice to see a list of available commands.

Copyright (c) 2012 Cloudera, Inc. All rights reserved.

(Shell build version: Impala Shell v2.0.0 (ecf30af) built on Sat Oct 11 13:5
6:06 PDT 2014)
[impala-proxy:21000] > show tables;
Query: show tables
```

```
+-----------+
| name      |
+-----------+
| sample_07 |
| sample_08 |
+-----------+
Fetched 2 row(s) in 0.16s
[impala-proxy:21000] >
```

If you're connecting to Impala using JDBC drivers, then you pass the username and password to the DriverManager when getting a connection. Example 11-18 shows how to connect using the JDBC driver with LDAP authentication.

Example 11-18. JDBC connection string for LDAP/Active Directory authentication

```
// Use the basic JDBC URL string
String url = "jdbc:hive2://impala-proxy.example.com:21050/default";

// Create the connection from the URL passing in the username and password
Connection con = DriverManager.getConnection(url, "alice", "secret");
```

Using SSL wire encryption with Impala

The methods described so far have covered different ways for clients to authenticate with Impala. It is also important to set up a protected channel for data transfers between clients and Impala. This is even more critical when the data processed by Impala is sensitive, such as data that requires at-rest encryption. Impala supports SSL wire encryption for this purpose. Example 11-19 shows the necessary startup flags.

Example 11-19. Configuring Impala with SSL

```
IMPALA_SERVER_ARGS="${IMPALA_SERVER_ARGS} \
  --ssl_client_ca_certificate=/etc/impala/ca.cer \
  --ssl_private_key=/etc/impala/impala.key \
  --ssl_server_certificate=/etc/impala/impala.cer
```

The `ssl_private_key`, `ssl_server_certificate`, and `ssl_client_ca_certificate` paths must all be readable by the `impala` user, and the certificates must be in PEM format. It is recommended to restrict the permissions of the private key to 400.

When Impala is set up with SSL, clients must also know how to connect properly. The `--ssl` option tells the `impala-shell` to enable SSL for the connection, and the `--ca_cert` argument specifies the certificate authority chain (in PEM format) to use to verify the certificate presented by the Impala daemon you are connecting to. Example 11-20 shows what this looks like when using both Kerberos authentication and SSL wire encryption.

Example 11-20. Impala shell with SSL and Kerberos

```
alice@hadoop01 ~]$ impala-shell -i impala-proxy -k --ssl --ca_cert /etc/impala/ca.pem
Starting Impala Shell using Kerberos authentication
SSL is enabled
Connected to impala-proxy:21000
Server version: impalad version 2.0.0 RELEASE (build ecf30af0b4d6e56ea80297d
f2189367ada6b7da7)
Welcome to the Impala shell. Press TAB twice to see a list of available commands.

Copyright (c) 2012 Cloudera, Inc. All rights reserved.

(Shell build version: Impala Shell v2.0.0 (ecf30af) built on Sat Oct 11 13:5
6:06 PDT 2014)
[impala-proxy:21000] > show tables;
Query: show tables
+-----------+
| name      |
+-----------+
| sample_07 |
| sample_08 |
+-----------+
Fetched 2 row(s) in 0.16s
[impala-proxy:21000] >
```

Hive

The old, deprecated Hive command-line tool, `hive`, does not support direct authentication or authorization with Hive. Instead, it either directly accesses data on HDFS or launches a MapReduce job to execute a query. This means it follows the same rules as the Hadoop commands described before and only supports Kerberos and delegation tokens. In general, the `hive` command is deprecated and users should use `beeline` instead.

When using `beeline` or JDBC drivers, users connect to the HiveServer2 daemon which handles query parsing and execution. HiveServer2 supports Kerberos, LDAP, and custom authentication plug-ins. Only one authentication provider can be configured at a time, so administrators need to choose the preferred authentication mechanism to use when configuring the HiveServer2 daemon. A workaround for this limitation is to run multiple HiveServer2 daemons that share the same Hive metastore. This requires that end users connect to the correct HiveServer2 depending on their authentication needs. The authentication mechanism for HiveServer2 is configured in the *hive-site.xml* file. See Table 11-2 for a description of the HiveServer2 authentication configuration properties.

Table 11-2. Configuration properties for HiveServer2 authentication

Property	Description
`hive.server2.authentication`	Client authentication type. Valid values: NONE, LDAP, KERBEROS, CUSTOM
`hive.server2.authentication.kerberos.principal`	The Kerberos principal for the HiveServer2 daemon
`hive.server2.authentication.kerberos.keytab`	The keytab used to authenticate with the KDC
`hive.server2.thrift.sasl.qop`	The SASL quality of protection to use with Kerberos connections; valid values are `auth` for authentication only, `auth-int` for authentication and integrity checks, and `auth-conf` for authentication, integrity, and confidentiality (encryption)
`hive.server2.use.SSL`	Set to *true* to enable TLS between clients the HiveServer2 daemon
`hive.server2.keystore.path`	The path to a Java keystore file with the private key to use with TLS
`hive.server2.keystore.password`	The password for the Java keystore file
`hive.server2.authentication.ldap.url`	The URL to the LDAP/Active Directory server; only used if `hive.server2.authentication` is set to LDAP
`hive.server2.authentication.ldap.Domain`	The Active Directory domain to authenticate against; only used if `hive.server2.authentication.ldap.url` points to an AD server
`hive.server2.authentication.ldap.baseDN`	The base distinguished name to use when `hive.server2.authentication.ldap.url` points to an OpenLDAP server
`hive.server2.custom.authentication.class`	The name of a class that implements the `org.apache.hive.service.auth.PasswdAuthenticationProvider` interface; used when `hive.server2.authentication` is set to CUSTOM

Using HiveServer2 with Kerberos authentication

Configuring HiveServer2 with Kerberos authentication follows the same pattern as with the core Hadoop services described in "Configuration" on page 83. Namely, we need to set the authentication type to Kerberos and set the Kerberos principal and keytab. When setting the Kerberos principal, we can use the *_HOST* wildcard placeholder. This will automatically be replaced with the fully qualified domain name of the server running the HiveServer2 daemon. An example snippet of the *hive-site.xml* file enabling Kerberos authentication is shown in Example 11-21.

Example 11-21. Configuration for Kerberos authentication with HiveServer2

```
<property>
  <name>hive.server2.authentication</name>
  <value>KERBEROS</value>
</property>
<property>
  <name>hive.server2.authentication.kerberos.principal</name>
  <value>hive/_HOST@EXAMPLE.COM</value>
</property>
<property>
  <name>hive.server2.authentication.kerberos.keytab</name>
  <value>/etc/hive/conf/hive.keytab</value>
</property>
```

JDBC clients connecting to a Kerberos-enabled HiveServer2 daemon need to have a valid Kerberos TGT, and need to add the principal of the HiveServer2 daemon to their connection string. Example 11-22 shows how to create a connection string for Kerberos authentication.

Example 11-22. JDBC connection string for Kerberos authentication

```
// Start with the basic JDBC URL string
String url = "jdbc:hive2://hive.example.com:10000/default";

// Add the Hive Kerberos principal name, including the FQDN and realm
url = url + ";principal=hive/hive.example.com@EXAMPLE.COM";

// Create the connection from the URL
Connection con = DriverManager.getConnection(url);
```

The Beeline shell uses the Hive JDBC driver to connect to HiveServer2. You need to obtain your Kerberos TGT using kinit and then connect using the same JDBC connection string shown earlier in order to use Kerberos authentication with Beeline. See Example 11-23 for an example. Even though you're using Kerberos for authentication, Beeline will prompt for a username and password. You can leave these blank and just hit Enter, as shown in the example.

Example 11-23. Beeline connection string for Kerberos authentication

```
[alice@hadoop01 ~]$ kinit
Password for alice@EXAMPLE.COM:
[alice@hadoop01 ~]$ beeline
Beeline version 0.13.1 by Apache Hive
beeline> !connect jdbc:hive2://hive.example.com:10000/default;principal=hive/hiv
e.example.com@EXAMPLE.COM
scan complete in 2ms
Connecting to jdbc:hive2://hive.example.com:10000/default;principal=hive/hive.ex
ample.com@EXAMPLE.COM
```

```
Enter username for jdbc:hive2://hive.example.com:10000/default;principal=hive/hi
ve.example.com@EXAMPLE.COM:
Enter password for jdbc:hive2://hive.example.com:10000/default;principal=hive/hi
ve.example.com@EXAMPLE.COM:
Connected to: Apache Hive (version 0.13.1)
Driver: Hive JDBC (version 0.13.1)
Transaction isolation: TRANSACTION_REPEATABLE_READ
0: jdbc:hive2://hive.example.com> show tables;
+-------------+--+
|  tab_name   |
+-------------+--+
| sample_07   |
| sample_08   |
+-------------+--+
2 rows selected (0.261 seconds)
0: jdbc:hive2://hive.example.com>
```

Using HiveServer2 with LDAP/Active Directory authentication

HiveServer2 also supports username/password authentication backed by LDAP. To use LDAP-based authentication, set the authentication type to LDAP, configure the LDAP URL, and then either set a domain name or base distinguished name for binding. The domain name is used when you're binding against an Active Directory server while the base DN is used for other LDAP providers such as OpenLDAP or freeIPA.

 By default, the connection between clients and HiveServer2 are not encrypted. This means that when you're using either LDAP or a custom authentication provider, the username and password could be intercepted by a third party. When using a non-Kerberos authentication provider, it's strongly recommended to enable HiverServer2 over-the-wire encryption using TLS, as shown in "HiveServer2 over-the-wire encryption" on page 269.

Regardless of the LDAP provider, it's strongly recommend that you use LDAPS (LDAP over SSL) rather than straight LDAP. This will ensure that communication between HiveServer2 and the LDAP server is encrypted. In order to use LDAPS, you need to make sure that LDAP server certificate or the CA signing certificate is loaded into a Java truststore. This can either be the system-wide Java truststore located at *$JAVA_HOME/jre/lib/security/cacerts* or a specific truststore for use with Hive. If using a specific truststore, you need to set the *javax.net.ssl.trustStore* and *javax.net.ssl.trustStorePassword* system properties. This can be done by setting the HADOOP_OPTS variable in the *hive-env.sh* file similar to Example 11-24.

Example 11-24. Setting the LDAPS truststore for Hive

```
HADOOP_OPTS="-Djavax.net.ssl.trustStore=/etc/pki/java/hive.truststore"
HADOOP_OPTS="${HADOOP_OPTS} -Djavax.net.ssl.trustStorePassword=secret"
```

 The truststore password used here will be visible to anyone that can perform a process listing on the server running HiveServer2. You must protect the truststore file itself with strong permissions to prevent users from modifying the truststore.

If you're configuring HiveServer2 to authenticate against an Active Directory server, then you need to set the `hive.server2.authentication.ldap.Domain` setting in *hive-site.xml* to your AD domain name in addition to the common LDAP settings. See Example 11-25 for an example configuration.

Example 11-25. Configuration for Active Directory authentication with HiveServer2

```
<property>
  <name>hive.server2.authentication</name>
  <value>LDAP</value>
</property>
<property>
  <name>hive.server2.authentication.ldap.url</name>
  <value>ldaps://ad.example.com</value>
</property>
<property>
  <name>hive.server2.authentication.ldap.Domain</name>
  <value>example.com</value>
</property>
```

If you're using another LDAP provider, such as OpenLDAP or freeIPA, then you need to set the `hive.server2.authentication.ldap.baseDN` property rather than the domain name. The base DN will depend on your environment, but the default for common OpenLDAP installations is `ou=People,dc=example,dc=com` where `dc=example,dc=com` will be replaced with your LDAP server's domain components. Typically, this is the domain name of the LDAP server. For freeIPA, the default base DN will be `cn=users,cn=accounts,dc=example,dc=com`. Again, substitute in the domain components for your environment. A complete configuration example is provided in Example 11-26.

Example 11-26. Configuration for LDAP authentication with HiveServer2

```
<property>
  <name>hive.server2.authentication</name>
  <value>LDAP</value>
</property>
```

```
<property>
  <name>hive.server2.authentication.ldap.url</name>
  <value>ldaps://ldap.example.com</value>
</property>
<property>
  <name>hive.server2.authentication.ldap.baseDN</name>
  <value>ou=People,dc=example,dc=com</value>
</property>
```

 Some versions of Hive (notably Hive 0.13.0 and 0.13.1) have a bug where they won't use Kerberos authentication to communicate with Hadoop when the authentication type is set to something other than *KERBEROS*. When using these versions of Hive, you should only use Kerberos for authentication.

Connecting to HiveServer2 when configured for LDAP/Active Directory authentication is easily handled by passing the username and password to the DriverManager when getting a connection. See Example 11-27 for an example.

Example 11-27. JDBC connection string for LDAP/Active Directory authentication

```
// Use the basic JDBC URL string
String url = "jdbc:hive2://hive.example.com:10000/default";

// Create the connection from the URL passing in the username and password
Connection con = DriverManager.getConnection(url, "alice", "secret");
```

Connecting with Beeline is much the same way. This time, you'll enter the username and password when prompted following the !connect command. See Example 11-28 for an example.

Example 11-28. Beeline connection string for LDAP/Active Directory authentication

```
[alice@hadoop01 ~]$ beeline
Beeline version 0.13.1 by Apache Hive
beeline> !connect jdbc:hive2://hive.example.com:10000/default
scan complete in 2ms
Connecting to jdbc:hive2://hive.example.com:10000/default
Enter username for jdbc:hive2://hive.example.com:10000/default: alice
Enter password for jdbc:hive2://hive.example.com:10000/default: ******
Connected to: Apache Hive (version 0.13.1)
Driver: Hive JDBC (version 0.13.1)
Transaction isolation: TRANSACTION_REPEATABLE_READ
0: jdbc:hive2://hive.example.com> show tables;
+-------------+--+
| tab_name  |
+-------------+--+
| sample_07  |
```

```
| sample_08  |
+------------+--+
2 rows selected (0.261 seconds)
0: jdbc:hive2://hive.example.com>
```

Using HiveServer2 with pluggable authentication

Hive has a pluggable interface for implementing new authentication providers. Hive calls this authentication mode `CUSTOM` and it requires a Java class that implements the `org.apache.hive.service.auth.PasswdAuthenticationProvider` interface. This interface defines an `authenticate(String user, String password)` method that you implement to verify the supplied username and password. As its name suggests, this pluggable interface only works with authentication providers that use usernames and passwords for authentication. You configure this mode by setting the authentication type to `CUSTOM` and setting the authentication class. You also have to add the JAR file with your class in it to Hive's classpath. The easiest way is to add the path to your JAR to the `hive.aux.jars.path` setting in *hive-site.xml*. This property takes a comma-delimited list of full paths to JARs. See Example 11-29 for an example configuration.

Example 11-29. Configuration for pluggable authentication with HiveServer2

```
<property>
  <name>hive.server2.authentication</name>
  <value>CUSTOM</value>
</property>
<property>
  <name>hive.server2.custom.authentication.class</name>
  <value>com.example.my.whizbang.AuthenticationProvider</value>
</property>
<property>
  <name>hive.aux.jars.path</name>
  <value>file:///opt/hive-plugins/whizbang-1.0.jar</value>
</property>
```

The connection settings for custom authentication is the same as for LDAP/Active Directory-based authentication. See Examples 11-18 and 11-28 for a illustration of this.

HiveServer2 over-the-wire encryption

The Hive JDBC driver supports two methods of enabling encryption over the wire. The method you use will depend on the method of authentication you're using and your version of Hive. When you use Kerberos authentication, the Hive JDBC driver uses SASL to perform the Kerberos authentication. SASL supports integrity checks and encryption when doing authentication based on a configuration setting called the *quality of protection*. To enable encryption, set the SASL QOP to `auth-conf`, which is short for authentication with confidentiality. See Example 11-30 to see how to configure HiveServer2 to use SASL for encryption.

Example 11-30. Configuring HiveServer2 to use SASL encryption

```
<property>
  <name>hive.server2.thrift.sasl.qop</name>
  <value>auth-conf</value>
</property>
```

When the SASL QOP is enabled on the server side, you need to make sure the client sets it to the same value. This can be done by adding the option `sasl.qop=auth-conf` to the JDBC URL. Example 11-31 shows how to use SASL encryption with Beeline.

Example 11-31. Beeline connection string with SASL encryption

```
[alice@hadoop01 ~]$ beeline
Beeline version 0.13.1 by Apache Hive
beeline> !connect jdbc:hive2://hive.example.com:10000/default;principal=hive/hiv
e.example.com@EXAMPLE.COM;sasl.qop=auth-conf
scan complete in 4ms
Connecting to jdbc:hive2://hive.example.com:10000/default;principal=hive/hive.ex
ample.com@EXAMPLE.COM;sasl.qop=auth-conf
Enter username for jdbc:hive2://hive.example.com:10000/default;principal=hive/hi
ve.example.com@EXAMPLE.COM;sasl.qop=auth-conf:
Enter password for jdbc:hive2://hive.example.com:10000/default;principal=hive/hi
ve.example.com@EXAMPLE.COM;sasl.qop=auth-conf:
Connected to: Apache Hive (version 0.13.1)
Driver: Hive JDBC (version 0.13.1)
Transaction isolation: TRANSACTION_REPEATABLE_READ
0: jdbc:hive2://hive.example.com> show tables;
+-------------+--+
|  tab_name   |
+-------------+--+
| sample_07   |
| sample_08   |
+-------------+--+
2 rows selected (0.261 seconds)
0: jdbc:hive2://hive.example.com>
```

If you've configured Hive to use username/password-based authentication, such as LDAP/Active Directory, then Hive will no longer use SASL to secure the connection. That means an alternative is needed to enable encryption. Starting with Hive 0.13 and later, you can configure Hive 0.13 or later to use TLS/SSL for encryption. Before you can configure Hive to use TLS, you need the private key and certificate for your server in a Java keystore file. Assuming that you already have your private key and certificate in a PKCS12 file, you can import them into a Java keystore following the process shown in Example 11-32. Hive requires that the private key's password be set to the same as the keystore's password. We handle that in the example by setting both -deststorepass and -destkeypass on the command line. In addition, we provided the -srcalias parameter for the key/certificate we're importing.

A note on Hive versions

Setting the SASL QOP property is only available in Hive 0.12.0 or later, and support for TLS encryption requires Hive 0.13.0 or later.

Example 11-32. Importing a PKCS12 private key into a Java keystore

```
[root@hive ~]# mkdir /etc/hive/ssl
[root@hive ~]# keytool -v -importkeystore \
  -srckeystore /etc/pki/tls/private/hive.example.com.p12 -srcstoretype PKCS12 \
  -destkeystore /etc/hive/ssl/hive.example.com.keystore -deststoretype JKS \
  -deststorepass secret -srcalias hive.example.com -destkeypass secret
Enter source keystore password:
[Storing /etc/hive/ssl/hive.example.com.keystore]
[root@hive ~]# chown -R hive:hive /etc/hive/ssl
[root@hive ~]# chmod 400 /etc/hive/ssl/*
[root@hive ~]# chmod 700 /etc/hive/ssl
```

After creating our Java keystore, we're ready to configure Hive to use it. Set the configuration properties shown in Example 11-33 in the *hive-site.xml* file for Hive-Server2.

Example 11-33. Configuring HiveServer2 to use TLS for encryption

```
<property>
  <name>hive.server2.use.SSL</name>
  <value>true</value>
</property>
<property>
  <name>hive.server2.keystore.path</name>
  <value>/etc/hive/ssl/hive.example.com.keystore</value>
</property>
<property>
  <name>hive.server2.keystore.password</name>
  <value>secret</value>
</property>
```

TLS cannot be configured when using Kerberos for authentication. If you're using Kerberos for authentication, then use SASL QOP for encryption and use TLS otherwise.

Finally, we need to enable TLS on the client side by adding `ssl=true` to the JDBC URL. If your certificate is not signed by a central certificate authority, then you also need to specify a truststore in the JDBC URL. When we configured Hive to use LDAPS, we created a truststore that we can reuse here by copying the truststore file to the client server and setting the `sslTrustStore` and `trustStorePassword` parameters in the JDBC URL. See Example 11-34 for a full example of using TLS for encryption with Beeline.

Example 11-34. Beeline connection string with TLS

```
[alice@hadoop01 ~]$ beeline
Beeline version 0.13.1 by Apache Hive
beeline> !connect jdbc:hive2://hive.example.com:10000/default;ssl=true;sslTrustS
tore=/etc/pki/java/hive.truststore;trustStorePassword=secret
scan complete in 3ms
Connecting to jdbc:hive2://hive.example.com:10000/default;ssl=true;sslTrustStore
=/etc/pki/java/hive.truststore;trustStorePassword=secret
Enter username for jdbc:hive2://hive.example.com:10000/default;ssl=true;sslTrust
Store=/etc/pki/java/hive.truststore;trustStorePassword=secret alice
Enter password for jdbc:hive2://hive.example.com:10000/default;ssl=true;sslTrust
Store=/etc/pki/java/hive.truststore;trustStorePassword=secret **********
Connected to: Apache Hive (version 0.13.1)
Driver: Hive JDBC (version 0.13.1)
Transaction isolation: TRANSACTION_REPEATABLE_READ
0: jdbc:hive2://hive.example.com> show tables;
+--------------+--+
|   tab_name   |
+--------------+--+
| sample_07    |
| sample_08    |
+--------------+--+
2 rows selected (0.261 seconds)
0: jdbc:hive2://hive.example.com>
```

WebHDFS/HttpFS

Hadoop has two methods of exposing a REST interface to HDFS: WebHDFS and HttpFS. Both systems use the same API so the same client can work with either; the difference is in how they're deployed and where the access to data lives. WebHDFS isn't actually a separate service and runs inside the NameNode and DataNodes. Because WebHDFS runs on the NameNode and DataNodes, it's not suitable for users that don't have direct access to the cluster. In practice, WebHDFS is most commonly used to provide version-independent access for bulk access utilities such as DistCp, the distributed copy command. See Example 5-10 in Chapter 5 for the example configuration for WebHDFS.

In contrast, HttpFS runs as a gateway service similar to the HBase REST gateway. The first step of configuring HttpFS with authentication is to configure HttpFS to use Kerberos to authenticate against HDFS:

```
<property>
  <name>httpfs.hadoop.authentication.type</name>
  <value>kerberos</value>
</property>
<property>
  <name>httpfs.hadoop.authentication.kerberos.principal</name>
  <value>httpfs/httpfs.example.com@EXAMPLE.COM</value>
</property>
<property>
  <name>httpfs.hadoop.authentication.kerberos.keytab</name>
  <value>httpfs.keytab</value>
</property>
```

Next, we set the authentication method that the HttpFS server will use to authenticate clients. Again we use Kerberos, which will be implemented over SPNEGO:

```
<property>
  <name>httpfs.authentication.type</name>
  <value>kerberos</value>
</property>
<property>
  <name>httpfs.authentication.kerberos.principal</name>
  <value>HTTP/httpfs.example.com@EXAMPLE.COM</value>
</property>
<property>
  <name>httpfs.authentication.kerberos.keytab</name>
  <value>httpfs.keytab</value>
</property>
<property>
  <name>httpfs.authentication.kerberos.name.rules</name>
  <value>DEFAULT</value>
</property>
```

Lastly, we need to configure HttpFS to allow the Hue user to impersonate other users. This is done with the typical proxy user settings—for example, the following settings will allow the hue user to impersonate users from any host and in any group:

```
<property>
  <name>httpfs.proxyuser.hue.hosts</name>
  <value>*</value>
</property>
<property>
  <name>httpfs.proxyuser.hue.groups</name>
  <value>*</value>
</property>
```

Summary

In this chapter, we took a deep dive into how clients access a Hadoop cluster to take advantage of the many services it provides and the data it stores. What is immediately obvious is that securing this access is a daunting task because of the myriad of access points available to clients. A key theme throughout, however, is that clients must obey the established authentication and authorization methods, such as those provided by Kerberos and LDAP.

We also spent some time on how users get data out of the cluster with Sqoop, Hive, Impala, WebHDFS, and HttpFS. While the Hadoop ecosystem itself has grown over the years, so too has the wide ecosystem of business intelligence, ETL, and other related tools that interact with Hadoop. For this reason, having a solid grasp on data extraction capabilities of the platform and the modes to secure them is critical for an administrator to understand.

## CHAPTER 12

Cloudera Hue

Hue is a web application that provides an end-user focused interface for a large number of the projects in the Hadoop ecosystem. When Hadoop is configured with Kerberos authentication, then Hue must be configured with Kerberos credentials to properly access Hadoop. Kerberos is enabled by setting the following parameters in the *hue.ini* file:

hue_principal
> The Kerberos principal name for the Hue, including the fully qualified domain name of the Hue server

hue_keytab
> The path to the Kerberos keytab file containing Hue's service credentials

kinit_path
> The path to the Kerberos kinit command (not needed if kinit is on the path)

reinit_frequency
> The frequency in seconds for Hue to renew its Kerberos tickets

These settings should be placed under the [[kerberos]] subsection of the [desktop] top-level section in the *hue.ini* file. See Example 12-1 for a sample Hue kerberos configuration.

Example 12-1. Configuring Kerberos in Hue

```
[desktop]
[[kerberos]]
hue_principal=hue/hue.example.com@EXAMPLE.COM
hue_keytab=/etc/hue/conf/hue.keytab
reinit_frequency=3600
```

Hue has its own set of authentication backends and authenticates against Hadoop and other projects using Kerberos. In order to perform actions on behalf of other users, Hadoop must be configured to trust the Hue service. This is done by configuring Hadoop's proxy user/user impersonation capabilities. This is controlled by setting the hosts Hue can run on and the groups of users that Hue can impersonate. Either value can be set to * to indicate that impersonation is enabled from all hosts or from all groups, respectively. Example 12-2 shows how to enable Hue to impersonate users when accessing Hadoop from the host *hue.example.com* and for users in the hadoop-users group.

Example 12-2. Configuring Hue User Impersonation for Hadoop in core-site.xml

```
<property>
  <name>hadoop.proxyuser.hue.hosts</name>
  <value>hue.example.com</value>
</property>
<property>
  <name>hadoop.proxyuser.hue.groups</name>
  <value>hadoop-users</value>
</property>
```

HBase and Hive use the Hadoop impersonation configuration, but Oozie must be configured independently. If you want to use Oozie from Hue, you must set the oozie.service.ProxyUserService.proxyuser.*<user>*.hosts and oozie.service.ProxyUserService.proxyuser.*<user>*.groups properties in the *oozie-site.xml* file. Example 12-3 shows how to enable Hue to impersonate users when accessing Oozie from the host hue.example.com and for users in the *hadoop-users* group.

Example 12-3. Configuring Hue user impersonation for Oozie in oozie-site.xml

```
<property>
  <name>oozie.service.ProxyUserService.proxyuser.hue.hosts</name>
  <value>hue.example.com</value>
</property>
<property>
  <name>oozie.service.ProxyUserService.proxyuser.hue.groups</name>
  <value>hadoop-users</value>
</property>
```

If you're using the Hue search application, you also need to enable impersonation in Solr. This is done by setting the SOLR_SECURITY_ALLOWED_PROXYUSERS, SOLR_SECURITY_PROXYUSER_*<user>*_HOSTS, and SOLR_SECURITY_PROX YUSER_*<user>*_GROUPS environment variables in the */etc/default/solr* file. See Example 12-4 for a sample configuration to enable impersonation from the host hue.example.com and for users in the *hadoop-users* group.

Example 12-4. Configuring Hue user impersonation for Solr in /etc/default/solr

```
SOLR_SECURITY_ALLOWED_PROXYUSERS=hue
SOLR_SECURITY_PROXYUSER_hue_HOSTS=hue.example.com
SOLR_SECURITY_PROXYUSER_hue_GROUPS=hadoop-users
```

Hue HTTPS

By default, Hue runs over plain old HTTP. This is suitable for proofs of concept or for environments where the network between clients and Hue is fully trusted. However, for most environments it's strongly recommended that you configure Hue to use HTTPS. This is especially important if you don't fully trust the network between clients and Hue, as most of Hue's authentication backends support entering in a username and password through a browser form.

Fortunately, Hue makes configuring HTTPS easy. To do so, you simply configure the `ssl_certificate` and `ssl_private_key` settings, which are both under the `desktop` section of the *hue.ini* file. Both files should be in PEM format and the private key cannot be encrypted with a passphrase. See Example 12-5 for a sample configuration.

Example 12-5. Configuring Hue to use HTTPS

```
[desktop]
ssl_certificate=/etc/hue/conf/hue.crt
ssl_private_key=/etc/hue/conf/hue.pem
```

 Hue does not currently support using a private key that is protected with a passphrase. This means it's very important that Hue's private key be protected to the greatest extent possible. Ensure that the key is owned by the `hue` user and is only readable by its owner (e.g., `chmod 400 /etc/hue/conf/hue.pem`). You might also configure filesystem-level encryption on the filesystem, storing the private key as described in "Filesystem Encryption" on page 205. In cases where Hue is on a server that has other resources protected by TLS/SSL, it's strongly recommended that you issue a unique certificate just for Hue. This will lower the risk if Hue's private key is compromised by protecting other services running on the same machine.

Hue Authentication

Hue has a pluggable authentication framework and ships a number of useful authentication backends. The default authentication backend uses a private list of usernames and passwords stored in Hue's backing database. The backend is configured by setting the `backend` property to `desktop.auth.backend.AllowFirstUserDjangoBackend` under the [[auth]] subsection of the [desktop] section. See Example 12-6 for a sample *hue.ini* file where the backend is explicitly set. Because this is the default, you can also leave this setting out entirely.

Example 12-6. Configuring the default Hue authentication backend

```
[desktop]
[[auth]]
backend=desktop.auth.backend.AllowFirstUserDjangoBackend
```

Hue also has support for using Kerberos/SPNEGO, LDAP, PAM, and SAML for authentication. We won't cover all of the options here, so refer to the config_help command for more information.[1]

SPNEGO Backend

Simple and Protected GSSAPI Negotiation Mechanism (SPNEGO)[2] is a GSSAPI pseudo-mechanism for allowing clients and servers to negotiate the choice of authentication technology. SPNEGO is used any time a client wants to authenticate with a remote server but neither the client nor the server knows in advance the authentication protocols the other supports. The most common use of SPNEGO is with the HTTP negotiate protocol first proposed by Microsoft.[3]

Hue only supports SPNEGO with Kerberos V5 as the underlying mechanism. In particular this means you can't use Hue with the *Microsoft NT LAN Manager* (NTLM) protocol. Configuring SPNEGO with Hue requires setting the Hue authentication backend to SpnegoDjangoBackend (see Example 12-7), as well as setting the KRB5_KTNAME environment variable to the location of a keytab file that has the key for the HTTP/*<fully qualified domain name>*@*<REALM>* principal. If you're starting Hue by hand on the server hue.example.com and your keytab is located in */etc/hue/conf/ hue.keytab*, then you'd start Hue as shown in Example 12-8.

Example 12-7. Configuring the SPNEGO Hue authentication backend

```
[desktop]
[[auth]]
backend=desktop.auth.backend.SpnegoDjangoBackend
```

---

1 You can execute the config_help command with either /usr/share/hue/build/env/bin/hue config_help or /opt/cloudera/parcels/CDH/lib/hue/build/env/bin/hue config_help depending on how Hue was installed.

2 See RFC 4178 (*http://tools.ietf.org/html/rfc4178*) for a description of the SPNEGO pseudo-mechanism.

3 See Microsoft's MSDN article (*http://msdn.microsoft.com/en-us/library/ms995329.aspx*) for details.

Example 12-8. Setting KRB5_KTNAME and starting Hue manually

```
[hue@hue ~]$ export KRB5_KTNAME=/etc/hue/conf/hue.keytab
[hue@hue ~]$ ${HUE_HOME}/build/env/bin/supervisor
```

In order to use SPNEGO, you also need to have a TGT on your desktop (e.g., by running `kinit`) and you need to use a browser that supports SPNEGO. Internet Explorer and Safari both support SPNEGO without additional configuration. If you're using Firefox, you first must add the server or domain name you're authenticating against to the list of trusted URIs. This is done by typing `about:config` in the URL bar, then searching for `network.negotiate-auth.trusted-uris`, and then updating that preference to include the server name or domain name. For example, if you wanted to support SPNEGO with any server on the `example.com` domain, you would set `network.negotiate-auth.trusted-uris=example.com`. If you see the message `401 Unauthorized` while trying to connect to Hue, you likely don't have your trusted URIs configured correctly in Firefox.

SAML Backend

Hue also supports using the *Security Assertion Markup Language* (SAML) standard for *single sign-on* (SSO). SAML works by separating *service providers* (SP) from *identity providers* (IdP). When you request access to a resource, the SP will redirect you to the IdP where authentication will take place. The IdP will then pass an assertion validating your identity to the SP who will grant access to the target resource. The Wikipedia article on SAML (*http://bit.ly/1GFpLur*) has more details, including a diagram showing the steps of the SAML process.

When configured with the SAML authentication backend, Hue will act as a service provider and redirect to your identity provider for authentication. Configuring Hue to use SAML is more complicated than the other authentication backends. Hue has to interact with a third-party identity provider so some of the details will depend on which identity provider you're using. Also, Hue doesn't ship with several of the dependencies required to use SAML. So we'll start by installing the required dependencies by following the steps in Example 12-9.

Example 12-9. Install dependencies for SAML authentication backend

```
[root@hue ~]# yum install swig openssl openssl-devel gcc python-devel
Loaded plugins: fastestmirror, priorities
Loading mirror speeds from cached hostfile
 * base: mirror.hmc.edu
 * extras: mirrors.unifiedlayer.com
 * updates: mirror.pac-12.org
...
Complete!
[root@hue ~]# yum install xmlsec1 xmlsec1-openssl
```

```
Loaded plugins: fastestmirror, priorities
Loading mirror speeds from cached hostfile
 * base: mirror.hmc.edu
 * extras: mirrors.unifiedlayer.com
 * updates: mirror.pac-12.org
...
Complete!
[root@hue ~]# $HUE_HOME/build/env/bin/pip install --upgrade setuptools
Downloading/unpacking setuptools from https://pypi.python.org/packages/sourc
e/s/setuptools/setuptools-7.0.tar.gz#md5=6245d6752e2ef803c365f560f7f2f940
  Downloading setuptools-7.0.tar.gz (793Kb): 793Kb downloaded
...
Successfully installed setuptools
Cleaning up...
[root@hue ~]# $HUE_HOME/build/env/bin/pip install -e \
  git+https://github.com/abec/pysaml2@HEAD#egg=pysaml2
Obtaining pysaml2 from git+https://github.com/abec/pysaml2@HEAD#egg=pysaml2
  Updating ./build/env/src/pysaml2 clone (to HEAD)
...
Successfully installed pysaml2 m2crypto importlib WebOb
Cleaning up...
[root@hue ~]# $HUE_HOME/build/env/bin/pip install -e \
  git+https://github.com/abec/djangosaml2@HEAD#egg=djangosaml2
Obtaining djangosaml2 from git+https://github.com/abec/djangosaml2@HEAD#egg=
djangosaml2
  Cloning https://github.com/abec/djangosaml2 (to HEAD) to ./build/env/src/d
jangosaml2
...
Successfully installed djangosaml2
Cleaning up...
```

This will install some development tools and then install the Python modules required to work with SAML. After installing the dependencies, you need to download the metadata file from your identity provider. The details will vary depending on which identity provider you're using. For the Shibboleth Identity Provider, you can use curl to download the metadata to */etc/hue/saml/metadata.xml*.

```
[root@hue ~]# mkdir /etc/hue/saml
[root@hue ~]# curl -k -o /etc/hue/saml/metadata.xml \
  https://idp.example.com:8443/idp/shibboleth
```

You also need a certificate and private key to sign requests with. This has to be a key trusted by your identity provider to sign requests, so you might not be able to just reuse the same key and certificate you used when enabling HTTPS for Hue. For our purposes, we'll assume that the key and certificate have been created and placed into the */etc/hue/saml/key.pem* and */etc/hue/saml/idp.pem* files, respectively. All that's left is to configure Hue itself. See Example 12-10 for the relevant sections from the */etc/hue/conf/hue.ini* file.

Example 12-10. Configuring the SAML Hue authentication backend

```
[desktop]
[[auth]]
backend=libsaml.backend.SAML2Backend

[libsaml]
xmlsec_binary=/usr/bin/xmlsec1
create_users_on_login=true
metadata_file=/etc/hue/saml/metadata.xml
key_file=/etc/hue/saml/key.pem
cert_file=/etc/hue/saml/idp.pem
```

There are additional optional configuration parameters that can be set in the `saml` configuration group. The full list of configuration parameters is shown here:

xmlsec_binary
> Path to the xmlsec1 binary, which is the executable used to sign, verify, encrypt, and decrypt SAML requests and assertions. Typically */usr/bin/xmlsec1*.

create_users_on_login
> Create Hue users upon login. Can be `true` or `false`.

required_attributes
> Attributes Hue demands from the IdP. Comma-separated list of attributes. Example: `uid,email`

optional_attributes
> Attributes Hue can handle from the IdP. Comma-separated list of attributes. Handled the same way as `required_attributes`.

metadata_file
> Path to the metadata XML file from the IdP. The file must be readable by the hue user.

key_file
> PEM-formatted key file.

cert_file
> PEM-formatted X.509 certificate.

user_attribute_mapping
> Maps attributes received from the IdP (specified in `required_attributes`, `optional_attributes`, and the IdP config) to Hue user attributes. Example: `{uid:'username', email: email}`

authn_requests_signed

> Sign authentication requests. Can be `true` or `false`. Check the documentation of your IdP to see if this setting is required.

logout_requests_signed

> Sign logout requests. Can be `true` or `false`. Check the documentation of your IdP to see if this setting is required.

LDAP Backend

The final authentication method we'll cover is using LDAP/Active Directory to verify usernames and passwords. There are two ways to configure Hue's LDAP backend. The first is to perform an LDAP search to find the distinguished names (DN) of users and then use the DN to bind to LDAP. The second is to provide Hue with a DN pattern which is filled in with a username, and then a bind is performed without a search.

When configuring Hue with search bind, you must set `search_bind_authentication` to `true`, `ldap_url`, and the `base_dn` setting in the `ldap` subsection of the `desktop` section. You also must set the `user_filter` and `user_name_attr` settings in the `users` subsection of the `ldap` subsection of the `desktop` section. You should also set the `group_filter`, `group_name_attr`, and `group_member_attr` settings in the `groups` subsection of the `ldap` subsection of the `desktop` section so that you can import LDAP groups as Hue groups.

A snippet of a *hue.ini* configuration file configured to do LDAP authentication with a search bind is shown in Example 12-11. In this example, the LDAP server is running with LDAPS on `ldap.example.com`. This LDAP server stores users and groups under a base DN of `cn=accounts,dc=example,dc=com`. Finally, user accounts are in `object Class=posixaccount` and groups are in `objectClass=posixgroup`. A complete description of all of the LDAP-related settings is shown in Table 12-1.

Example 12-11. Configuring the LDAP Hue authentication backend with search bind

```
[desktop]
[[auth]]
backend=desktop.auth.backend.LdapBackend

[[ldap]]
ldap_url=ldaps://ldap.example.com
base_dn="cn=accounts,dc=example,dc=com"
search_bind_authentication=true
ldap_cert=/etc/hue/conf/ca.crt
use_start_tls=false
create_users_on_login=true
```

```
[[[users]]]
user_filter="objectClass=posixaccount"
user_name_attr="uid"

[[[groups]]]
group_filter="objectClass=posixgroup"
group_name_attr="cn"
group_member_attr="member"
```

If you prefer to use a direct bind, then you must set search_bind_authentication to false and set either nt_domain or ldap_username_pattern depending on whether you're using Active Directory or another LDAP provider, respectively. You must still configure the search-related settings (e.g., user_filter, user_name_attr, etc.) as those will be used when syncing users and groups from LDAP. If we want to use the same server setup as before but use direct bind instead of search bind, we would use a configuration similar to Example 12-12. Again, the full set of LDAP configuration parameters is shown in Table 12-1.

Example 12-12. Configuring the LDAP Hue authentication backend with direct bind

```
[desktop]
[[auth]]
backend=desktop.auth.backend.LdapBackend

[[ldap]]
ldap_url=ldaps://ldap.example.com
base_dn="cn=accounts,dc=example,dc=com"
search_bind_authentication=false
ldap_username_pattern="uid=<username>,cn=users,cn=accounts,dc=example,dc=com"
ldap_cert=/etc/hue/conf/ca.crt
use_start_tls=false
create_users_on_login=true

[[[users]]]
user_filter="objectClass=posixaccount"
user_name_attr="uid"

[[[groups]]]
group_filter="objectClass=posixgroup"
group_name_attr="cn"
group_member_attr="member"
```

Table 12-1. Configuration properties for Hue LDAP authentication

Section	Property	Description
desktop.auth	backend	The authentication backend to use (set to `desktop.auth.backend.LdapBackend`)
desktop.ldap	ldap_url	The LDAP server URL (use `ldaps://` for secure LDAP)
desktop.ldap	base_dn	The base LDAP distinguished name to use for LDAP search
desktop.ldap	bind_dn	The distinguished name to bind as when searching LDAP; only required when anonymous searching is disabled on your LDAP server
desktop.ldap	bind_password	The password for the bind_dn user; only required when anonymous searching is disabled on your LDAP server
desktop.ldap	create_users_on_login	Set to true to create users the first time they login; if this is set to false, an administrator will have to manually add a user to Hue before they can log in with their LDAP credentials
desktop.ldap	search_bind_authentication	Set to `true` to use search bind; false enables direct bind
desktop.ldap	ldap_username_pattern	The pattern used to construct distinguished names from usernames—it must contain the string *<username>*, which will be replaced with the username of the user to construct the final DN; only used when you configure Hue with direct bind (i.e., `search_bind_authentication=`*false*)
desktop.ldap	nt_domain	The NT domain of the Active Directory server; only used when you configure Hue with direct bind (i.e., `search_bind_authentication=`*false*)
desktop.ldap	ldap_cert	The location of the CA certificate used to verify the LDAP server's certificate
desktop.ldap	use_start_tls	Set to true to use StartTLS; set to false when using an `ldaps://` URL for `ldap_url`
desktop.ldap.users	user_filter	The base filter to use when searching for users

Section	Property	Description
desktop.ldap.users	user_name_attr	The username attribute in the LDAP schema (this is typically sAMAccountName for Active Directory and uid for other LDAP directories)
desktop.ldap.groups	group_filter	The base filter to use when searching for groups
desktop.ldap.groups	group_name_attr	The group name attribute in the LDAP schema (this is typically cn)
desktop.ldap.groups	group_member_attr	The LDAP attribute that specifies members of a group (this is typically member)

One thing you'll notice in Examples 12-11 and 12-12 is that we set ldap_cert to point to a CA certificate. This is needed because we configured the LDAP URL using the *ldaps://* scheme. It's strongly recommended that you use either LDAPS or StartTLS. When using StartTLS, configure the LDAP URL with the *ldap://* scheme and set use_start_tls to true.

Hue Authorization

Hue has two types of user accounts: regular users and superusers. Regular users are governed by an access control list (ACL)–based authorization system that controls which application permissions are available to which groups. Hue superusers can:

- Add and delete users
- Add and delete groups
- Assign permissions to groups
- Change a user into a superuser
- Import users and groups from an LDAP server
- Install the example queries, tables, and data
- View, submit, and modify any Oozie workflow, coordinator, or bundle
- Impersonate any user when viewing and modifying Sentry permissions
- Impersonate any user when viewing and modifying HDFS ACLs

The Hue superuser is *not* the same as the HDFS superuser. The HDFS superuser is the user that runs the NameNode daemon, typically `hdfs`, and has permission to list, read, and write any HDFS files and directories. If you want to perform HDFS superuser actions from Hue, you need to add a user with the same username as the HDFS superuser. Alternatively, you can set the HDFS super group to assign a group of users HDFS superuser privileges. See "HDFS Authorization" on page 97.

Each Hue application defines one or more actions that users can perform. Authorization is controlled by setting an ACL per action that lists the groups that can perform that action. Every application has an action called "Launch this application" which controls which users can run that application. Several applications define additional actions that can be controlled.

The permissions granted in Hue only grant privileges to *invoke* the given action from the given Hue app. The user performing an action will still need to be authorized by the service they're accessing. For example, a user might have permissions for the "Allow DDL operations" in the Metastore app, but if she doesn't have the ALL privilege on the database in Sentry, she won't be able to create tables.

The HBase app defines the "Allow writing in the HBase app" action, which gives permissions to add rows, add cells, edit cells, drop rows, and drop cells from the HBase app. The Metastore app defines the "Allow DDL operations" action, which gives permission to create, edit, and drop tables from the metastore browser. The Oozie app defines the "Oozie Dashboard read-only user for all jobs," which grants permission to have read-only access to all workflows, coordinators, and bundles, regardless of whether they're shared. The Security app defines the "Let a user impersonate another user when listing objects like files or tables" action. This action lets the user impersonate other users and see what tables, files, and directories that user has access to.

Granting permission for the "Let a user impersonate another user when listing objects like files or tables" can expose information that would otherwise not be available. In particular, it allows a user to impersonate a user that has access to see files in a directory for which the logged-in user is not authorized. Permissions to perform this action should be granted sparingly. It's also worth warning that Hue superusers also have access to impersonate users in the Security app. Thus care should also be taken in making a user a Hue superuser.

The Useradmin app defines the "Access to profile page on User Admin" action, but this action is deprecated and can be safely ignored.

Hue SSL Client Configurations

In this Hue section, we have covered a lot of pertinent security configurations, but certainly have not exhaustively covered how to set up and configure Hue in the general case, which we deem out of scope for this book. However, one important aspect to explain is how to properly set up Hue when the various underlying components are set up with SSL wire encryption. If Hadoop, Hive, and Impala have SSL enabled, Example 12-13 shows the snippets that are necessary.

Example 12-13. Hue SSL client configurations

```
# Non-SSL configurations omitted for brevity
[beeswax]
[[ssl]]
enabled=true
cacerts=/etc/hue/ca.cer
key=/etc/hue/host.key
cert=/etc/hue/host.cer
validate=true
[impala]
[[ssl]]
enabled=true
cacerts=/etc/hue/ca.cer
key=/etc/hue/host.key
cert=/etc/hue/host.cer
validate=true
```

In both the Hive and Impala configurations, the `validate` option specifies whether Hue should check that the certificates presented by those services are signed by an authority in the configured certificate authority chain.

In addition to what is shown in the example, an environment variable `REQUESTS_CA_BUNDLE` needs to point to the location on disk where the SSL certificate authority chain file is (in PEM format). This is used for the Hadoop SSL client to HDFS, MapReduce, YARN, and HttpFS.

Summary

In this chapter, we took a close look at Hue's important role in allowing end users to access several different ecosystem components through a centralized web console. With Hue, users are able to log in once to a web console, with the rest of their cluster actions performed via impersonation from a Hue system user.

This chapter closes our review of data security components. From here, we can take what we have learned throughout the book and put it all together by walking through case studies using real-world scenarios.

## PART IV

Putting It All Together

## CHAPTER 13

Case Studies

In this chapter, we present two case studies that cover many of the security topics in the book. First, we'll take a look at how Sentry can be used to control SQL access to data in a multitenancy environment. This will serve as a good warmup before we dive into a more detailed case study that shows a custom HBase application in action with various security features in place.

Case Study: Hadoop Data Warehouse

One of the key benefits of big data and Hadoop is the notion that many different and disparate datasets can be brought together to solve unique problems. What comes along with this are different types of users that span multiple lines of business. In this case study, we will take a look at how Sentry can be used to provide strong authorization of data in Hive and Impala in an environment consisting of multiple lines of business, multiple data owners, and different analysts.

First, let's list the assumptions we are making for this case study:

- The environment consists of three lines of business, which we will call `lob1`, `lob2`, and `lob3`
- Each line of business has analysts and administrators
  - The analysts are defined by the groups `lob1grp`, `lob2grp`, and `lob3grp`
  - The administrators are defined by the groups `lob1adm`, `lob2adm`, and `lob3adm`
  - Administrators are also in the analysts groups
- Each line of business needs to have its own sandbox area in HDFS to do ad hoc analysis, as well as to upload self-service data sources

- Each line of business has its own administrators that control access to their respective sandboxes
- Data inside the Hive warehouse is IT-managed, meaning only noninteractive ETL users add data
- Only Hive administrators create new objects in the Hive warehouse
- The Hive warehouse uses the default HDFS location */user/hive/warehouse*
- Kerberos has already been set up for the cluster
- Sentry has already been set up in the environment
- HDFS already has extended ACLs enabled
- The default umask for HDFS is set to 007

Environment Setup

Now that we have the basic assumptions, we need to set up the necessary directories in HDFS and prepare them for Sentry. The first thing we will do is lock down the Hive warehouse directory. HiveServer2 impersonation is disabled when enabling Sentry, so only the hive group should have access (which includes the hive and impala users). Here's what we need to do:

```
[root@server1 ~]# kinit hive
Password for hive@EXAMPLE.COM:
[root@server1 ~]# hdfs dfs -chmod -R 0771 /user/hive/warehouse
[root@server1 ~]# hdfs dfs -chown -R hive:hive /user/hive/warehouse
[root@server1 ~]#
```

As mentioned in the assumptions, each line of business needs a sandbox area. We will create the path */data/sandbox* as the root directory for all the sandboxes, and create the associated structures within it:

```
[root@server1 ~]# kinit hdfs
Password for hdfs@EC2.INTERNAL:
[root@server1 ~]# hdfs dfs -mkdir /data
[root@server1 ~]# hdfs dfs -mkdir /data/sandbox
[root@server1 ~]# hdfs dfs -mkdir /data/sandbox/lob1
[root@server1 ~]# hdfs dfs -mkdir /data/sandbox/lob2
[root@server1 ~]# hdfs dfs -mkdir /data/sandbox/lob3
[root@server1 ~]# hdfs dfs -chmod 770 /data/sandbox/lob1
[root@server1 ~]# hdfs dfs -chmod 770 /data/sandbox/lob2
[root@server1 ~]# hdfs dfs -chmod 770 /data/sandbox/lob3
[root@server1 ~]# hdfs dfs -chgrp lob1grp /data/sandbox/lob1
[root@server1 ~]# hdfs dfs -chgrp lob2grp /data/sandbox/lob2
[root@server1 ~]# hdfs dfs -chgrp lob3grp /data/sandbox/lob3
[root@server1 ~]#
```

Now that the basic directory structure is set up, we need to start thinking about what is needed to support Hive and Impala access to the sandbox. After all, these sandboxes are the place where all the users will be doing their ad hoc analytic work. Both the hive and impala users need access to these directories, so let's go ahead and set up HDFS-extended ACLs to allow the hive group full access:

```
[root@server1 ~]# hdfs dfs -setfacl -m default:group:hive:rwx /data/sandbox/lob1
[root@server1 ~]# hdfs dfs -setfacl -m default:group:hive:rwx /data/sandbox/lob2
[root@server1 ~]# hdfs dfs -setfacl -m default:group:hive:rwx /data/sandbox/lob3
[root@server1 ~]# hdfs dfs -setfacl -m group:hive:rwx /data/sandbox/lob1
[root@server1 ~]# hdfs dfs -setfacl -m group:hive:rwx /data/sandbox/lob2
[root@server1 ~]# hdfs dfs -setfacl -m group:hive:rwx /data/sandbox/lob3
[root@server1 ~]#
```

Remember, the default ACL is only applicable to directories, and it only dictates the ACLs that are copied to new subdirectories and files. Because of this fact, the parent directories still need a regular access ACL.

The next part we need to do is to make sure that regardless of who creates new files, all the intended accesses persist. If we left the permissions as they are right now, new directories and files created by the hive or impala users may actually be accessible by the analysts and administrators in the line of business. To fix that, let's go ahead and add those groups to the extended ACLs:

```
[root@server1 ~]# hdfs dfs -setfacl -m default:group:lob1grp:rwx \
  /data/sandbox/lob1
[root@server1 ~]# hdfs dfs -setfacl -m default:group:lob1adm:rwx \
  /data/sandbox/lob1
[root@server1 ~]# hdfs dfs -setfacl -m default:group:lob2grp:rwx \
  /data/sandbox/lob2
[root@server1 ~]# hdfs dfs -setfacl -m default:group:lob2adm:rwx \
  /data/sandbox/lob2
[root@server1 ~]# hdfs dfs -setfacl -m default:group:lob3grp:rwx \
  /data/sandbox/lob3
[root@server1 ~]# hdfs dfs -setfacl -m default:group:lob3adm:rwx \
  /data/sandbox/lob3
[root@server1 ~]# hdfs dfs -setfacl -m group:lob1grp:rwx /data/sandbox/lob1
[root@server1 ~]# hdfs dfs -setfacl -m group:lob1adm:rwx /data/sandbox/lob1
[root@server1 ~]# hdfs dfs -setfacl -m group:lob2grp:rwx /data/sandbox/lob2
[root@server1 ~]# hdfs dfs -setfacl -m group:lob2adm:rwx /data/sandbox/lob2
[root@server1 ~]# hdfs dfs -setfacl -m group:lob3grp:rwx /data/sandbox/lob3
[root@server1 ~]# hdfs dfs -setfacl -m group:lob3adm:rwx /data/sandbox/lob3
[root@server1 ~]#
```

Now that we have all the extended ACLs set up, let's take a look at one of them:

```
[root@server1 ~]# hdfs dfs -getfacl -R /data/sandbox/lob1
# file: /data/sandbox/lob1
```

```
# owner: hdfs
# group: lob1grp
user::rwx
group::rwx
group:hive:rwx
group:lob1adm:rwx
group:lob1grp:rwx
mask::rwx
other::---
default:user::rwx
default:group::rwx
default:group:hive:rwx
default:group:lob1adm:rwx
default:group:lob1grp:rwx
default:mask::rwx
default:other::---
[root@server1 ~]#
```

We have handled all of the tenants in the cluster, so let's make sure we also create a space in HDFS for the ETL noninteractive user to use:

```
[root@server1 ~]# hdfs dfs -mkdir /data/etl
[root@server1 ~]# hdfs dfs -chown etluser:hive /data/etl
[root@server1 ~]# hdfs dfs -chmod 770 /data/etl
[root@server1 ~]# hdfs dfs -setfacl -m default:group:hive:rwx /data/etl
[root@server1 ~]# hdfs dfs -setfacl -m group:hive:rwx /data/etl
[root@server1 ~]# hdfs dfs -setfacl -m default:user:etluser:rwx /data/etl
[root@server1 ~]# hdfs dfs -setfacl -m user:etluser:rwx /data/etl
[root@server1 ~]# hdfs dfs -getfacl /data/etl
# file: /data/etl
# owner: etluser
# group: hive
user::rwx
user:etluser:rwx
group::rwx
group:hive:rwx
mask::rwx
other::---
default:user::rwx
default:user:etluser:rwx
default:group::rwx
default:group:hive:rwx
default:mask::rwx
default:other::---
[root@server1 ~]#
```

The next step is to start doing some administration tasks in Hive using the beeline shell. We will use the hive user, because by default it is a Sentry administrator, and can thus create policies.

You can use a properties file for `beeline` to specify connection information. This makes it much easier than remembering the syntax or looking at your bash history.

The *beeline.properties* file we will use is shown in Example 13-1. Note that the username and password are required but unused for the actual authentication because Kerberos is enabled.

Example 13-1. beeline.properties file

```
ConnectionURL=jdbc:hive2://server1.example.com:10000/;principal=
  hive/server1.example.com@EXAMPLE.COM
ConnectionDriverName=org.apache.hive.jdbc.HiveDriver
ConnectionUserName=.
ConnectionPassword=.

    [root@server1 ~]# kinit hive
    Password for hive@EXAMPLE.COM:
    [root@server1 ~]# beeline
    ...
    beeline> !properties beeline.properties
    ...
    > CREATE ROLE sqladmin;
    > GRANT ROLE sqladmin TO GROUP hive;
    > GRANT ALL ON SERVER server1 TO ROLE sqladmin;
    > CREATE DATABASE lob1 LOCATION '/data/sandbox/lob1';
    > CREATE DATABASE lob2 LOCATION '/data/sandbox/lob2';
    > CREATE DATABASE lob3 LOCATION '/data/sandbox/lob3';
    > CREATE DATABASE etl LOCATION '/data/etl';
```

Now that we have the administrator role and databases created, we can set up the Sentry policies that will provide authorization for both Hive and Impala to end users:

```
    > CREATE ROLE lob1analyst;
    > GRANT ROLE lob1analyst TO GROUP lob1grp;
    > GRANT ALL ON DATABASE lob1 TO ROLE lob1analyst;
    > CREATE ROLE lob1administrator;
    > GRANT ROLE lob1administrator TO GROUP lob1adm WITH GRANT OPTION;
    > GRANT ALL ON DATABASE lob1 TO role lob1administrator;
    > CREATE ROLE lob2analyst;
    > GRANT ROLE lob2analyst TO GROUP lob2grp;
    > GRANT ALL ON DATABASE lob2 TO ROLE lob2analyst;
    > CREATE ROLE lob2administrator;
    > GRANT ROLE lob2administrator TO GROUP lob2adm WITH GRANT OPTION;
    > GRANT ALL ON DATABASE lob2 TO ROLE lob2administrator;
    > CREATE ROLE lob3analyst;
    > GRANT ROLE lob3analyst TO GROUP lob3grp;
    > GRANT ALL ON DATABASE lob3 TO role lob3analyst;
    > CREATE ROLE lob3administrator;
```

```
> GRANT ROLE lob3administrator TO GROUP lob3adm WITH GRANT OPTION;
> GRANT ALL ON DATABASE lob3 TO ROLE lob3administrator;
> CREATE ROLE etl;
> GRANT ROLE etl TO GROUP etluser;
> GRANT ALL ON DATABASE etl TO ROLE etl;
```

Another important requirement we listed in the assumptions is that users should able to upload self-service files to their respective sandboxes. To allow users to leverage these files in Hive and Impala, they also need some URI privileges. We will also go ahead and provide write privileges so that users can also extract data out of Hive and into the sandbox area for additional non-SQL analysis:

```
> GRANT ALL ON URI 'hdfs://nameservice1/data/etl' TO ROLE etl;
> GRANT ALL ON URI 'hdfs://nameservice1/data/sandbox/lob1' TO ROLE lob1analyst;
> GRANT ALL ON URI 'hdfs://nameservice1/data/sandbox/lob1'
  TO ROLE lob1administrator;
> GRANT ALL ON URI 'hdfs://nameservice1/data/sandbox/lob2' TO ROLE lob2analyst;
> GRANT ALL ON URI 'hdfs://nameservice1/data/sandbox/lob2'
  TO ROLE lob2administrator;
> GRANT ALL ON URI 'hdfs://nameservice1/data/sandbox/lob3' TO ROLE lob3analyst;
> GRANT ALL ON URI 'hdfs://nameservice1/data/sandbox/lob3'
  TO ROLE lob3administrator;
```

The URI paths shown use the HDFS HA nameservice name. If you do not have HA set up, you will need to specify the NameNode fully qualified domain name explicitly, including the port (8020).

User Experience

With the environment fully up, ready, and outfitted with our full set of HDFS privileges and Sentry policies, let's look at what end users see with these enforcements in place. First, we will look at what a user in the sqladmin role sees:

```
[root@server1 ~]$ kinit hive
Password for hive@EXAMPLE.COM:
[root@server1 ~]$ beeline
...
> !properties beeline.properties
...
> SHOW DATABASES;
+----------------+
| database_name  |
+----------------+
| default        |
| etl            |
| lob1           |
| lob2           |
| lob3           |
+----------------+
```

```
> quit;
[root@server1 ~]$
```

As you can see, the `sqladmin` role is allowed to see every database that we set up. This is expected because the `sqladmin` role has been granted full access to the `SERVER` object. Next, we will take a look at what a user assigned the `etl` role sees:

```
[root@server1 ~]$ kinit etluser
Password for etluser@EXAMPLE.COM:
[root@server1 ~]$ beeline
...
> !properties beeline.properties
...
> SHOW DATABASES;
+----------------+
| database_name  |
+----------------+
| default        |
| etl            |
+----------------+
> USE lob1;
Error: Error while compiling statement: FAILED: SemanticException
 No valid privileges (state=42000,code=40000)
> quit;
[root@server1 ~]$
```

This time, the user does not see the full list of databases in the metastore. Instead, the user sees only the databases that contain objects that they have some access to. The example shows that not only are objects the user does not have access to hidden from the user, but that they are denied access even if the user requests the object by name. This is exactly what we expect to happen.

Now let's say that the table `sample_07` in the `etl` database needs to be made available to the `lob1analyst` role. However, the caveat is that not all of the columns can be shared. For that, we need to create a view that contains only the columns we intend to make visible to the role. After creating this view, we grant access to it for the `lob1analyst` role:

```
[root@server1 ~]$ kinit hive
Password for hive@EXAMPLE.COM:
[root@server1 ~]$ beeline
...
> !properties beeline.properties
...
> USE etl;
> CREATE VIEW sample_07_view AS SELECT code, description, total_emp
  FROM sample_07;
> GRANT SELECT ON TABLE sample_07_view TO ROLE lob1analyst;
> quit;
[root@server1 ~]$
```

After completing these tasks, we can test access with a user that is assigned to the
lob1analyst role:

```
[root@server1 ~]$ kinit lob1user
Password for lob1user@EXAMPLE.COM:
[root@server1 ~]$ beeline
...
> !properties beeline.properties
...
> SHOW DATABASES;
+----------------+
| database_name  |
+----------------+
| default        |
| etl            |
| lob1           |
+----------------+
> USE etl;
> SHOW TABLES;
+-----------------+
|    tab_name     |
+-----------------+
| sample_07_view  |
+-----------------+
> SELECT * FROM sample_07 LIMIT 1;
Error: Error while compiling statement: FAILED: SemanticException
 No valid privileges (state=42000,code=40000)
> quit;
[root@server1 ~]$ hdfs dfs -ls /data/etl
ls: Permission denied: user=lob1user, access=READ_EXECUTE, inode="/data/etl":
 etluser:hive:drwxrwx---:group::---,group:hive:rwx,
 default:user::rwx,default:group::---,default:group:hive:rwx,
 default:mask::rwx,default:other::---
[root@server1 ~]$
```

As shown, the lob1user is able to see the etl database in the listing. However, notice
that within the database only the sample_07_view object is visible. As expected, the
user is unable to read the source table either with SQL access, or from direct HDFS
access. Because we saw some "access denied" messages in this example, let's inspect
what shows up in the logfiles, starting with the HiveServer2 log:

```
2015-01-13 19:31:40,173 ERROR org.apache.hadoop.hive.ql.Driver: FAILED:
 SemanticException No valid privileges
org.apache.hadoop.hive.ql.parse.SemanticException: No valid privileges
        at org.apache.sentry.binding.hive.HiveAuthzBindingHook.
         postAnalyze(HiveAuthzBindingHook.java:320)
        at org.apache.hadoop.hive.ql.Driver.compile(Driver.java:457)
        at org.apache.hadoop.hive.ql.Driver.compile(Driver.java:352)
        at org.apache.hadoop.hive.ql.Driver.compileInternal
         (Driver.java:995)
        at org.apache.hadoop.hive.ql.Driver.compileAndRespond
         (Driver.java:988)
```

```
    at org.apache.hive.service.cli.operation.SQLOperation.prepare
     (SQLOperation.java:98)
    at org.apache.hive.service.cli.operation.SQLOperation.run
     (SQLOperation.java:163)
    at org.apache.hive.service.cli.session.HiveSessionImpl.
     runOperationWithLogCapture(HiveSessionImpl.java:524)
    at org.apache.hive.service.cli.session.HiveSessionImpl.
     executeStatementInternal(HiveSessionImpl.java:222)
    at org.apache.hive.service.cli.session.HiveSessionImpl.
     executeStatement(HiveSessionImpl.java:204)
    at org.apache.hive.service.cli.CLIService.executeStatement
     (CLIService.java:168)
    at org.apache.hive.service.cli.thrift.ThriftCLIService.
     ExecuteStatement(ThriftCLIService.java:316)
    at org.apache.hive.service.cli.thrift.TCLIService$Processor
     $ExecuteStatement.getResult(TCLIService.java:1373)
    at org.apache.hive.service.cli.thrift.TCLIService$Processor
     $ExecuteStatement.getResult(TCLIService.java:1358)
    at org.apache.thrift.ProcessFunction.process
     (ProcessFunction.java:39)
    at org.apache.thrift.TBaseProcessor.process(TBaseProcessor.java:39)
    at org.apache.hadoop.hive.thrift.HadoopThriftAuthBridge20S$Server
     $TUGIAssumingProcessor.process(HadoopThriftAuthBridge20S.java:608)
    at org.apache.thrift.server.TThreadPoolServer$WorkerProcess.run
     (TThreadPoolServer.java:244)
    at java.util.concurrent.ThreadPoolExecutor.runWorker
     (ThreadPoolExecutor.java:1145)
    at java.util.concurrent.ThreadPoolExecutor$Worker.run
     (ThreadPoolExecutor.java:615)
    at java.lang.Thread.run(Thread.java:745)
Caused by: org.apache.hadoop.hive.ql.metadata.AuthorizationException:
     User lob1user does not have privileges for QUERY
    at org.apache.sentry.binding.hive.authz.HiveAuthzBinding.authorize
     (HiveAuthzBinding.java:317)
    at org.apache.sentry.binding.hive.HiveAuthzBindingHook.
     authorizeWithHiveBindings(HiveAuthzBindingHook.java:502)
    at org.apache.sentry.binding.hive.HiveAuthzBindingHook.
     postAnalyze(HiveAuthzBindingHook.java:312)
    ... 20 more
```

Next, we see the access-denied audit event that showed up in the NameNode audit log:

```
2015-01-13 20:01:15,005 INFO FSNamesystem.audit: allowed=false
  ugi=lob1user@EXAMPLE.COM (auth:KERBEROS)
  ip=/10.6.9.73
  cmd=listStatus src=/data/etl dst=null perm=null
```

Summary

This basic case study has shown how to look at protecting data with both Sentry policies coupled with HDFS-extended ACLs. This example is purposefully basic, but it still illustrates how it is necessary to think about data organization as a key factor in multitenancy. Having a clear structure of how data resides in HDFS makes for easy security administration.

Case Study: Interactive HBase Web Application

A common use case for Hadoop is to build scale-out web applications. HBase has a number of features that make it ideal for interactive scale-out applications:

- A flexible data model that supports complex objects with rapidly evolving schemas
- Automatic repartitioning of data as nodes are added or removed from the cluster
- Integration with the rest of the Hadoop ecosystem allowing offline analysis of transactional data
- Intra-row ACID transactions
- Advanced authorization capabilities for various applications

For our purposes, we're most interested in the last feature in the list. For interactive applications, you often have to control which users have access to which datasets. For example, an application like Twitter has messages that are fully public, messages that are restricted to a whitelist of authorized users, and messages that are fully private. Being able to flexibly manage authorization in the face of such dynamic security requirements requires the use of a database that is equally dynamic.

In this case study, we'll take a look at an application for storing and browsing web page snapshots. This case study is built on top of an open source, HBase-based web application example (*https://github.com/kite-sdk/kite-spring-hbase-example*) from The Kite SDK (*http://kitesdk.org*). The original example works in a standalone development mode, as an application deployed on OpenShift, and as a production application deployed on an HBase cluster. Due to limitations of the MiniHBaseCluster class that is used for development mode and OpenShift deployments, our version will only work on production, secured HBase clusters. The full source code for our version of the example is available in the GitHub source code repository (*https://github.com/hadoop-security/kite-spring-hbase-example*) that accompanies this book.

Design and Architecture

Let's start by taking a look at the architecture of the web page snapshot demo shown in Figure 13-1. The web application gets deployed to an edge node. The user connects to the application through their browser and provides a URL to either take a new snapshot or view existing snapshots. When a new snapshot is taken, the web application downloads the web page and metadata and stores them in HBase. When a snapshot is viewed, the web application retrieves the page metadata and the snapshot of the page contents from HBase and displays it in the browser.

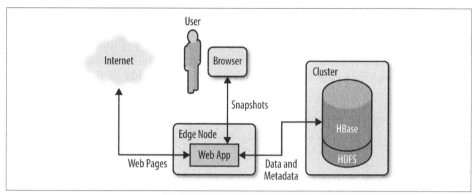

Figure 13-1. Web application architecture

Before we dive into the security requirements, let's take a look at the data model used by the example. Each web page is uniquely identified by a URL and each snapshot is further identified by the time the page was fetched. The full list of fields in the data model are shown in Table 13-1.

Table 13-1. Web page snapshot data model

Field	Type	Description
url	String	The URL of the web page
fetchedAt	long	The UTC time that this page was fetched
fetchTimeMs	int	The amount of time it took to fetch the web page, in ms
size	int	The size of the web page
title	String	The title of the HTML page, if one exists
description	String	The description from the HTML meta tag
keywords	List<String>	The keywords from the HTML meta tag
outlinks	List<String>	The URLs of pages this page links to
content	String	The content of the web page

HBase stores data as a multidimensional sorted map. This means we need to map the fields of our records to the row key, column family, and column-qualifier keys that

HBase uses to sort data. For our use case, we want each row in HBase to be keyed by URL and the time the snapshot was fetched. In order to make the most recent snapshot sort first, we will reverse the order of the fetchedAt timestamp before using it in the row key by subtracting it from Long.MAX_VALUE, and we show that as <rev fetch edAt> in Figure 13-2. Each field will correspond to a single column in HBase so we define a mapping from each field name to a column family and column qualifier. Figure 13-2 shows how the row key is mapped and a sample of field mappings to HBase columns.

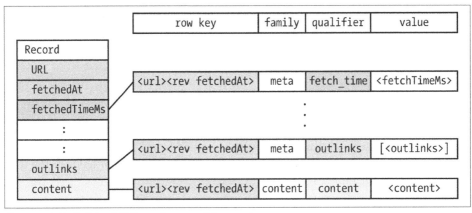

Figure 13-2. Original HBase data model mapping

Security Requirements

At this point, we're ready to add security features to the demo. By default, all of the fields in the snapshots are accessible to any user. For our use case, we want to lock down the content of the pages by default and only allow access if we request a snapshot to be made public. We could use cell-level security and keep the same data model that we used before, but that is probably overkill for our use case. Instead, we'll modify the data model slightly.

In particular, we'll add a field to our model called contentKey. The contentKey will be used as the column qualifier for storing content. We'll use the username as the contentKey for private snapshots and the special value public for public snapshots. We're now want to store the content of each snapshot under a potentially different column qualifier, so we'll change the type of the content field to Map<String, String>. The updated mapping configuration is shown in Figure 13-3.

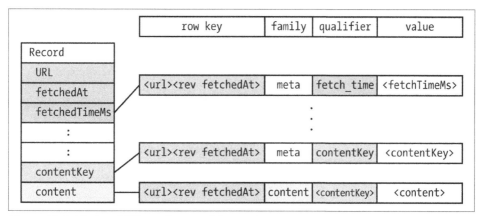

Figure 13-3. Updated HBase data model mapping

Before continuing, let's come up with a list of the security requirements we want to enforce in our application:

1. The content of private snapshots is only accessible by the user who took the snapshot

2. The content of public snapshots is visible to all users

3. The metadata of all snapshots is visible to all users

4. Users authenticate with the application using HTTP basic authentication

5. The application impersonates the authenticated user when communicating with HBase

6. Authorization is enforced at the HBase level

Cluster Configuration

With these requirements in hand, we can start configuring our cluster. Requirement five (5) implies that the application needs to authenticate with HBase. In order for HBase authentication to be enabled, we must first enable Hadoop authentication. To meet requirement six (6), we also have to enable HBase authorization. HBase authorization is also required to meet requirements one (1) and two (2). Requirement three (3) implies that we'll allow all users access to the metadata fields. The fourth (4) requirement applies to the web application itself and the application server, Tomcat for our purposes, used. We're now ready to plan our configuration steps:

1. Configure Hadoop authentication (see "Configuration" on page 83)

2. Configure HBase authentication (refer to "Securing Apache HBase" (*http://hbase.apache.org/book.html#security*) in *The Apache HBase Reference Guide* (*http://hbase.apache.org/book.html*))

3. Configure HBase authorization by adding the following to *hbase-site.xml*:

```
<property>
  <name>hbase.coprocessor.region.classes</name>
  <value>
    org.apache.hadoop.hbase.security.access.AccessController,
    org.apache.hadoop.hbase.security.token.TokenProvider
  </value>
</property>
<property>
  <name>hbase.coprocessor.master.classes</name>
  <value>
    org.apache.hadoop.hbase.security.access.AccessController
  </value>
</property>
<property>
  <name>hbase.coprocessor.regionserver.classes</name>
  <value>
    org.apache.hadoop.hbase.security.access.AccessController
  </value>
</property>
<property>
  <name>hbase.security.exec.permission.checks</name>
  <value>true</value>
</property>
```

4. Create a Kerberos principal to perform HBase administration functions:

```
kadmin: addprinc hbase@EXAMPLE.COM
WARNING: no policy specified for hbase@EXAMPLE.COM; defaulting to no \
policy
Enter password for principal "hbase@EXAMPLE.COM":
Re-enter password for principal "hbase@EXAMPLE.COM":
Principal "hbase@EXAMPLE.COM" created.
kadmin:
```

5. Create a Kerberos principal for the application and export the key to a keytab:

```
kadmin: addprinc web-page-snapshots@EXAMPLE.COM
WARNING: no policy specified for web-page-snapshots@EXAMPLE.COM;
defaulting to no policy
Enter password for principal "web-page-snapshots@EXAMPLE.COM":
Re-enter password for principal "web-page-snapshots@EXAMPLE.COM":
Principal "web-page-snapshots@EXAMPLE.COM" created.
kadmin: ktadd -k app.keytab web-page-snapshots
Entry for principal web-page-snapshots with kvno 4, encryption type
des3-cbc-sha1 added to keytab WRFILE:app.keytab.
Entry for principal web-page-snapshots with kvno 4, encryption type
```

```
arcfour-hmac added to keytab WRFILE:app.keytab.
Entry for principal web-page-snapshots with kvno 4, encryption type
des-hmac-sha1 added to keytab WRFILE:app.keytab.
Entry for principal web-page-snapshots with kvno 4, encryption type
des-cbc-md5 added to keytab WRFILE:app.keytab.
kadmin:
```

6. Copy the *keytab* file into the home directory of the application user

7. Grant the application principal create table permissions:

```
[app@snapshots ~]$ kinit hbase
Password for hbase@ENT.CLOUDERA.COM:
[app@snapshots ~]$ hbase shell
14/11/13 14:45:53 INFO Configuration.deprecation: hadoop.native.lib is
deprecated. Instead, use io.native.lib.available
HBase Shell; enter 'help<RETURN>' for list of supported commands.
Type "exit<RETURN>" to leave the HBase Shell
Version 0.98.6, rUnknown, Sat Oct 11 15:15:15 PDT 2014

hbase(main):001:0> grant 'web-page-snapshots', 'RWXCA'
0 row(s) in 4.0340 seconds

hbase(main):002:0>
```

8. Create the HBase tables:

```
[app@snapshots ~]$ kinit -kt ~/app.keytab web-page-snapshots
[app@snapshots ~]$ export KITE_USER_CLASSPATH=/etc/hadoop/conf
[app@snapshots ~]$ export \
ZK=zk1.example.com,zk2.example.com,zk3.example.com
[app@snapshots ~]$ kite-dataset create \
  dataset:hbase:${ZK}:2181/webpagesnapshots.WebPageSnapshotModel \
  -s src/main/avro/hbase-models/WebPageSnapshotModel.avsc
[app@snapshots ~]$ kite-dataset create \
  dataset:hbase:${ZK}:2181/webpageredirects.WebPageRedirectModel \
  -s src/main/avro/hbase-models/WebPageRedirectModel.avsc
[app@snapshots ~]$
```

9. Grant users *alice* and *bob* access to the public tables/columns:

```
[app@snapshots ~]$ kinit -kt ~/app.keytab web-page-snapshots
[app@snapshots ~]$ hbase shell
14/11/13 14:45:53 INFO Configuration.deprecation: hadoop.native.lib is
deprecated. Instead, use io.native.lib.available
HBase Shell; enter 'help<RETURN>' for list of supported commands.
Type "exit<RETURN>" to leave the HBase Shell
Version 0.98.6, rUnknown, Sat Oct 11 15:15:15 PDT 2014

hbase(main):001:0> grant 'alice', 'RW', 'webpagesnapshots', 'content',
'public'
0 row(s) in 2.9580 seconds
```

```
hbase(main):002:0> grant 'alice', 'RW', 'webpagesnapshots', '_s'
0 row(s) in 0.1640 seconds

hbase(main):003:0> grant 'alice', 'RW', 'webpagesnapshots', 'meta'
0 row(s) in 0.2100 seconds

hbase(main):004:0> grant 'alice', 'RW', 'webpagesnapshots', 'observable'
0 row(s) in 0.1600 seconds

hbase(main):005:0> grant 'alice', 'RW', 'webpageredirects'
0 row(s) in 0.1600 seconds

hbase(main):006:0> grant 'alice', 'RW', 'managed_schemas'
0 row(s) in 0.1570 seconds

hbase(main):007:0> grant 'bob', 'RW', 'webpagesnapshots', 'content',
'public'
0 row(s) in 0.1920 seconds

hbase(main):008:0> grant 'bob', 'RW', 'webpagesnapshots', '_s'
0 row(s) in 0.1510 seconds

hbase(main):009:0> grant 'bob', 'RW', 'webpagesnapshots', 'meta'
0 row(s) in 0.2100 seconds

hbase(main):010:0> grant 'bob', 'RW', 'webpagesnapshots', 'observable'
0 row(s) in 0.1640 seconds

hbase(main):011:0> grant 'bob', 'RW', 'webpageredirects'
0 row(s) in 0.1590 seconds

hbase(main):012:0> grant 'bob', 'RW', 'managed_schemas'
0 row(s) in 0.1870 seconds

hbase(main):013:0>
```

10. Grant *alice* and *bob* access to their private columns:

```
[app@snapshots ~]$ kinit -kt ~/app.keytab web-page-snapshots
[app@snapshots ~]$ hbase shell
14/11/13 14:45:53 INFO Configuration.deprecation: hadoop.native.lib is
deprecated. Instead, use io.native.lib.available
HBase Shell; enter 'help<RETURN>' for list of supported commands.
Type "exit<RETURN>" to leave the HBase Shell
Version 0.98.6, rUnknown, Sat Oct 11 15:15:15 PDT 2014

hbase(main):001:0> grant 'alice', 'RW', 'webpagesnapshots', 'content',
'alice'

0 row(s) in 2.8890 seconds
```

```
hbase(main):002:0> grant 'bob', 'RW', 'webpagesnapshots', 'content',
'bob'
0 row(s) in 0.1600 seconds

hbase(main):003:0>
```

11. Add the following parameters to *hbase-site.xml* on all of the HBase nodes to enable user impersonation by the web-page-snapshots principal:

```
<property>
  <name>hadoop.proxyuser.web-page-snapshots.groups</name>
  <value>*</value>
</property>
<property>
  <name>hadoop.proxyuser.web-page-snapshots.hosts</name>
  <value>*</value>
</property>
```

 There are additional application configuration steps that are unique to the design and implementation of the demo application. The full set of steps for running the demo are available in the project's README on GitHub (*https://github.com/hadoop-security/kite-spring-hbase-example*).

Implementation Notes

In adding security to our application, we made a number of implementation changes. The full set of changes can be viewed by comparing our demo with the original Kite SDK example, but we'll summarize the key changes here. The first modification was the addition of a Kerberos login module to obtain a Kerberos TGT using the application's keytab. This module is loaded by Spring before initializing the rest of the web application. Here is an abbreviated version of the module without logging or error checking:

```
public class KerberosLoginService {

  public KerberosLoginService(String applicationPrincipal,
      String applicationKeytab) throws IOException {

    if (UserGroupInformation.isSecurityEnabled()) {
      UserGroupInformation.loginUserFromKeytab(applicationPrincipal,
          applicationKeytab);
    }
  }
}
```

The key takeaways are that we first check that security on our cluster has been enabled before using the loginUserFromKeytab() method on the UserGroupInforma tion class. This method will obtain our Kerberos TGT using the keytab file.

The second change required from a Hadoop security standpoint is modifying the Web PageSnapshotService to impersonate the authenticated user when communicating with HBase. To accomplish, this we use the doAs() method of the UserGroupInforma tion object that represents the proxy user we want to impersonate. Here is an example of adding impersonation to one of the methods of the WebPageSnapshotService:

```
private WebPageSnapshotModel getWebPageSnapshot(String url,
    final long ts, final String user) throws IOException {
  WebPageSnapshotModel snapshot = null;
  final String normalizedUrl = normalizeUrl(url, user);

  UserGroupInformation ugi = UserGroupInformation.createProxyUser(user,
      UserGroupInformation.getLoginUser());
  snapshot = ugi.doAs(new PrivilegedAction<WebPageSnapshotModel>() {

    @Override
    public WebPageSnapshotModel run() {
      Key key = new Key.Builder(webPageSnapshotModels(user))
          .add("url", normalizedUrl)
          .add("fetchedAtRevTs", Long.MAX_VALUE - ts).build();
      return webPageSnapshotModels(user).get(key);
    }
  });

  return snapshot;
}
```

The final required modification is to switch from using a single, shared connection to HBase to creating a connection per user. This is required due to the way the HBase client caches connections. The most important takeaways are to create per-user connections and to set the hbase.client.instance.id to a unique value in the Configu ration object that HBase will end up using. For this application, we created a utility method to create and cache our connections:

```
private synchronized RandomAccessDataset<WebPageSnapshotModel>
    webPageSnapshotModels(String user) {

  RandomAccessDataset<WebPageSnapshotModel> dataset =
      webPageSnapshotModelMap.get(user);

  if (dataset == null) {
    Configuration conf = new Configuration(
        DefaultConfiguration.get());
    conf.set("hbase.client.instance.id", user);
    DefaultConfiguration.set(conf);
```

```
      dataset = Datasets.load(webPageSnapshotUri,
          WebPageSnapshotModel.class);
      webPageSnapshotModelMap.put(user, dataset);
  }

  return dataset;
}
```

Summary

In this case study, we reviewed the design and architecture of a typical interactive HBase application. We then looked at the security considerations (authentication, authorization, impersonation, etc.) associated with our use case. We also described changes to the data model necessary to support our authorization model. Next, we summarized the security requirements that we wanted to add to the application, followed by the steps necessary to configure our cluster to meet our security requirements. Finally, we described elements of the application implementation that required changes to support the security requirements.

Afterword

Hadoop has come a long way since its inception. As you have seen throughout this book, security encompasses a lot of material across the ecosystem. With the boom of big data and the impact it's having on businesses that quickly adopt Hadoop as their data platform of choice, it is no wonder that Hadoop and its wide ecosystem have moved rapidly. That being said, Hadoop is still very much in its infancy. Even with the many security configurations available, Hadoop has much to do until it's on the level of relational databases and data warehouses to fully meet the needs of enterprises that have billions of dollars on the line with their data management.

The good news is that because of Hadoop's massive growth in the marketplace, security deficits in the product are rapidly being filled. We leave you with some things that are either in development right now (possibly even completed by the time this is published), as well as features on the horizon that will be a part of the Hadoop ecosystem in the not too distant future.

Unified Authorization

One of the hardest jobs a Hadoop security administrator has is to keep track of how the myriad of components handles access controls. While we dedicated a good deal of coverage to Apache Sentry as a centralized authorization component for Hadoop, it is not there yet in terms of providing authorization across the entire ecosystem. This will happen in the long term—and it needs to. Security administrators and auditors alike need to have a single place they can go to view and manage all policies related to user authorization controls. Without this, it is simply too easy to make mistakes along the way.

In the very near term, Apache Sentry will have authorization integration for HDFS. This will allow for a unified way to define policies for data access when data is shared between components. For example, if data is loaded into the Hive warehouse and is controlled by Sentry policies, how is that handled with MapReduce access? As we saw in Chapter 13, this involved using HDFS-extended ACLs. With HDFS integration with Sentry, this is not necessary. Instead, HDFS paths can be specified as controlled by Sentry, thus authorization decisions are determined by Sentry policies, not standard POSIX permissions or extended ACLs.

Also on the horizon for Sentry is integration with HBase. We saw in Chapter 6 that authorization policies are stored in a special table in HBase, and managed via the HBase shell by default. This is a good candidate to migrate the policy store to Sentry instead.

Data Governance

This book did not cover the larger topic of data governance, but it did go into a subtopic of it that relates to accounting. As we saw in Chapter 8, there are audit logs in many different places that capture activity in the cluster. However, there is not a centralized place to capture auditing holistically, nor is there a place to perform general data governance tasks such as managing business metadata, viewing linkages and lineage, or managing data retention. These features are prominently covered in the traditional data warehouse. For Hadoop to reach the next level of security as a whole, data governance needs to be addressed far better than it is today.

Native Data Protection

In addition to encryption, Hadoop needs native methods for masking and tokenization. While masking can be done creatively using UDFs or specialized views, it makes more sense to provide the ability to mask data on the fly based on predefined policies. This is available today from other commercial products, but we believe a native capability should be included as part of Hadoop. Tokenization is not currently possible at all in Hadoop without commercial products. Tokenization is important for data scientists especially because they might not need to see specific values of data, but do need to preserve linkages and other statistical properties in order to do analysis. This is not possible with masking, but is possible with tokenization.

Final Thoughts

Hadoop and big data are exciting markets to be in. While it might be a bit scary for some, especially seasoned security professionals who are accustomed to more unified security features, we hope this book has shed some light on the state of Hadoop security and shown that even a large Hadoop cluster with many components can be protected using a well-planned security architecture.

Index

About the Authors

Ben Spivey is currently a solutions architect at Cloudera. During his time with Cloudera, he has worked in a consulting capacity to assist customers with their Hadoop deployments. Ben has worked with many Fortune 500 companies across multiple industries, including financial services, retail, and health care. His primary expertise is the planning, installation, configuration, and securing of customers' Hadoop clusters.

Prior to Cloudera, Ben worked for the National Security Agency and with a defense contractor as a software engineer. During this time, Ben built applications that, among other things, integrated with enterprise security infrastructure to protect sensitive information.

Joey Echeverria is a software engineer at Rocana where he builds the next generation of IT Operations Analytics on the Apache Hadoop platform. Joey is also a committer on the Kite SDK, an Apache-licensed data API for the Hadoop ecosystem. Joey was previously a software engineer at Cloudera where he contributed to a number of ASF projects including Apache Flume, Apache Sqoop, Apache Hadoop, and Apache HBase.

Colophon

The animal on the cover of *Hadoop Security* is a *Japanese badger* (*Meles anakuma*), in the same family as weasels. As its name suggests, it's endemic to Japan; it is found on Honshu, Kyushu, Shikoku, and Shodoshima.

Japanese badgers are small compared to its European counterparts. Males are about 31 inches in length and females are a little smaller at an average of 28 inches. Other than the size of their canine teeth, males and females don't differ much physically. Adults weigh about 8.8 to 17.6 pounds, and have blunt torsos with short limbs. The badger has powerful digging claws on its front feet and smaller hind feet. Though not as distinct as on the European badger, the Japanese badger has the characteristic black and white stripes on its face.

Japanese badgers are nocturnal and hibernate during the winter. Once females are two years old, they mate and birth litters up to two or three cubs in the spring. Compared to their European counterparts, Japanese badgers are more solitary; mates don't form pair bonds.

Japanese badgers inhabit a variety of woodland and forest habitats, where they eat an omnivorous diet of worms, beetles, berries, and persimmons.

Many of the animals on O'Reilly covers are endangered; all of them are important to the world. To learn more about how you can help, go to *animals.oreilly.com*.

The cover image is from loose plates, source is unknown. The cover fonts are URW Typewriter and Guardian Sans. The text font is Adobe Minion Pro; the heading font is Adobe Myriad Condensed; and the code font is Dalton Maag's Ubuntu Mono.

Get even more for your money.

Join the O'Reilly Community, and register the O'Reilly books you own. It's free, and you'll get:

- $4.99 ebook upgrade offer
- 40% upgrade offer on O'Reilly print books
- Membership discounts on books and events
- Free lifetime updates to ebooks and videos
- Multiple ebook formats, DRM FREE
- Participation in the O'Reilly community
- Newsletters
- Account management
- 100% Satisfaction Guarantee

Signing up is easy:

1. Go to: oreilly.com/go/register
2. Create an O'Reilly login.
3. Provide your address.
4. Register your books.

Note: English-language books only

To order books online:
oreilly.com/store

For questions about products or an order:
orders@oreilly.com

To sign up to get topic-specific email announcements and/or news about upcoming books, conferences, special offers, and new technologies:
elists@oreilly.com

For technical questions about book content:
booktech@oreilly.com

To submit new book proposals to our editors:
proposals@oreilly.com

O'Reilly books are available in multiple DRM-free ebook formats. For more information:
oreilly.com/ebooks

O'REILLY®

Lightning Source UK Ltd.
Milton Keynes UK
UKOW07f1831280615

254238UK00001B/1/P